American Reformers, 1870–1920

American Reformers, 1870–1920

Progressives in Word and Deed

Steven L. Piott

ROWMAN & LITTLEFIELD PUBLISHERS, INC.
Lanham • Boulder • New York • Toronto • Oxford

ROWMAN & LITTLEFIELD PUBLISHERS, INC.

Published in the United States of America
by Rowman & Littlefield Publishers, Inc.
A wholly owned subsidary of The Rowman & Littlefield Publishing Group, Inc.
4501 Forbes Boulevard, Suite 200, Lanham, Maryland 20706
www.rowmanlittlefield.com

PO Box 317
Oxford
OX2 9RU, UK

British Library Cataloguing in Publication Information Available

Library of Congress Cataloging-in-Publication Data

American reformers, 1870–1920 : progressives in word and deed / Steven L. Piott.
    p. cm.
  Includes bibliographical references and index.
  ISBN-13: 978-0-7425-2762-1 (cloth : alk. paper)
  ISBN-10: 0-7425-2762-X (cloth : alk. paper)
  ISBN-13: 978-0-7425-2763-8 (pbk. : alk. paper)
  ISBN-10: 0-7425-2763-8 (pbk. : alk. paper)
  1. United States—History—1865–1921—Biography. 2. United States—Social
conditions—1865–1918. 3. United States—Politics and government—1865–1933. 4.
Progressivism (United States politics) 5. Populism—United States. 6. Reformers—
United States—Biography. 7. Social reformers—United States—Biography. 8. Political
activists—United States—Biography. 9. Social change—United States—History. I.
Piott, Steven L.
E663.A47 2006
303.48'4092273—dc22   2005027554

Printed in the United States of America

The paper used in this publication meets the minimum requirements of American
National Standard for Information Sciences—Permanence of Paper for Printed Library
Materials, ANSI/NISO Z39.48-1992.

To Cindy

Contents

Introduction

The period from 1870 to 1920 has been described as the rise of industrial America. This time of remarkable industrial growth did much to increase the wealth and improve the lives of many Americans. A number of factors contributed to this growth: an abundance of raw materials, the construction of national transportation and communications networks, an increasing supply of labor, a burst of technological innovation, an emerging entrepreneurial class of businessmen, and an expanding domestic market for manufactured goods. The federal government assisted this process by offering loans, tax breaks, and land grants to railroads; tariff protection to manufacturers; and homesteads to potential market-oriented farmers. As the nation committed itself to economic development, the need for investment capital became especially crucial. Increasingly, large investment banking houses like J. P. Morgan and Co. played a dominant role as they marketed investment opportunities through the buying and selling of corporate bonds and stocks. The influence of these new financiers drew increasing concern from many Americans who began to develop a general distrust of the growing economic power of Wall Street.

Railroads pioneered the growth of big business and were followed by iron, steel, and petroleum. These large business concerns soon developed new forms of corporate organization and began to rationalize their operations through forms of vertical integration (controlling the various aspects on which a corporation relies for its primary function). In refined form this involved controlling every step of the production process beginning with the acquisition of raw material resources and continuing forward to include the merchandising and marketing of products. Corporations also engaged in horizontal integration (combining a number of firms engaged in the same enterprise into a single corporation or trust). By the end of the nineteenth century, 1 percent of all corporations in America controlled more than 33 percent of all manufacturing. As smaller competitors increasingly clamored for protection against such domination, Congress began to establish federal regulatory agencies like the Interstate Commerce Commission (1887) and enact regulatory legislation like the Sherman Antitrust Act (1890) in an attempt to protect or restore competition. Although the growth of large-scale industrial capitalism contributed substantially to the nation's economic growth, it also triggered a heated debate over the implications of rising corporate power (often referred to loosely in public discourse as "monopoly") not just on the economy but on the political system as well.

Not everyone benefited equally from these economic advances. Many workers and farmers looked at a future of diminishing rather than advancing returns. They sensed that society's wealth was not being distributed equitably. Ironically, as the nation's wealth-producing power had increased, so too had the difficulties of the masses to earn a decent living. How had that happened? The United States had been a land of opportunity because of its vast acres of public lands. Was that no longer true? Had the government used up much of the public domain because of settlement? Had the government lavished it too freely on railroads and speculators who took advantage of that largesse to monopolize land? Had the government wrongly encouraged inequality through land and tax laws that allowed various individuals to acquire personal wealth at the expense of society? If this had indeed happened, maybe the government could restore the imbalance by adopting new tax laws to restore the opportunity that had historically resided in available land.

Workers experienced their own unique set of problems as a result of the growth of industrialization. The rise of big business, which increasingly utilized machines to mass-produce goods, directly affected both the size and composition of the workforce and the nature of work itself. As the number of manufacturing workers doubled between 1880 and 1900, dependent wage earners quickly replaced independent artisans. Technological innovations and division of labor further diminished the position of skilled workers. Employers increasingly utilized lower-paid, semiskilled and unskilled laborers, an increasing number of which were immigrants, to fill factory positions. Although most American workers toiled in factories, many worked in sweatshops in dimly lit second-floor lofts or basements or "finished" work in their own cramped tenement apartments. In many cases, volume, not hours, determined pay as workers labored for piecework rates. When contractors reduced rates, workers had to speed up to maintain the same pay. The workdays were long—usually ten hours a day (twelve hours in the steel industry) for six days a week. The working environment was often unhealthy and unsafe. Regulated working environments were uncommon, and even in the few states with factory regulations, inspection was sporadic and enforcement difficult. Employers had almost no legal responsibilities for an employee's safety or health.

Wages were another concern. Although real wages rose during the last four decades of the nineteenth century, increases for skilled workers were much higher than for unskilled. For workers with unsteady or seasonal employment, increases in real wages seemed meaningless. Severe economic depressions, as occurred between 1873 and 1879 and between 1893 and 1897, meant reduced wages or layoffs for both skilled and unskilled workers. Because unemployment insurance did not exist, workers had no cushion against economic insecurity. The decreasing need for skilled workers encouraged some employers to use women and children whom they could hire at lower wages than men who worked the same jobs. By 1900, 20 percent of all manufacturing jobs were done by women who worked at wages well below the minimum needed for survival. In addition, nearly two million children under the age of sixteen worked in factories and fields. Like many women, they worked to supplement meager family incomes or to help cope with the immediate threat of poverty.

The world of the farmer changed with that of the industrial worker. As transportation facilitated access to the growing market economy, farmers increasingly specialized. Farmers on the Great Plains grew wheat, midwesterners raised corn, and southerners continued to cultivate cotton. As farmers specialized in cash crops, they became increasingly dependent on others. Bankers controlled access to credit, buyers dictated prices, and railroads set the transportation rates on goods being sent to market. In the more geographically isolated South, small farmers, tenants, and sharecroppers found themselves buying supplies on credit from "furnishing merchants" at exorbitant interest charges so that they could plant next year's crop and support their families until harvest time. Under this system, merchants dictated the nature of a farmer's crop, demanded that he not incur financial obligations from another merchant, and required him to sign a lien on his future crop as collateral. When farmers sold their crops, they most often found that they had not earned enough to pay off the merchant. As a result, the struggling farmer often found himself trapped in a never-ending cycle of debt peonage.

Trying to understand abstract economic forces proved difficult. As farmers increasingly utilized machinery to expand the amount of land under cultivation, they found that gains in productivity worked only to force down commodity prices. Corn that had sold for seventy-eight cents a bushel in 1867 could only command twenty-three cents in 1889. Likewise, wheat that sold for $2 a bushel in 1867 brought only seventy cents in 1889, while cotton dropped from eleven cents a pound in 1875 to less than five cents a pound in the early 1890s. Although high tariffs protected manufacturers against foreign competition (allowing higher prices on finished goods), farmers had to sell their produce in an unprotected international market where competition further reduced prices. Compounding the farmer's problems was deflation, which increased the value of real debts. As debt obligations mounted, farmers became increasingly interested in various inflationary panaceas, such as issuing "greenbacks" (paper dollars) or, later, coining silver dollars in addition to gold as a possible way of expanding the money supply and easing financial burdens. Accompanying these suggestions was usually some plan for the government to make capital available at low rates of interest so that hard-pressed producers could circumvent usurious lenders and realize economic opportunity.

As agricultural problems intensified after the Civil War, farmers increasingly looked for ways to eliminate their economic dependence. One solution was to organize. Beginning with the creation of the Patrons of Husbandry or Grange in 1867, they began to promote farmer-owned cooperatives to handle buying and selling. During the 1880s, a new organization, the Farmers' Alliance, absorbed existing farm groups, established new locals (suballiances), and developed a captivating vision of a national cooperative program. In doing so, Alliance members hoped to sidestep existing marketing practices by establishing an independent, member-owned enterprise to direct the selling and purchasing of products. They also began to call on the federal government to abandon its laissez-faire philosophy that seemed to ignore farm problems.

During the last half of the nineteenth century, the urban population in the United States grew rapidly. Swelling the population density of America's cities were numerous African Americans fleeing poverty and racial violence in the South and many rural agriculturalists looking to abandon unprofitable farms and escape suffocating debts. The most important source of this tremendous growth in the urban population, however, which jumped from 20 percent of the total U.S. population to 40 percent between 1860 and 1900, was the large number of new immigrants. These newcomers, increasingly from southern and eastern Europe, tended to settle in crowded industrial cities where they confronted nativistic biases while they eked out an existence working at low-paying jobs. Many labored in sweatshops where seasonal work was often done in cramped working conditions for long hours and at piecework rates or in exploitative factory environments. Immigrants also tended to gravitate to ethnic enclaves (ghettos) in the inner city where they rented housing. Many lived in crowded tenements—substandard apartments in buildings that lacked sufficient light and ventilation, had little or no plumbing or heating, and were often served by inadequate sewage systems. Outdoor privies or shared water closets in the hallways were common. Water often came from outdoor hydrants or central faucets in the hallways. Inconvenient access or inadequate water pressure to the upper floors of the tenements often meant that women had to carry water for cooking, washing, and cleaning. Because the general environment was unhealthy, urban death rates and infant mortality rates were high.

Responding to these growing social problems were groups of men and women who became known as settlement house workers. Like their religious counterparts in the Protestant Church, the social gospelers, they challenged the dominant cultural thinking that regarded poverty as the direct result of personal failure and adopted the belief that environmental factors were more important in shaping human development. To alleviate the distress of poverty, ways of improving the environment would have to be designed. One such way was the settlement house, which served as a center of activity in the community. The idea was to help immigrants adjust to urban life by providing advice, care, and education. The individuals who came to the settlements had a view of society properly oriented toward cooperation rather than competition, where self-sacrifice would rule over self-interest. In working to solve the social problems generated by life in a big city, settlements also placed an emphasis on the scientific gathering of facts to provoke legislative action. Such information would be useful in battles to establish building codes for tenements, regulate sweatshops, outlaw child labor, improve working conditions, and underscore the need for government to broaden its responsibility for human welfare.

The rise of industrial capitalism generated its own rationale, one that served to legitimize success, confirm individual virtues, and justify capitalism's disparities. Relying on the old ideology of individualism, this rationale argued that opportunities existed for anyone to get ahead by hard work and ingenuity. Those who succeeded deserved their success. Those who did not had only themselves to blame for being lazy, careless, or thoughtless. These assumptions became the basis for Herbert Spencer's popular social theory, social Darwinism, which applied Charles Darwin's evolutionary laws of natural selection as set forth in his influential *The Origin of Species* (1859) to human society. Only the fittest individuals would survive and flourish in the competitive world. The human struggle that Spencer, William Graham Sumner, and even Andrew Carnegie described had important benefits. Society would improve by eliminating the weak and unfit and allowing the strong and talented to survive. The state's role in this inevitable process was negative. It simply should not interfere. To attempt to enact paternalistic legislation designed to help the poor would be detrimental to hardworking, middle-class citizens (the class that would have to foot the bills for such legislation) and, in the long run, futile. Similarly, any attempt to restrict the strong with regulations would only retard society's destined evolutionary development. Allied with these beliefs in the minds of most social Darwinists was the assumption that the Anglo-Saxon race, having evolved to the highest level of social evolution, was superior. Such assumptions were also used to justify racial supremacy and sanction imperialism.

The conservative thinking that underscored social Darwinism also governed late nineteenth-century race relations, the law, and religion. As the United States emerged as an industrial power and workers and farmers strove to survive amidst the growing disparity between rich and poor, another group of Americans struggled against institutionalized economic, political, and social oppression. The most glaring failure of Reconstruction was that it did not, despite its guarantees of citizenship rights and the vote, secure civil rights or legal protections for African Americans, nor did it promote economic independence or provide material resources to guarantee them real equality. When the Republican Party, the original sponsor of the rights of freed blacks, withdrew federal troops in 1877 in favor of "home rule" for the Democratic South, it left blacks to fend for themselves as a racial minority.

The courts soon abandoned blacks as well. Congress enacted a civil rights act in 1875 to protect blacks from racial discrimination in public accommodations. In 1883, however, the Supreme Court overturned that law and ruled that civil rights protections under the Fourteenth Amendment prohibited racial discrimination only by states. In other words, the federal government no longer had the right to involve itself in race relations between individuals, private corporations, or organizations. The courts further circumscribed the meaning of equality by validating state laws that imposed segregation in transportation as well. Many trains had first- and second-class cars that already established a degree of racial separation based on the price of a ticket. After the state of Tennessee mandated that railroads maintain separate first-class cars for blacks and whites in 1881, other southern states soon adopted statutes requiring passengers to occupy the car set aside for their race. When Louisiana enacted such a law in 1890, it was challenged in court. In *Plessy v. Ferguson* (1896), the Supreme Court ruled that separate accommodations did not deprive blacks of equal rights if those accommodations were equal. Soon a system of "Jim Crow" laws officially divided the country into white America and "colored" America. Blacks and whites could not stay in the same hotels; eat in the same restaurants; sit in the same theaters and railway waiting rooms; enjoy the same parks, playgrounds, and beaches; or even use the same drinking fountains and washrooms.

This legalized system of segregation had a political dimension as well as southerners cleverly schemed to deny African Americans the franchise. Prohibited from denying anyone the right to vote because of race by the Fifteenth Amendment, southern states resorted to a number of devices to evade that federal mandate. Two of the methods used included the requirement that voters pay a poll tax or that they show proof of property ownership as a precondition for voting. Few blacks were prosperous enough to meet such qualifications. Another method was the literacy test, by which potential voters were required to demonstrate the ability to read. This method would conceivably disenfranchise any illiterate voter, but an "understanding clause" gave white registrars leeway to allow an illiterate white man to vote if, in their opinion, he could satisfactorily interpret a passage from the state constitution that was read to him. Legal challenges followed, but in the case of *Williams v. Mississippi* (1898), the Supreme Court approved a Mississippi plan that utilized a combination of poll tax, literacy test, and residency requirement to exclude blacks from voting. Over a twenty-year period between 1890 and 1910, similar amendments to southern state constitutions effectively disenfranchised African Americans.

As race relations deteriorated in the late nineteenth century, violence against African Americans increased. The worst such violence, the lynching of blacks by white mobs, reached staggering levels. During the 1890s, there occurred on average 187 lynchings per year, of which over 80 percent were in the South. The vast majority of the victims were black. Those who took part in lynchings often legitimized their actions as a form of law enforcement and often as a necessary response to allegations of rape. In the process, lynching became a means by which whites further controlled the black population through intimidation and fear.

The Supreme Court's narrowing definition of constitutional guarantees of racial equality during the last three decades of the nineteenth century reflected its overall tendency to view the law from an increasingly conservative perspective. Accepting the doctrine of laissez-faire, the Supreme Court modified its interpretation of the Fourteenth Amendment in yet another unique way. Arguing that government intervention in business deprived corporations of their property without due process of law, jurists came to regard corporations as individuals and, as such, equally entitled to the same protections as individuals under the law. In a similar manner, the Court limited the police powers reserved to states and used the doctrine of liberty of contract to stifle protective labor legislation. In the legal mind, workers were seen as free agents able to choose their employment and individually bargain with their employers concerning the contractual terms of their employment. What right did a state have to set maximum hours on the workday or to define the length of the workweek or to set limitations on the labor of women or children? In tending to view the law as static and refusing to acknowledge the existence of change, the Court regarded suggestions that the law be used to guarantee human rights, protect workers, or promote social welfare as unconstitutional. To an increasing number of legal jurists, however, the law had not kept pace with what Justice Oliver Wendell Holmes called the "felt necessities of the time" and had come to stand in the way of social progress.

For an increasing number of Americans, the Protestant Church seemed to have lost step with a changing world as much as the law. To many, institutionalized religion seemed to be losing its vitality, its meaning, and its relevancy to a society plagued with modern, urban social problems. Compounding this religious disconnection was the growing perception that organized religion had allowed itself to become controlled by wealth and had aligned itself with conservative or reactionary forces that stood as defenders of the status quo. In accepting the notion that laissez-faire capitalism would solve all social problems, the church ignored the voices of religious critics who accused it of pandering to an individual's selfish quest for salvation and asked it to exhibit a broader moral leadership. Declining church membership among the working class only seemed to underscore the failure of organized religion to articulate a relevant Christian message. Beset by ever-worsening social and economic conditions, especially in the inner cities, the working class seemed to find the complacency of the church and its refusal to entertain reform ideas that might improve the quality of their lives increasingly objectionable. The question confronting Protestant ministers was how to revitalize Christianity and make it relevant to urban/industrial problems.

In a laissez-faire political environment that seemed to eschew rules and regulations and encourage an entrepreneurial "get ahead" spirit and a Darwinian social environment that appeared guided by the tooth-and-claw dictates of natural law, late nineteenth-century America had apparently lost its moral compass. What had happened to the ideals of public morality and business ethics? Guided by the civil service–minded "mugwumps" who complained vociferously that city governments had fallen under the control of boss-directed, machine-controlled political parties that fostered graft and vice while they exploited newly arrived immigrants, Gilded Age critics lamented the debilitating effect that political patronage had on honest, efficient government. Overlooked in the mugwump critique of popular politics, however, was any analysis of what caused corruption (beyond the assumption that unscrupulous politicians and compliant immigrants were to blame) and the apparent decline in public morality. It was not too long, however, before a more sophisticated analysis suggested that businessmen, in need of low tax assessments or prized municipal contracts (franchises), might be corrupting politics for their own selfish ends. The suggestion that such a business–political alliance existed, that a city's "best" citizens were often in league with its "worst," raised questions about modern-day ethics and the depth and extent of both municipal and state corruption. If corruption had become systematized and institutionalized and the public trust truly betrayed, then what were the implications of this apparent debasement for democratic government?

Such questioning, which would be raised by the more perceptive turn-of-the-century investigative journalists known as muckrakers, foreshadowed a growing unease with ethical standards in business itself. One area of growing concern was the preparation of food and drugs. As food processing shifted from the home to the factory, competition intensified. In the process, ethical standards declined, and companies adulterated their goods in an effort to maximize profits and stay competitive. Food manufacturers added impurities and chemical preservatives to their products to lower costs and reduce spoilage. Drug manufacturers sold medicines that contained dangerous habit-forming ingredients (product labeling of ingredients was nonexistent) and dishonestly advertised them. Meat packers sold spoiled or diseased meat that had been treated to restore color and preserved with ammonia. Such fraud and deception in the industry underscored the need to protect the interests of consumers in the preparation of food and drugs. Shortly after the turn of the century, reformers would intensify their claim that it was both unhealthy and wrong to add certain preservatives to food, that it was unethical to make unfounded claims for ineffectual drugs, and that it was immoral to add drugs to compounds that might have harmful or addictive consequences for consumers. The Pure Food and Drug Act of 1906 was in many ways a testament to their efforts.

As Americans struggled with the economic transformation of an emerging industrial society, many felt increasingly ignored as participants in the political system. In their minds, policymakers displayed a general unresponsiveness to the needs of workers, farmers, consumers, and taxpayers and an increasing susceptibility to the influence of economic power. Exacerbating these problems was a feeling that the political system was dominated by political parties. There had been an earlier campaign to establish the secret ballot, but maybe party rule could be broken by expanding the power of voters at the polls by allowing them to bypass unresponsive or irresponsible party-dominated legislative bodies and express their will directly. Known as direct democracy or direct legislation, the core reforms were the initiative, referendum, and recall. The initiative would allow a given percentage of voters to propose a law on the ballot subject to voter approval, while the referendum would allow a given percentage of voters to request that a law passed by a lawmaking body be submitted to the voters for approval. The recall would allow a given percentage of voters to demand, by petition and then by voter approval, that a public official be removed from office in a special election. With the initiative and referendum, voters could gain control over the political process and set their own reform agenda. With the recall, they could force officeholders to be more accountable. The process offered the potential of political empowerment as a means for bringing about social change.

Perhaps no group in the country understood the meaning of empowerment more than women. The fight for woman suffrage during the Progressive Era was the culmination of a long struggle to obtain basic political rights. Nineteenth-century suffragists argued that the vote was a natural right denied them and that, to be considered citizens, women must have the same rights as men. A woman's role as mother and wife was secondary. At the same time, many in society had accepted the idea that women should be assigned a separate "sphere" in which, it was argued, they would find fulfillment as mothers, wives, and home managers. Antisuffragists, both men and women, successfully blocked efforts by women to gain the vote for decades. Frustrated by the determined nature of the opposition, suffragists shifted their rights-denied approach to one that was more pragmatic—arguing that female enfranchisement would benefit society as a whole. Women's virtue would help solve society's problems. Led by the National American Woman Suffrage Association (NAWSA), women became better organized and more politically savvy. The movement slowly began to move forward.

One group of women who grew impatient with the slow progress of the suffrage fight and felt restricted by NAWSA's conservative leadership broke away from the national organization in 1916 to form the National Woman's Party. Believing that a more militant approach should be used in the suffrage campaign, this relatively small group of dedicated activists picketed the White House, chained themselves to fences, and blocked public streets. Arrested for obstructing the sidewalk, they staged prison hunger strikes in protest. They also challenged the established political culture in ways that were equally confrontational. They carried banners that held President Woodrow Wilson personally responsible for legislative inaction, refused to defer their campaign while the nation was at war, and burned Wilson's speeches in public bonfires to underscore the hypocrisy of fighting for democracy abroad while denying it at home.

With the ratification of the Nineteenth Amendment, many women felt that their goal had been achieved and retired from further activism. Others did not. A few women regarded securing the vote as a victory but a triumph that stopped short of establishing full equality for women. Their new cause was to lobby for an equal rights amendment to the Constitution to do just that. Angering earlier women reformers who had worked to gain protective labor legislation for women, they argued that the establishment of a special status for women workers actually demeaned them and allowed states to pass laws that discriminated against women. Prior crusades for empowerment and protection had been superceded by a new one that sought to ensure a woman's dignity as a human being. These new feminists wanted to redefine gender in order to equalize power relations in American society. Because society was structured to deny women basic liberties, rights, and responsibilities, women were prohibited from becoming fully human. They envisioned a society in which women no longer confronted legal, economic, and professional disabilities and inequities that relegated them to second-class citizenship.

When reformers called for change in the late nineteenth and early twentieth century, they challenged one or more of the dominant "truths" that held sway over American society. As historian Eric Goldman noted, the ideas that dominated the era "were no deliberate contrivance on the part of evil men. The dominant groups in America had simply done what dominant groups usually do. They had, quite unconsciously, picked from among available theories the ones that best protected their position and had impressed these ideas on the national mind as Truth."[1] These truths functioned as a self-serving prophecy: liberty was equated with the right of an individual to acquire property and keep it without interference by government, the law, or a union; natural laws (devoid of natural rights) governed economics; law rested on the Constitution (a near-sacred document); inbred characteristics (hereditary traits) dictated economic circumstance; the role of the church was to ensure individual salvation; innate gender, ethnic, and racial inferiority naturally created inequalities of power; society was an organism that evolved by a process of natural selection (not a mechanism that people could control and direct by rational action); the role of the state should be minimal (maintain law and order and leave business alone); amorality governed business and politics; selfishness (not fairness) governed the political economy; and human nature dictated that politics would have to be exclusive. In a metaphor that has stood the test of time, Goldman referred to these so-called truths as the "steel chain of [conservative] ideas." Between 1870 and 1920, reformers began to break that chain one link at a time.

NOTE

1. Eric F. Goldman, *Rendezvous with Destiny: A History of Modern American Reform* (New York: Random House, 1977), 85.

1

Lester Frank Ward and Reform Darwinism

Few today have ever heard of Lester Frank Ward, let alone have a sense of his place in late nineteenth-century America or his significance to the topic of American reform. He was, however, one of the most diverse and widely read intellectuals of his day in both the natural and the social sciences. He was a botanist, a geologist, a paleontologist, a social statistician, a linguistics expert (he could read Hebrew, Sanskrit, and Latin as well as modern European languages), a social philosopher, and one of the founders of modern sociology. His importance for this study, however, is as a social philosopher and the first of a number of late nineteenth-century thinkers to challenge the assumptions of social Darwinism and laissez-faire individualism that dominated intellectual discourse in the Gilded Age. In doing so, he was able to posit an expansive social theory that others would adapt to their own reform efforts.

The formation of Ward's social philosophy was, to a great extent, molded by his life experiences. As one biographer noted, the "gulf between the dream and the reality of American experience formed the creative tension within which Ward lived and thought."[1] His life was in many ways a constant struggle to overcome environmental obstacles. His ultimate success enabled him to see himself as the personification of his own democratic social theory. He was born in 1841 as the tenth child of peripatetic parents along America's rapidly expanding Middle Western frontier. His father, Justus Ward, a mechanic, millwright, and wheelwright by trade, migrated from New York to Illinois in the mid-1830s to help build locks on the Illinois and Michigan Canal that was being constructed between Lake Michigan and La Salle, Illinois. Settling in the small canal town of Joliet, Justus contracted to supply stones for canal construction and, later, to build a towpath bridge over the Des Plaines River swamps. But the entrepreneurial-minded father never kept his family in one place for long and variously worked as a sawmill operator and farmer as he moved his family from Joliet to Cass (now Downer's Grove) to St. Charles, Illinois, in search of a better opportunity. Having served briefly in the War of 1812, the elder Ward applied for a land grant as a veteran under a revised land law of 1850 and gained title to a 160-acre tract of land in Buchanan County in eastern Iowa. In true pioneer style, the family made the trip in a covered wagon. Ward later remembered this childhood experience in Iowa as idyllic but intellectually stultifying. The isolation bore the potential of limiting his future prospects:

> Roaming wildly over the boundless prairies of northern Iowa in the fifties, interested in every animal, bird, insect, and flower I saw, but not knowing what science was, scarcely having ever heard of zoology, ornithology, entomology, or botany, without a single book on any of those subjects, and not knowing a person in the world who could give me the slightest information with regard to them, what chance was there of my becoming a naturalist?[2]

The death of Lester's father in 1857, after only two summers in Iowa, forced his mother to move the family back to St. Charles, where there were greater opportunities for an inquisitive teenager.

The return to St. Charles offered Lester the advantages of at least a minimal education. After boarding out during the crop season at local farms where he worked doing odd chores and harvesting wheat and corn, Lester attended grammar school during the winter. He remembered the time as one in which he began to read voraciously—school primers; French, Greek, and Latin readers; newspapers; and popular dime novels. He even began to keep a diary in French to assist him in mastering the language. When an older brother needed help in his small wagon-hub factory in Myersburg, Pennsylvania, seventeen-year-old Lester, excited by the prospects of economic advancement and broader educational opportunities, decided to move east.

The anticipated opportunities waiting in northeastern Pennsylvania, however, proved disappointing. The recession of 1858–1859 closed his brother's shop, and Lester had to take back pay in wagon hubs that he tried to sell or barter for necessities. Lester returned to work as an itinerant agricultural laborer until he was able to find a job as a teacher in a township school in 1860. The position paid only $6 a month with boarding privileges, but the money he earned, along with loans from relatives, enabled him to attend the Susquehanna Collegiate Institute in nearby Towanda, Pennsylvania, for four terms beginning in 1861. During that time, the young Ward poured himself into his studies, fell in love, and made plans to attend Lafayette University in Easton, Pennsylvania, to study law, although he had doubts that he could find a way to obtain the funds to do so. As the nation slipped more deeply into civil war, Ward made a decision that would ultimately change the direction of his life. He decided to volunteer for the Union army and, on August 12, 1862, enlisted in the 141st Regiment of the Pennsylvania Volunteers. The following day, he married his sweetheart, Elizabeth "Lizzie" Vought, and a week later reported for duty.

Ward's service in the army was tragically short lived, but he was able to use the experience to his advantage. At the battle of Chancellorsville, on May 3, 1863, Ward suffered severe wounds when he was shot three times in the legs. After a summer's convalescence in a Union hospital and a brief medical furlough, Ward was transferred to the Veteran's Reserve Corps, whose duties entailed guarding the nation's capital and assisting in the movement of military supplies. The time spent in Washington, D.C., convinced Ward that there were professional opportunities available. After leaving the army on a medical discharge in 1864, Lester and Lizzie settled in Washington. Ward immediately began to press his case for a governmental appointment and, after a great deal of persistence, finally gained a job as a clerk (grade 1) in the Treasury Department examining quartermaster's accounts. In doing so, he began what would be a twenty-five-year career in the Washington bureaucracy.

Ward's new job offered him more than just security and the possibility of advancement. It also provided him time to read, write essays, and satisfy his growing intellectual curiosity. He joined the temperance society, various debate clubs, and the (Woman) Suffrage League. At home, he and Lizzie played the piano, and Ward learned the violin. The couple read the classics to each other and enjoyed going out to listen to speakers and congressional debates. Life was enjoyable, and Ward, with intelligence and a strong Protestant work ethic, moved rapidly up the bureaucratic ladder. In 1872, he gained promotion to librarian (grade 4) in the Bureau of Statistics, a position he would hold for the next ten years.

As Ward advanced professionally, he also formally resumed his education at night, gaining a bachelor of arts degree from Columbian College (now George Washington University) in 1869, a bachelor of laws degree in 1871, and a master of arts degree with an emphasis on science and certification to practice medicine in 1872. The more Ward learned, the more he wanted to learn. He also began to write articles and to sketch out the foundation for a book on education that he intended to call "The Great Panacea." Stealing time from his writing during 1869–1871, Ward joined the National Liberal Reform League, "an ambitious secret society which began with six members and died a few months later with four." The members devoted themselves to "the dissemination of liberal sentiment; the opposition to all forms of superstition; the

exposition of all fallacious moral and religious doctrines, and the establishment of the principles of mental, moral, and religious liberty, as embodied in
the Declaration of Independence."[3] They also encouraged the fellowship of
"Liberals, Skeptics, Infidels, Secularists, Utilitarians, Socialists, Positivists,
Spiritualists, Deists, Theists, Pantheists, Atheists, [and] Freethinkers."[4] In addition, Ward assumed, in January 1870, the editorship of *The Iconoclast*, the
League's journal of opinion. His participation in the League suggests a perception of himself as a freethinker sympathetic to newer trends of thought.
But his brief tenure as an editor goading the public to abandon old and embrace new modes of thinking proved to be disappointing and seems to have
convinced Ward that it was not the best method to effect social change. Perhaps wrongheaded thinking could better be undermined by the dissemination
of knowledge through scholarly writing and teaching rather than direct public exhortation.

Lester Frank Ward's life took a slightly different turn in 1872, when his
wife died suddenly from an attack of appendicitis. To combat his depression,
Ward started taking long walks on the outskirts of the city and began to
collect botanical and zoological specimens. His interest piqued, he began to
intensify his reading in the biological sciences. In 1873, Ward married Rose
Simons Pierce, a widow with interests similar to his own, who helped him
collect and label his growing collection. As a natural progression of his expanding interest in the natural sciences, he joined the Potomac Naturalist
Club. Active membership in the organization brought him into closer contact
with the local scientific community.

One of those whom Ward met at the Naturalist Club was Major John
Wesley Powell, whose explorations of the lower Colorado River in 1869
had made him a national celebrity. Ward and Powell had a good deal in
common—both Illinois natives, Civil War veterans (Powell had lost an arm
at the battle of Shiloh), and ardent naturalists. They soon became close
friends. When Powell won authorization for another expedition to the
Wasatch Mountains of Utah in 1875, he procured a summer transfer for Ward
to serve as botanist on the trip. Ward's job was to collect specimens for a scientific display at the Centennial Exposition in Philadelphia the following
year. Cutbacks in funding for the national surveys, however, prevented Powell from offering Ward permanent employment, but their association enabled
him to become a member of Washington's Biological, Anthropological, and
Philosophical Societies as well as the elite Cosmos Club, which joined members of the various societies socially.

While Ward worked at the Bureau of Statistics, he continued to use his free
time to write. By 1879, he finally had a finished manuscript titled "Dynamic
Sociology" ready for publication. It was an endeavor that had taken him al-

most fifteen years to complete. With Powell's help, Ward eventually found a publisher for his book, but only after the struggling author agreed to pay nearly $2,300 of his own money to cover initial printing costs. Ward's two-volume treatise was finally published in 1883. In *Dynamic Sociology*, Ward outlined a new positivist–humanitarian approach to the study of human society that stressed the importance of human intelligence in allowing man to control his own evolution and argued that progress could be socially engineered to create a planned society directed by a benevolent government. "Intelligence," said Ward, "far more than necessity, is the mother of invention."[5]

Ward's association with John Wesley Powell benefited him again in 1881, when the famous explorer became director of a newly reorganized Geological Survey and immediately offered Ward a position in the new bureau. Ward actually had his choice of two positions—geologist in the Survey or linguist in the Bureau of Ethnology, also headed by Powell. He chose geology with the understanding that he could eventually move into paleobotany, the study of fossilized plants. The field was a new one, and Ward hoped to make a name for himself as a scientist. At age forty, after nearly sixteen years of tedious work at the Bureau of Statistics, Ward now felt like he had found a true vocation. Given free rein to pursue his research, the period from 1881 until political pressure forced Powell to resign as director in 1893–1894 was the happiest of his life. It also enabled him to develop a broad view of scientific research for the public good. Powell's grand vision of mapping the West and suggesting the most rational ways of utilizing the region's natural resources fit nicely with Ward's own developing view of the role of the federal government and scientific expertise in directing natural forces.

Never really able to stem an intellectual curiosity that constantly pulled him in new directions, Ward began to spend more and more of his off-duty time reading social philosophy. As part of this intellectual progression, he joined the new American Economic Association formed by Professor Richard T. Ely of nearby Johns Hopkins University. Ely and other economists had become disenchanted with the so-called Manchester School of laissez-faire economics. In contrast, they pushed for the application of scientific procedures to the study of the political economy and argued that an activist federal government could be used to improve the economy. Ely, a fellow member of the Cosmos Club, introduced Ward to Professor Albion Small of Colby College. Small was a professor of sociology and assigned Ward's *Dynamic Sociology* in his courses. The two soon became friends and encouraged each other in their sociological studies. Sociology was only just becoming a recognized academic subject, but growing social concerns attached to intensified industrialization, urbanization, and immigration made this discipline increasingly popular. When Small, who eventually moved to the University of Chicago to establish a new department of sociology, began to shape the new discipline by creating the *American Journal of Sociology* in 1895, he invited Ward to become an advisory editor.

As Ward's interest in sociology increased, so too did his writing in that area. Sales of *Dynamic Sociology* had been disappointing (only 500 copies in ten years), and he hoped that by writing a new book he could more clearly explain his growing interest in the possibilities of rational social control. The product of his thinking, *Psychic Factors of Civilization*, appeared in 1893. Ward followed this with *Outlines of Sociology* (1898), *Pure Sociology* (1903), and *Applied Sociology* (1906). The general theme in all Ward's books remained unchanged: the potential for human intelligence to direct natural and social forces for the benefit of society.

In formulating his own social and political philosophy, Ward was influenced by the writings of the renowned British social philosopher Herbert Spencer, whose espousal of social or "conservative" Darwinism dominated intellectual discourse during the 1870s and 1880s. Spencer argued that society evolved much like an organism in nature and could be analyzed in terms similar to the biological world as described by Charles Darwin in his pathbreaking study *The Origin of Species* (1859). To Spencer, progress was the result of a process of natural selection or natural competition that weeded out the weak and selected the strong. It was, in popular phraseology, "the survival of the fittest." The result was an evolutionary progression of society/civilization in the general direction of higher forms of structure, refinement, and organization. Change and progress would derive from the natural course of evolution. As man evolved, so too would his nature and his social arrangements, which would become more ethical. Importantly, society would approach its ideal stage as a result of changes in man's nature, not from changes in man's institutions. Because the natural laws that shaped organisms were immutable, man risked interfering with them at his own peril. As a result, governmental interference should be kept to a minimum. "Laissez-faire" should be the government's guiding philosophy.

While Ward found Spencer's evolutionary theories agreeable, he rejected his conclusions. In particular, Ward challenged the applicability of Darwinism to society and contested Spencer's emphasis on the benefits to be derived from unfettered competition and the negative view of the role of government. Ward found "natural" competition to be wasteful and argued that it inhibited the maximum development of a species. In advancing the doctrine that society was governed by fixed and immutable laws and that man was powerless to control his fate, Ward felt that Spencer (and later his American disciple William Graham Sumner) advocated a pessimistic social philosophy that destroyed hope and paralyzed effort. In contrast, Ward argued that the evolution of a society was not identical with that of an organism. Society was, instead, a mechanism, a product of man's ingenuity. Social Darwinists were so mesmerized by the forces of nature that they had overlooked the "psychic" factors that could influence and, ultimately, control natural forces. The mind was, to Ward, a factor in the evolutionary process. As a result, society did not have to be "static" as the social Darwinists perceived it; it could be "dynamic." Man could direct evolution intelligently. "[E]very implement or utensil," said Ward, "every mechanical device, every object of design, skill, and labor, every artificial thing that serves a human purpose, is a triumph of mind over the physical forces of nature in ceaseless and aimless competition."[6]

Man differed from the natural world because of his intelligence, his capacity for rational thought. Ward termed this intellectual potential "telesis." But there were two kinds of telic action: individual and social. The first used intelligence for personal self-gain. The second used rational thought for the good of society. Although man had not yet reached this second stage of development, he had the potential to do so. Rejecting the rigid determinism of Spencer and other social Darwinists and drawing on his firm faith in the potentiality of the human mind, Ward embraced a more optimistic view of man's destiny. Man did not have to conform to the laws of nature. He could direct them and transform society (environment) in the process, and government could be an agency for that direction. Moral progress, for the most part, would result not from a change in man's character but from the improvement in human institutions. After all, man had adopted ethics and morality as the means to suppress his animalistic nature. Man did not live in a jungle.

Ward also took issue with the social Darwinists' views on education. Because they believed that evolution took long periods of time to show results and that the evolutionary process acted independently of human actions, they believed that education was not an important factor in human progress. Teachers could provide information or knowledge that would help individuals adapt to their current environment, but one's environment would have to wait on evolutionary progress to change. Ward disagreed. He adhered to an environmentalist philosophy rooted in an unwavering belief in the value of education. He felt it was important to encourage the infusion of information throughout society and that, by popularizing knowledge, society could improve itself. Education would provide the foundation for progress. In contrast to many privately schooled social Darwinists like Herbert Spencer who felt that state-supported public education would undermine parental freedom and infect the social order with the virus of public welfare, Ward thought education should be open to all. Only through such accessibility would talented but "submerged" individuals be allowed to gain the opportunity to realize cherished democratic ideals. Ward truly believed that everyone was educable. It was the means by which individuals would find satisfaction in self-development, increased comforts, and greater happiness. It was also the way in which the average citizen would become more sympathetic to new ideas and social experimentation and more willing to support intelligent legislation. Society would benefit from an accelerated rate of social progress that would be shared by all. Ward had a firm faith in the perfectibility of human life and society's institutions through intellectual effort and human control of the environment. In the end, improved social conditions could be secured only by the wide dissemination of knowledge through education. To Ward, the ideal citizen was truly an informed one.

Ward's educational theories reflected his own social background and life experience. He wanted others who came from common backgrounds as he did to have the same opportunity for intellectual development and expression that he demanded for himself. Ward possessed a strongly developed sense of class that viewed education as power. Without it, the uneducated were at the mercy of the educationally privileged. The latter possessed power and advantage, while the former were unable to secure the knowledge that could gain them opportunity.

Ward was also forced to contest social Darwinian views regarding the impossibility of promoting social welfare by state action. Social Darwinist William Graham Sumner, for one, argued rather persuasively that the general nature of Gilded Age politics precluded enlightened social policy. To Sumner, politics was a morass of spoils, patronage, lobbying, and corruption. "The activity of the State," said Sumner, "shows itself every year more at the mercy of clamorous factions, and legislators find themselves constantly under greater pressure to act . . . against their judgment of public interests."[7] How could it be otherwise? Officials were either appointed by party leaders as a reward for dutiful partisan service or elected by ill-informed voters and then thrust into a political culture actuated by the drive for power, compromised by political bargaining, and manipulated by special interests. Furthermore, the complexity of society required that the architects of programs designed to promote social welfare possess exceptional wisdom and insight combined with an unwavering resolve to serve the general good. To Sumner, such individuals did not exist.

While Ward was certainly aware of the weaknesses of federal *legislation* during the scandal-ridden Gilded Age, he still trusted government and believed that there were men (like himself) of talent, intelligence, and benevolence within the federal bureaucracy to plan for the *administration* of programs (like public education) that would fairly and responsibly advance social welfare. On the basis of his belief in the capacity of the human mind, Ward countered the social Darwinists by constructing a theory of positive action that explained the proper role of the government in an increasingly scientific age. The view would still be evolutionary (that is, Darwinian), but the outlook would be that of a "reform" Darwinist. Whereas William Graham Sumner had argued that it was "folly" for man to try to plan out a new social world, Ward felt it would be just as foolish not to plan. But how would this be done?

The most important function that the government could provide, beyond the protection of its people, was the improvement of social conditions, and Ward firmly believed that a strong central government could plan for the economic well-being of society. Central to this would be an expanded governmental bureaucracy that would be refined to increase its reliance on experts, technocrats, and statisticians. Because the key to good government was knowledge and understanding the working of society was a key component of that knowledge, Ward favored the establishment of a national academy of the social sciences that would train public administrators and study social problems. Sufficiently educated and professionally trained, this new bureaucracy would begin to design scientifically formulated legislation to respond to basic social and economic problems. As Ward envisioned it,

> Legislation will consist in a series of exhaustive experiments on the part of true scientific sociologists and sociological inventors working on the problems of social physics from the practical point of view. It will undertake to solve not only questions of general interest to the State, . . . but questions of social improvement, the amelioration of the condition of all the people, the removal of whatever privations may still remain, and the adoption of means to the positive increase of the social welfare, in short the organization of human happiness.[8]

To Ward, the list of possibilities was limitless. Food and drugs could be subjected to quality controls, diseases investigated to discover causes and suggest cures, disaster relief programs formulated, and transportation, communication, insurance, banking, and public utilities regulated. Social welfare legislation would protect the weak, and regulatory statutes would restrain the strong. Used intelligently, government would function as a form of social engineering that could, in theory, serve as an agency of social progress in eliminating poverty and economic insecurity. As the administrative branch of government perfected the application of science to government, legislators would also increasingly see themselves as professional bureaucrats did: as public servants working for the good of society.

A government that promoted the general welfare of its citizenry by positive action Ward called a "sociocracy." This view, according to Ward, stood in stark contrast to the type of government advocated by Adam Smith, Herbert Spencer, William Graham Sumner, and others who believed that the primary function of government is to maintain the natural liberty of "individuals." As they saw it, industry and commerce should be immune from governmental interference. State intervention would disrupt natural laws, infringe on individual rights, inhibit free competition, and compromise the most efficient system (free-market capitalism) yet developed for the production and distribution of wealth. Ward termed this type of laissez-faire government a "physiocracy" and likened its proponents to advocates of a doctrine of despair and inaction. Equally damaging to the public interest were the members of an economic elite who exploited the economic system (and the legislative system) for their own selfish interests. To Ward, this "plutocracy" thrived on weak government and, whenever possible, tried to influence public opinion to fear strong government. The result was luxury and power for the few and misery and drudgery for the many. In a sociocracy, Ward was certain, economic planning by trained experts would create greater efficiency. Poverty and the social conflict it generated would be eliminated. With the state viewed as a positive agency for the public welfare, a desire for public service would be instilled. Under Ward's educational system, positions in the new bureaucracy would go to individuals from all socioeconomic backgrounds. In the end, as Ward had learned from his days as editor of *The Iconoclast*, progressive advances came about when popular attitudes and ideas changed. That type of fundamental change required education and proven practical demonstration.

In 1906, at the age of sixty-five, Ward accepted his first full-time academic teaching position at Brown University. That same year, he became president of the American Sociological Society. But the lasting satisfaction that might have been realized at an earlier point in his life was never really fulfilled. During his first year in Providence, his wife's health failed. A paralyzing stroke two years later placed her under the permanent care of her sister living in Washington, D.C. To economize on his $2,000-a-year salary, Ward moved into one of the student rooming houses. Lonely and increasingly introspective, he turned to the idea of completing a "mental biography." This work, his last, was to be a collection of all his published articles, lesser writings, and autobiographical information that might allow readers to better understand the development of his thought. Envisioned as a twelve-volume collection to be titled *Glimpses of the Cosmos*, the full study was never completed. Vacationing in Washington, D.C., in the spring of 1913 and struggling with his own health, Ward suffered a heart attack and died. His death came the day after the first volume of his final treatise appeared in print. The remaining volumes in the series (reduced from twelve to six in number) appeared posthumously.

Ward's contributions to the furtherance of American reform during the 1870–1920 period are significant on several levels. Although his treatise *Dy-*

namic Sociology was not widely read, Ward did reach a larger public with a series of magazine articles written in the late 1880s, and his influence on the new
generation of social scientists who were gaining a voice during the 1890s was
considerable. After all, his interest in the promotion of social progress, his advocacy of the application of scientific techniques to the study of social problems,
and his theory of the state as a positive agency for the development of the public welfare were the ideas that were becoming the new basis of intellectual discussion. As a social planner, Ward's emphasis on the positive role of government
placed him ahead of his time as an advocate of governmental paternalism. His
vision of a working alliance between trained experts and politicians suggested
both the "Wisconsin Idea" of Governor Bob La Follette (that emphasized the
theme of government in the public interest and relied heavily on university faculty such as Richard T. Ely and Frederick Jackson Turner to design and admin-
ister reform laws) and the "Brain Trust" behind President Franklin Roosevelt's
New Deal and, ultimately, the creation of the early welfare state.

Ward was not, however, without his blind spots. His view of human nature
was naively positive. He had an exaggerated faith in the good intentions of
individuals in general to conduct affairs unselfishly, broad-mindedly, and intelligently and in the ability of planners to perfect social institutions scientifically. He also placed too much emphasis on the importance of education as
a socioeconomic cure-all.

Despite Ward's intellectual naïveté, his progressive assumptions and boldly
stated reform rationale served to inspire those who were gaining their own expansive sense of economic, social, and political possibilities and a belief that
government should use its power for reform. In directly and forcefully confronting social Darwinism and laissez-faire individualism, Ward helped to
redirect intellectual discourse during the last half of the nineteenth century. In
challenging the dominant value system of conservative thinkers and the rigid
orthodoxy of modern natural science, Ward encouraged individuals to question economic "realities" and scientific "truths" and to dispute the increasingly pessimistic view of opportunity.

NOTES

1. Clifford H. Scott, *Lester Frank Ward* (Boston: Twayne Publishers, 1976), 167.

2. Ralph Henry Gabriel, *The Course of American Democratic Thought* (Westport, Conn.: Greenwood Press, 1986), 215.

3. Gabriel, *The Course of American Democratic Thought*, 216.

4. Page Smith, *The Rise of Industrial America: A People's History of the Post-Reconstruction Era* (New York: Penguin Books, 1990), 919.

5. Gabriel, *The Course of American Democratic Thought*, 219.

6. John A. Garraty, *The New Commonwealth, 1877–1890* (New York: Harper and Row, 1968), 329.

7. Robert Green McCloskey, *American Conservatism in the Age of Enterprise, 1865–1910* (New York: Harper and Row, 1951), 59–60.

8. Gabriel, *The Course of American Democratic Thought*, 220.

SOURCES

Cohn, Jules. "The Political Philosophy of Lester Frank Ward." Ph.D. diss., Rutgers University, 1953.

Commager, Henry Steele. *The American Mind: An Interpretation of American Thought and Character since the 1880s*. New Haven, Conn.: Yale University Press, 1950.

———, ed. *Lester Ward and the Welfare State*. Indianapolis: Bobbs-Merrill, 1967.

Gabriel, Ralph Henry. *The Course of American Democratic Thought*. Westport, Conn.: Greenwood Press, 1986.

Garraty, John A. *The New Commonwealth, 1877–1890*. New York: Harper and Row, 1968.

Goldman, Eric F. *Rendezvous with Destiny: A History of Modern American Reform*. New York: Random House, 1977.

Hofstadter, Richard. *Social Darwinism in American Thought*. Boston: Beacon Press, 1955.

Kimball, Elsa Peverly. *Sociology and Education: An Analysis of the Theories of Spencer and Ward*. New York: AMS Press, 1932.

Nelson, Alvin F. *The Development of Lester Ward's World View*. Fort Worth, Tex.: Branch-Smith, 1968.

Scott, Clifford. *Lester Frank Ward*. Boston: Twayne Publishers, 1976.

Smith, Page. *The Rise of Industrial America: A People's History of the Post-Reconstruction Era*. New York: Penguin Books, 1990.

Ward, Lester Frank. *Dynamic Sociology*. New York: Johnson Reprint Corp., 1968.

2

Henry George's Democratic Economics

In the opening lines of *Progress and Poverty* (1879), one of the most influential books of the late nineteenth century, Henry George described the great problem facing modern society: the paradox of advancing wealth and intensifying poverty. "The present century has been marked," he said, "by a prodigious increase in wealth-producing power." To George, it was not unnatural to suppose that this new power "would make real poverty a thing of the past." But things did not work out as expected. "Disappointment has followed disappointment. . . . We plow new fields, we found new cities; we girdle the land with iron roads and lace the air with telegraph wires; we add knowledge to knowledge, and utilize invention after invention . . . yet it becomes no easier for the masses of our people to make a living. On the contrary, it is becoming harder. . . . The gulf between the employed and the employer is growing wider; social contrasts are becoming sharper; as liveried carriages appear, so do barefooted children."[1] The scourge of modern civilization, George truly believed, was the unequal distribution of wealth. The solution to that dilemma was the point of George's famous treatise and the promotion of social progress his life's work. Like his contemporary, Lester Frank Ward, George applied science (economics) to the study of social problems and in doing so challenged the pessimistic views of the classical economists. He also developed a reform Darwinian view of the state as a positive agency for advancing public welfare and broadening economic opportunities. And, like Ward, he envisioned a society of human fulfillment.

Henry George was born in Philadelphia in 1839, the second of ten children of Richard and Catherine Pratt George. His paternal grandfather had been a sea captain, while his father worked as a clerk in the Philadelphia Customs

Henry George, circa 1897. Library of Congress, Prints & Photographs Division.

House. When the Second Great Awakening began to spread its influence, Richard George quit his job to open a small printing office and bookshop that distributed texts for the Protestant Episcopal Church. He continued in this business during Henry's formative years until difficult economic times in the late 1850s forced him to resume his position at the customs house. Raised in a devout Episcopalian family, young Henry quickly became familiar with the Bible, the Book of Common Prayer, and various Episcopal Sunday school readers. Even though Henry had his rebellious moments as a youth, he never abandoned his staunch Protestant sensibilities. Despite the family's lower-middle-class economic status, Henry's parents strove to give their oldest son a proper Christian education. Disappointing for them, Henry never seemed at ease or intellectually satisfied in any formal educational environment. After three years at a private school, a year in public school, a short stint at the prestigious Episcopal Academy, two more years of private tutorials, and five months at a public high school, Henry George quit school, his formal education over at the age of thirteen.

For the next several years, Henry struggled to find some direction in his life. Jobs as a stock boy with a china and glass importing firm at two dollars a week and then as a handyman in a marine insurance adjuster's office near the Philadelphia waterfront seemed to offer very little. Although Henry had left school for good, he continued on a course of self-education by reading in the library of the Franklin Institute, where he also attended occasional lectures, and borrowing books from the Apprentice's Library. It was the job near the waterfront, however, that seemed to connect Henry to the sea and remind him of the stories his father had told him about his grandfather's seagoing exploits. Intrigued by the opportunity for adventure—and certainly in search of himself—he decided, at the age of sixteen, to sign on as a cabin boy aboard the *Hindoo*, captained by a friend of his father's. Carrying a Bible and a copy of *James' Anxious Enquirer*, Henry George set out for New York to join the crew of a merchant ship bound for Melbourne and Calcutta.

Henry's voyage to the antipodes served to broaden his perspective of the world and reinforce his independence, even if it did not persuade him that a life on the sea was his calling. Ironically, it was George's first adventure under sail that forced him to begin to write. Keeping a journal for the entire fourteen months spent at sea, the young cabin boy vividly recorded the events and impressions that affected him most: an unsuccessful sailor's strike over conditions and treatment during the voyage, severe unemployment in Melbourne, and poverty, starvation, and official indifference to human suffering in Calcutta. When the ship returned to New York in June 1857, George had back pay in his pocket but once again faced the dilemma of earning a livelihood. After six months without work, Henry's father found him a job in a printing house. Work as a typesetter's apprentice provided him with a valuable, marketable skill; served to improve his spelling and punctuation; and further broadened his education as he absorbed the information being set in type and engaged in discussions with others in the print shop. But nine months later, after a quarrel with his shop foreman, he was again out of work. With the local and national economy suffering through the Panic of 1857,

George found his prospects bleak. As he related in correspondence with a friend, "The times here are very hard and are getting worse and worse every day, factory after factory suspending and discharging its hands. There are thousands of hard-working mechanics now out of employment in this city."[2] After hearing from family friends who had moved to Oregon that opportunities were more plentiful on the West Coast, George decided to follow his acquisitive inclination. Signing on as a ship's steward aboard the steamer *Shubrick* bound for San Francisco, George imagined the golden opportunities that awaited him.

In May 1858, after a voyage of five months, George entered the open, semideveloped, frontier environment that characterized California only ten years after the Gold Rush. It seemed ideally suited for a young man determined to "get ahead." Rumors of a gold strike on the Frazer River in British Columbia, however, captured his imagination on arrival in San Francisco and allowed him to defer any difficult career decisions as he rushed north with thousands of other would-be gold seekers determined to strike it rich. When floods interrupted mining operations in the gold fields, George took a job in a cousin's mining supply store where he worked long hours outfitting other treasure seekers before trying his own luck. But after several months of fruitless digging and tent life in a mining camp, George returned to San Francisco penniless.

During the next two years, George eked out a living. An assortment of odd jobs that included typesetting and, for a while, a stint as a weigher in a rice mill led to nothing permanent. In between jobs, he set out once again for the gold fields in California but never even made it to his destination. After six months spent tramping the countryside, sleeping in barns, and doing odd jobs for subsistence, he again returned to San Francisco a dejected young dreamer. Fortunately, his experience as a typesetter landed him a job working for the *California Home Journal*. He was soon earning enough money to live at the What Cheer House, a respectable hotel with a rather good library where he could read freely and widely. In the spring of 1861, George abandoned the *Journal* and invested his entire savings of $100 in a partnership with five other printers to purchase the San Francisco *Daily Evening Journal*. The venture, however, collapsed by the early fall of that year, a victim of competition from other newspapers that subscribed to the new Associated Press wire service. In a revealing letter to his sister just after his twenty-second birthday, George verbalized his personal anguish during a moment of self-doubt. "How I long for the Golden Age—for the promised Millennium, when each one will be free to follow his best and noblest impulses, unfettered by the restrictions and necessities which our present state of society imposes upon him—when the poorest and the meanest will have a chance to use all his God-given faculties, and not be forced to drudge away the best part of his time in order to supply wants but little above those of the animal."[3] George's often-referred-to "millennial" letter went beyond mere poignant introspection and actually suggested, at an early age, a vision of his ideal world.

Jobless, in debt, and struggling to maintain his spirit, George entered into an impetuous courtship with Annie Fox, the eighteen-year-old daughter and orphan of John Fox, a former major in the British army. When Annie's uncle-guardian concluded that a shabbily dressed, unemployed printer was a poor match for his niece and refused to give his approval for courtship, the couple eloped in December 1861. In a story he often told, George remembered that on the night he proposed, he took a single coin from his pocket and solemnly declared, "Annie, that is all the money I have in the world. Will you marry me?"[4] George was so poor that he had to borrow clothes for the wedding ceremony. After the wedding, Henry worked as a substitute typesetter until he found regular employment at a newspaper in Sacramento. But soon after he had managed to set a little money aside, he lost everything speculating in mining stock. Making matters worse, an argument with his foreman again cost Henry his job and forced the couple to move back to San Francisco, where they hoped to weather the difficult economic times that plagued California during the Civil War years. While Annie pawned her few pieces of jewelry and did needlework to supplement the family income, Henry engaged in a series of part-time jobs that included selling newspaper subscriptions and peddling clothes wringers. When even this sporadic work ran out, Henry was forced to print advertising cards that he swapped for food. Finally, in the spring of 1865, with his family starving and his second child about to be born, Henry George hit bottom. Frantic for money to feed his family and haunted by the possibility that he might not be able to procure it, he decided to stop the first man on the street whose appearance suggested he might have money to give. When a likely prospect happened by, Henry explained his circumstances and begged for five dollars. The stranger, apparently moved by the story, gave him the money. "If he had not," George later recalled, "I think I was desperate enough to have killed him."[5]

Interestingly, as George sank deeper into the abyss, he articulated his despair in language reminiscent of Horatio Alger. Internalizing rather than externalizing the reasons for his failure in life, George blamed himself for lacking the personal qualities (character) necessary for success and began recording notes in his diary that suggest he had consciously dedicated himself to self-improvement. An entry for December 25, 1864, reads, "cultivate habits of determination, energy and industry . . . must use my utmost effort to keep afloat and go ahead."[6] In February 1865 he notes, "I have been unsuccessful in everything. I wish to profit by my experience and . . . cultivate those qualities necessary to success in which I have been lacking."[7] Then again, in March 1865, "[c]oncluded that the best thing I could do would be to go home and write a little. Came home and wrote for the sake of practice an essay on the 'Use of Time.'"[8] In that essay, he vowed that he would seek to better discipline his mind through writing. "I will endeavour to acquire facility and elegance in the expression of my thought by writing essays. . . . [I]n this practice it will be well to aim at mechanical neatness and grace, as well as at proper and polished language."[9] He soon began submitting freelance articles to local journals and newspapers. His big break came after submitting a lengthy eulogy for Abraham Lincoln to the *Alta Californian* the day after the president's assassination. The publication led to a job offer as a reporter. Without perhaps realizing it at the time, George was about to begin a career as an impassioned writer and seminal thinker.

For the next eighteen months, George continued his freelance work as an essayist. Writing under the pen name "proletarian," he increasingly turned his attention to labor questions. In November 1866, he joined the staff of the *San Francisco Times* and in less than a year worked his way up to managing editor. Editorial work deepened his interest in the political economy, and his columns began to reflect a concern that speculation in land was undermining opportunity and that a continued erosion of the public domain would eventually curtail the pursuit of happiness. After leaving the *Times* in August 1868, George further refined his thinking on the speculative aspects of landownership and focused his attention on the railroad and its role as a land monopolist. He soon published his first major article, "What the Railroad Will Bring Us," a 7,000-word essay that appeared in the *Overland Monthly*'s October issue. In summarizing his economic views and boldly challenging conventional economic thinking, George argued that "the completion of the transcontinental railroad and consequent great increase of business and population [in California] will not be a benefit to all of us, but only to a portion. As a general rule . . . those who have, it will make wealthier; for those who have not, it will make it more difficult to get." The "haves" in this reference were the owners of lands, mines, and established businesses, while the "have-nots" were the workers who possessed only their own labor. Simply put, progress exacted a high human cost: an increase in poverty. As the growth in population drove up land values and as competition for jobs reduced wages, labor would be at a disadvantage. Reduced earning power and rising land prices would make it more difficult to own land or go into business. Indicating that his own economic thinking was beginning to coalesce, George offered a cautionary note regarding "progress." "[A]s California becomes prosperous and rich;" he warned, "let us not forget that the character of a people counts more than their numbers; that the distribution of wealth is even a more important matter than its production." The question of how to enjoy progress without intensifying poverty would control George's thinking for the next ten years.[10]

In December 1868, John Nugent, the owner of the recently reestablished *San Francisco Herald*, asked George to become his business agent. The *Herald* was one of several struggling California newspapers that had not been admitted to the California Press Association. The association controlled access to the Associated Press news service and its national news wire and essentially determined whether a newspaper could stay in business. George's role as Nugent's representative was to travel to New York City to obtain membership in the Associated Press. Failing that, George was instructed to organize an independent news service as a way to circumvent the Associated Press monopoly. When the Associated Press rejected his request, George arranged through a friend at the *Harrisburg (Pa.) Patriot and Union* to access that newspaper's Associated Press dispatches as soon as they were received. Then, through a fee arrangement with Western Union (another communications monopoly), he had those news dispatches immediately sent on to the *Herald* offices in San Francisco. However, when the Associated Press learned of the arrangement and pressured Western Union to terminate it, he was defeated. To George, freedom of the press and the right of everyone to access public information (news), as well as the opportunity for small businesses to compete, had been egregiously denied. He had learned a lesson about the power of monopoly and its antidemocratic consequences.

George's connection with the *San Francisco Herald* was short lived, but his acquaintance with Democratic Governor Henry H. Haight helped him obtain a position as editor of the *Oakland Daily Transcript* in September 1869. There, he quickly resumed his outspoken attacks on monopolies in land and transportation. The following spring, Governor Haight, looking to generate support for legislation that would limit the power of the Central Pacific Railroad and hoping to channel popular resentment against the railroad trust to support his bid for reelection, asked George to assume the editorship of the party's flagship newspaper, the *Sacramento Reporter*. Now the party's point man on the antimonopoly issue, George began to attack the government's railroad subsidy policy that showered land grants, bonds, and money on the major railroad corporations. In response to that policy, George advocated the end of all federal and state subsidies, especially to the granting of public lands. He also moved closer to the conclusion that public transportation and public communication should not be left in private hands but regulated by the government for the public good. Looking to silence its severest critic and mute the political aspirations of Governor Haight, the Central Pacific arranged for a third party to purchase the *Reporter* and refashion its editorial policy in support of the railroad. Henry George was once again out of a job.

During his time at the *Reporter*, George wrote "Our Land and Land Policy," a forty-eight-page pamphlet that included a map showing the extent of railroad land grants in California. More important as a refinement of his economic thinking than as a political tract to aid the Democratic Party in that year's state campaign, it included the major outlines of the argument he would later make in *Progress and Poverty*. The central concern confronting civilization was the problem of the proper distribution of wealth. Because state and federal governments had recklessly given away public lands, they had allowed natural resources to be exploited and landownership to be concentrated in the hands of corporate land monopolists and greedy speculators. As a result, those interests had reaped the lion's share of the benefits of economic progress. A remedy, however, was still possible. If the land held by such monopolizers was heavily taxed, the benefits of progress could be channeled to the many instead of the few. What George had in mind was a tax on the *value* of land itself, not on any improvements that had been made to it. Simply put, the holder of land would have to pay the same tax as the user of land. If that could be done, he argued, land monopolization and land speculation would no longer pay. "Millions and millions of acres from which settlers are now shut out," George reasoned, "would be abandoned by their present owners, or sold to settlers on nominal terms."[11] Important as the pamphlet was intellectually in advancing George's "land thesis," it received little attention and sold poorly. Nevertheless, George learned a valuable lesson from the effort. For the public to take note, his economic theory would have to be explained more thoroughly.

In need of a livelihood as he continued to formulate his grand theory, George again invested his meager capital in another newspaper partnership with two friends and launched the *San Francisco Daily Evening Post*. For the next four years, the *Post* provided George, as editor, with a forum for his views on national issues. With a reform vision, a strong attachment to the state Democratic Party, and a working-class bias, the *Post* supported liberal campaigns against wide-open gambling, crime, corruption, and the ill treatment of seamen. As the nation sank deeper into the depression of the 1870s, George missed no opportunity to talk about the widening gap in the distribution of wealth and his proposed solution. In a characteristic editorial titled "A Problem for the Working Man" written in April 1874, George restated his now well-known position: "Why is it, then," he questioned, "as population increases, and wealth increases, that the largest class of the community not only do not get any of the benefit, but become actually poorer?" The explanation, as he had suggested many times before, resided in the fact that as "population increases, land, and hardly anything else but land, becomes valuable" and landownership "levies its tax upon all the productive classes." The remedy, argued George, was self-evident. "To make land-owners bear the common burden—tax land and exempt everything else." Unfortunately for George, the economic depression that intensified his critique of the political economy soon claimed him as a victim as well. Unable to pay their debts, the partners relinquished the operation of the newspaper to their creditors in 1875 without any compensation. Out of work once again and with a growing family to support, George used his connections to the Democratic Party and his influence with Governor William S. Irwin, whom the *Post* had supported, to gain a political appointment as state inspector of gas meters. A patronage position requiring little work, the sinecure provided George with a modest but steady income and the time he desperately needed for writing.[12]

As George prepared to write his major treatise, economic depression evolved into industrial crisis. When railroad workers could no longer tolerate wage cuts, layoffs, and increased workloads, they struck. During the summer, the Great Railroad Strike of 1877 proved by the number of its participants, the scope of confrontation, and the intensity of its violence that the paradox of misery amidst abundance had reached a breaking point. Events in California mirrored the rest of the nation. Hard times, drought, declining industrial production, wage cuts, layoffs, and nativistic resentment against Chinese laborers for accepting substandard wages and undermining unionism caused workers to hold protest meetings, threaten violence, and eventually organize their own Workingmen's Party under the leadership of the demagogic Dennis Kearney. In the midst of this upheaval (September 1877), George began to write *Progress and Poverty: An Inquiry into the Cause of Industrial Depressions and of Increase of Want with Increase of Wealth . . . the Remedy.*

Work on the book proceeded slowly. George's style of composition remained casual despite the current national turmoil. Smoking his cigar, he would lie on his couch watching the plumes of smoke waft upward until he grasped an idea. He would then bolt up, rush to his desk, write vigorously for an hour or so, and then return to the couch and await further inspiration. A meticulous wordsmith, George would often polish each piece of his argument before progressing to the next stage. As the income from reading gas meters dwindled to a trickle and debts again began to mount, George would often put the manuscript aside to lecture for a fee. When friends encouraged him to form the Land Reform League of California as a vehicle to spread his ideas, George acquiesced, motivated primarily by the potential monetary rewards that a lecture series arranged by the League might bring. However, when his first lecture, "Why Work Is Scarce, Wages Low and Labour Restless," barely turned up enough listeners to pay for the costs of the hall, he abandoned the hope of collecting riches from the podium.

As George became absorbed with his writing, he increasingly began to see himself as a teacher motivated by something akin to divine inspiration, a mediator among contending economic classes, a messiah who might guide a troubled society toward a more blissful Eden. Spurred by that feeling, George agreed to give an instructive talk to the Young Men's Hebrew Association of California on the topic of Moses. George envisioned Moses in heroic terms as the prophet who had led his people on a pilgrimage from a land of oppression to a land of abundance. Moses had recognized the evils of private property and understood the community's claim to land. "Everywhere in the Mosaic institutions," said George, "the land [is] treated as the gift of the Creator to His common creatures, which no one had the right to monopolise. Everywhere it is, not your estate, or your property, not the land which you bought, or the land which you conquered, but 'the land which the Lord thy God giveth thee'—'the land which the Lord lendeth thee.'" As George interpreted scripture, Moses realized that what had enslaved the masses of Egypt had produced enslavement everywhere. The problem resulted when one class in society gained possession of the land from which all people must live. In George's mind, Moses understood that "to permit in land the same unqualified private ownership that by natural right attaches to the things produced by labour, would be inevitably to separate the people into the very rich and the very poor, inevitably to enslave labour—to make the few the masters of the many, no matter what the political forms; to bring vice and degradation, no matter what the religion." To George, the aim of the Mosaic code was not the protection of property but the protection of humanity. "Its sanctions," he said, "are not directed to securing the strong in heaping up wealth so much as to preventing the weak from being crowded to the wall." This talk on Moses, given while George was earnestly at work on his great book, foreshadowed the spirit of *Progress and Poverty*—a blend of Protestant Christianity, Jefferson's philosophy of natural rights, and the desire to humanize and democratize the political economy.[13]

With *Progress and Poverty*, George brought the various strands of his thinking together in a unified treatise. In doing so, he again challenged the prevailing classical economic explanations for the causes of poverty (especially the wages-fund theory of employment and the Malthusian theory of population growth) and boldly suggested an alternative interpretation. The cause of the want and suffering that prevailed among the working classes; the recurring, often violent dislocations caused by industrial depression; the scarcity of employment; and the persistent, downward tendency of wages that manifested themselves more strongly with each passing year could be traced to the fact that land had become monopolized by a relative few. To George, such ownership denied a basic natural right—the right of the people to use the land. "The laws of nature," he argued in true Jeffersonian style, "are the decrees of the Creator. There is written in them no recognition of any right save that of labor; and in them is written broadly and clearly the equal right of all men to the use and enjoyment of nature; to apply to her by their exertions, and to receive and possess her reward." Because George believed that nature recognized only the claim of labor, it was only natural to advance his own version of the labor theory of value and argue that no one was entitled to own anything that was not the product of his labor. To do so was both wrong and unfair. No one should be allowed to appropriate unto himself the means by which his fellow men must live. But when confronted with the logic that property should therefore be confiscated and redistributed to restore this right, George qualified his intention:

> I do not propose either to purchase or confiscate private property in land. The first would be unjust; the second, needless. Let the individuals who now hold it still retain . . . possession of what they are pleased to call *their* land. . . . Let them buy and sell, and bequeath and devise it. We may safely leave them the shell, if we take the kernel. *It is not necessary to confiscate land; it is only necessary to confiscate rent.*

By "rent," George meant the increase in the value of land that occurred as settlement increased. Because speculators held vacant land off the market until the settlements that grew up around it increased its value, they were gaining a reward to which they were not entitled. As George saw it, "rent" had been stolen from the community, and it would have to be returned for the common good.[14]

George believed that landownership and economic opportunity were linked and that the way to create opportunity was to make land available. Because speculators had prevented this by holding land idle while they waited for community development to increase its value, they would have to be penalized. If the federal government levied a prohibitive tax on the increased value (what George called the "unearned increment") of all monopolized, unimproved land, no one could afford to keep land solely for speculation. The ownership of land would stay the same, but those who speculated would be left with the options of paying the tax, selling the land, or developing it. As collection of this "single tax" would be more than sufficient to meet all the expenses of government, all other taxes could be abolished.

George envisioned that his great panacea, the single tax, would have a liberating effect on society as a whole. The elimination of the monopoly in land would create new economic opportunities. Workers could buy land and become farmers, demand for labor would increase, unemployment would end, and wages would rise. The elimination of the current burden of taxation would energize capital investment (some workers could start their own businesses and workshops) and lead to an increase in the production of wealth. If the community appropriated "rent" via taxation, wealth would naturally be redistributed and equality promoted. "Give labor a free field and its full earnings," said George, "take for the benefit of the whole community that fund which the growth of the community creates, and want and fear of want would be gone." Free of the worry of finding employment and released from the preoccupation of obtaining basic necessities, man could enjoy increased comfort, leisure, and independence. He could improve himself intellectually and culturally. George also believed that the liberating effect of the single tax would lead to the ennoblement of society. "The wrong that produces inequality," he argued, "the wrong that in the midst of abundance tortures men with want or harries them with the fear of want; that stunts them physically, degrades them intellectually, and distorts them morally, is what alone prevents harmonious social development." In his mind, man was made for cooperation. Given the opportunity, man would express a new social intelligence and replace selfishness with humanism. He would become a new citizen.[15]

That new consciousness would emerge as part of a larger structural transformation. The adoption of the single tax and the elimination of all other taxes would allow for the streamlining of government and the elimination of unneeded bureaucracy. The simplification of existing governmental operations would allow for new initiatives. The government could run the telegraph and mail systems and build and operate the railroads. Revenue derived from the single tax would also allow for increased spending for the public benefit in the form of public baths, museums, libraries, gardens, lecture halls, music and dancing auditoriums, playgrounds, and gymnasiums. Municipal utilities such as heating, lighting, and transportation could be publicly operated. Scientific investigations could increase with government support. Once opportunity was restored for all citizens, the possibilities were limitless.

When George finished *Progress and Poverty* in the spring of 1879, he knew he had written an important book. The work had taken hold of him emotionally. "[W]hen I had finished the last page in the dead of night," he later recalled, "I flung myself on my knees and wept like a child. The rest was in the Master's hands."[16] He admitted the book had affected him psychologically and likened the writing process to that of a religious conversion experience. In his own way, George was expressing what readers would soon discover for themselves. *Progress and Poverty* was more than a study of the political economy; it was a powerful emotional plea for Christian thinking and action written by a Protestant reformer. The book's appeal and popularity would derive as much from its religious spirit as it would from its economic panacea. Readers steeped in the evangelical Protestant Christian tradition of the nineteenth century, as George himself was, would find his impassioned call to improve the human condition and uplift civilization as appealing as the hope that economic opportunity could be restored with magical simplicity.

Buoyed by the anticipation of positive reviews of his book (like Lester Frank Ward, George had to supply printing plates for the book before a publisher would agree to assume the cost of printing it), George moved to New York City to see how he could best spread his gospel. When Michael Davitt, the organizational leader of the Irish Land League, urged him to adapt his land reform ideas to address current problems in Ireland (landless Catholic tenants were being forced off the land by a few wealthy Protestant landowners), George was amenable. The result, a 100-page pamphlet, *The Irish Land Question*, wedded him to the cause of Irish nationalism and economic reform. In September 1881, George accepted an offer to travel to Ireland as a correspondent for the *Irish World*, a radical New York newspaper that advocated nationalizing land in both Ireland and the United States. When George returned home a year later, he found that he had become something of a celebrity.

In 1883 after publishing *Social Problems*, a collection of new articles, and making two more lecture tours in Great Britain in that year and the next, George was approached by the Central Labor Union (CLU) of New York and asked to run for mayor of New York City as an independent candidate on a labor ticket. The publication of *Progress and Poverty*, his writings on the Irish land question, and public knowledge that he had recently joined the Knights of Labor, an organization that advocated equal rights to the land as part of its platform, had led workers to identify George as an ally of the labor movement in this country. When the CLU produced a petition bearing 34,000 signatures as proof of his popular support among the working classes in the city, George abandoned his initial reluctance for the opportunity to explain his ideas on land reform before an attentive populace. "[T]he campaign will bring the land question into practical politics," George told a friend, "and will do more to popularize its discussion than years of writing would do."[17] After middle-class reformers nominated George as well, he incorporated both groups of supporters under the banner of the United Labor Party (ULP).

Enthusiastically entering the fray, George spoke up to a dozen times a day to predominantly working-class audiences in which he stressed his own program for economic equality based on the single tax on land values. Facing the dilemma of a legitimate political challenger and looking for a way to diminish that threat, the city's Democratic machine tried to capitalize on the popular revulsion to anarchism only five months after the Haymarket bombing by denouncing George as a fomenter of class hatreds, a destroyer of property, and an instigator of mob rule. In the end, amidst cries of voting fraud, George lost to Democrat Abram S. Hewitt by over 22,000 votes, although he bested by nearly 8,000 votes the youthful, aristocratic Republican candidate, Theodore Roosevelt, who came in third. The impact of this colorful example of Gilded Age politics on Henry George's career is debatable. But the event registered an importance beyond its impact on George personally. Years later, American Federation of Labor leader Samuel Gompers insightfully recalled the moment's significance in broader terms. "The campaign was notable," said Gompers, "in that . . . it proved a sort of vestibule school for many who later undertook practical work for human betterment. Many leaders in the constructive work of the following years were recruits of the Henry George campaign."[18] As a statement of protest against existing economic conditions, the failed campaign of 1886 was actually more of a beginning than an end. The ideas of Henry George, through word and action, were starting to serve as a touchstone for a growing body of incipient reformers.

The final years of his life, however, must have unfolded as somewhat of a disappointment to George. Any hopes that the ULP would continue to strengthen as a political force ended during the New York state campaign in 1887. When socialists tried to push George and the ULP leftward to advocate the abolition of all private property in the means of production, he severed all political connections with them. George widened this breach with organized labor when he switched his position in support of clemency for the Haymarket anarchists to accepting the more popular conclusion that they had engaged in a conspiracy that caused the bomb to be thrown and, therefore, were guilty under Illinois law. The former apostle of the working class was now viewed as a traitor. Still popular among middle-class reformers who continued to find his tax program preferable to socialism or class conflict, George continued to promote the single tax editorially in his newspaper, *The Standard* (1887–1892). He also promoted the organization of single tax clubs. By 1889, there were 131 of these clubs scattered across the country. But after the early 1890s, the movement began to lose steam in the United States. George continued to give lectures, and he conducted successful speaking tours to the United Kingdom in 1888 and 1889 and to Australia and New Zealand in 1890. But in a way, his continued popularity abroad served to underscore his inability to sustain similar popular interest at home.

In 1890, George suffered a serious stroke. Although he recovered rapidly, the attack weakened him physically and mentally. At the time, he had begun work on a new book, *The Science of Political Economy*. It was to be his grand synthesis, a final summation, an opportunity to clarify and reiterate ideas he felt had become distorted in the popular press. The unfinished manuscript, which his son published posthumously, was a disconnected collection of analysis, examples, anecdotes, and autobiographical information that was more an affirmation of his failing abilities than a successor to *Progress and Poverty*. In 1897, in the midst of working on his manuscript and in rapidly failing health, George made what amounted to a conscious decision for martyrdom at the age of fifty-nine. He agreed to run for mayor of New York City in a four-party contest he knew he could not win. In response to a doctor's warning that such exertion would probably kill him, George is reported to have said, "How can I die better than serving humanity? Besides, so dying will do more for the cause than anything I am likely to be able to do in the rest of my life."[19] Calling this final protest against economic injustice and thwarted economic opportunity "The Party of Thomas Jefferson," George stood on a simple platform of home rule, municipal ownership, and tax reform. Five days before the election, after a strenuous day of campaigning, George suffered a fatal heart attack.

Academic critics dealt harshly with Henry George's economic theories both before and after his death. His analysis, they said, was one dimensional. He oversimplified how all the inequities in wealth, power, and privilege could be derived simply from the ability of a few to monopolize the rising value of land. In doing so, he overlooked other causes for society's plight. Offended not only by his simplistic solution for the paradox of poverty amidst plenty, critics also objected to his censorious tone. They accused George of being a moralist who dabbled in economics and of letting his Christian ethics compromise his science.

To the general readership, however, the book struck a chord. Although George's single-tax idea fascinated them, it was the spirit of the book—the promise of a better life—that swept them away. What George offered these individuals was an image of America's unrealized potential and hope that the harsh realities of economic life could be adjusted. Fertile farmlands and abundant natural resources should have offered opportunity to every producer. Industrialization and the advance of new technologies should have created affordable goods for every consumer. A heritage of relatively democratic political institutions should have continued to empower the individual voter and make the will of the majority a reality. But things had not worked out as anticipated. Some individuals had obtained monopolies in land that denied others the means by which to experience freedom and pursue happiness. The government had encouraged this process through land and tax laws that allowed various special interests to take advantage of legislative privileges that advanced their own personal fortunes at the expense of society. But what had been stolen could be restored. By expropriating the monopolist's unearned reward, the community could still reclaim the wealth that progress and civilization had created. Poverty need not accompany progress.

George's importance to the history of American reform goes beyond his contribution of the single tax to the list of late nineteenth-century reform panaceas. *Progress and Poverty* precipitated new ways of thinking among a surprising number of men and women who would later emerge as reform leaders during the Progressive Era. In pointing out the inequities of American society, George offered an environmental explanation for social ills. The conditions under which people lived, not heredity or individual character, determined the outcomes of their lives. In suggesting the possibility of state action to improve social well-being, George inspired a generation of reformers to view the state as an agency of change. In redefining the role of government, they would attempt to fulfill George's dream to "humanize and democratize [the] political economy, that it might serve social ends rather than class exploitation."[20] Tax laws could be used as a means to redistribute wealth. Inspired by George's ethical approach to economics, a new school of social scientists would soon advocate mechanisms such as income, inheritance, land, franchise, and corporation taxes as the means by which the economically privileged would be required to contribute to the welfare of all. Similarly, social justice legislation could improve living and working conditions, while municipal ownership of public utilities could reduce costs and enhance efficiency in basic consumer services.

It was but a small step for the followers of George to conclude that if certain individuals or corporations received special privileges from government and used them to promote monopoly and thwart opportunity, then those same privileged individuals and corporations perverted democracy as well. As a result, political conceptions, just like economic ones, would have to evolve with changing social conditions. New participatory mechanisms—the initiative, referendum, recall, direct primary, woman suffrage, and the direct election of senators—would have to be adopted to enable the majority to reclaim political power. George, like Lester Frank Ward, truly believed that the good of society must take precedence over individual greed, governmental grants of special privilege, and the influence of special interests. His legacy was to inspire others to think likewise.

NOTES

1. Eric F. Goldman, *Rendezvous with Destiny: A History of Modern American Reform* (Chicago: Ivan R. Dee, 2001), 32–33.

2. Henry George Jr., *The Life of Henry George* (New York: Robert Schalkenbach Foundation, 1960), 50.

3. George, *The Life of Henry George*, 171.

4. George, *The Life of Henry George*, 123.

5. George, *The Life of Henry George*, 149.

6. John L. Thomas, *Alternative America: Henry George, Edward Bellamy, Henry Demarest Lloyd and the Adversary Tradition* (Cambridge, Mass.: Harvard University Press, 1983), 16.

7. Thomas, *Alternative America*, 16.

8. George, *The Life of Henry George*, 154.

9. George, *The Life of Henry George*, 158.

10. George, *The Life of Henry George*, 178–79.

11. George, *The Life of Henry George*, 226.

12. Edward J. Rose, *Henry George* (New York: Twayne Publishers, 1968), 48–49.

13. Rose, *Henry George*, 55–56.

14. Henry George, *Progress and Poverty: An Inquiry into the Cause of Industrial Depressions and of Increase of Want with Increase of Wealth . . . the Remedy* (New York: Robert Schalkenbach Foundation, 1971), 336, 403, 405.

15. George, *Progress and Poverty*, 461, 463.

16. George, *The Life of Henry George*, 311–12.

17. Thomas, *Alternative America*, 222–23.

18. Samuel Gompers, *Seventy Years of Life and Labor: An Autobiography*, vol. 1 (New York: A. M. Kelley, 1967), 313.

19. Thomas, *Alternative America*, 338.

20. Vernon Louis Parrington, *The Beginnings of Critical Realism in America: 1860–1920* (New York: Harcourt, Brace and World, 1958), 132.

SOURCES

Aaron, Daniel. *Men of Good Hope: A Story of American Progressives*. New York: Oxford University Press, 1951.

Barker, Charles Albro. *Henry George*. New York: Oxford University Press, 1955.

De Mille, Anna George. *Henry George: Citizen of the World*. Chapel Hill: University of North Carolina Press, 1950.

Geiger, George Raymond. *The Philosophy of Henry George*. New York: Macmillan, 1933.

George, Henry. *Progress and Poverty: An Inquiry into the Cause of Industrial Depressions and of Increase of Want with Increase of Wealth . . . the Remedy*. New York: Robert Schalkenbach Foundation, 1971.

George, Henry, Jr. *The Life of Henry George*. New York: Robert Schalkenbach Foundation, 1960.

Goldman, Eric F. *Rendezvous with Destiny: A History of Modern American Reform*. Chicago: Ivan R. Dee, 2001.

Parrington, Vernon Louis. *The Beginnings of Critical Realism in America: 1860–1920*. New York: Harcourt, Brace and World, 1958.

Rose, Edward J. *Henry George*. New York: Twayne Publishers, 1968.

Thelen, David P. "Progressivism as a Radical Movement." In *Main Problems in American History*, vol. 2, ed. Howard H. Quint, Milton Cantor, and Dean Albertson. Homewood, Ill.: Dorsey Press, 1972.

Thomas, John L. *Alternative America: Henry George, Edward Bellamy, Henry Demarest Lloyd and the Adversary Tradition*. Cambridge, Mass.: Harvard University Press, 1983.

3

Charles W. Macune's Cooperative Vision

When members of the Texas Farmers' Alliance gathered at a specially called conference in Waco in January 1887, they confronted an organizational crisis. The body lacked a dominant, forceful leader, and, while desperation had driven thousands to join the Alliance, factionalism threatened to pull it apart. Impatient farmers wanted a clear course of action, but the organization seemed to lack direction. How should the Alliance proceed? Should it continue to follow an alternative economic path rooted in the farm cooperative whereby farmers would own and operate their own commercial enterprises to facilitate the production, distribution, and sale of farm products for their mutual benefit, or should it begin a process of political education and activism that might provide the foundation for independent political action? On the second day of the conference, C. W. Macune offered a radical proposal. Looking to transform the existing debate, he suggested that delegates focus their attention on solving the farmers' persistent problems of credit and prices by creating a giant cooperative agency. At the same time, he urged the delegates to convert the Alliance into a national agrarian association.

Central to his program was a Farmers' Alliance Exchange of Texas—a central cooperative that would direct the marketing of the cotton crops of all Alliance members and serve as the purchasing agency for goods needed by Texas farmers. "I hold," said Macune, "that cooperation . . . will place a limit to the encroachments of organized monopoly, and will be the means by which the mortgage-burdened farmers can assert their freedom from the tyranny of organized capital, and obtain the reward for honesty, industry, and frugality, which they so richly deserve, and which they are now so unjustly denied."[1] But to be able to confront the power of existing marketing and banking monopolies effectively, Macune told the delegates that it would also be necessary to organize all the states of the cotton belt and create a southern monopoly of organized agriculture. Macune's emergence as a man of action with the vision to chart a course of escape from the economic ills that plagued them united the delegates. They voted to accept his program and unanimously elected him as their new president.

The man who seized the moment at Waco was anything but a typical cotton farmer. Charles W. Macune was born in Kenosha, Wisconsin, in 1851, the only son of William and Mary Macune. His father, a restless Canadian of Scotch-Irish descent, worked as a blacksmith and served as the local Methodist minister. While migrating to California in 1852, Charles's father died from cholera at Fort Laramie. His death forced the family to turn back and settle in Freeport, Illinois. Difficult economic circumstances ultimately forced Charles to drop out of school when he was ten and begin work as a farmhand. When he turned eighteen, he left home looking for a better opportunity. Traveling to California in 1869, he tried ranching. A year later, he moved to Kansas, where he joined a circus and then signed on as a cattle driver. At some point in the early 1870s, he moved to Burnet, Texas, where he launched unsuccessful ventures in newspaper publishing and hotel ownership. While in Burnet, however, he met and married Sally Vickery, and the couple soon relocated to San Saba, Texas. There, Macune studied medicine with a local doctor and read law. After moving again to Milam County, the Macunes finally settled down. Charles practiced medicine, continued to read law books, and dabbled in the study of monetary theory and greenbackism. Life seemed to progress routinely.

At some point during the winter of 1885–1886, Charles Macune joined the rapidly growing Texas Farmers' Alliance. It was a time of intense activity in the state, which, in turn, caused many citizens to become politicized. The noted Knights of Labor strike against the Gould railroad system at that time aroused agrarian sympathies with the struggle of workers against an obvious symbol of the power of monopoly in the state. Organizers vigorously encouraged farmers to join the Alliance and engage in cooperative ventures, establish "antimonopoly leagues" to nominate candidates for office, and participate in a program of food relief for farmers hard hit by drought. Macune himself had lost a portion of his land holdings in Milam County to foreclosure at the time he joined the Texas Alliance. Handsome, gregarious, a natural booster and promoter, and an authoritative public speaker, Macune exuded a great deal of personal magnetism. Coupled with a keen grasp of the political economy (and a strong sense of a moral economy), he rose quickly in the ranks of the organization and gained election as chairman of the executive committee of the Texas State Alliance within his first year of membership.

Caught up in the whirlwind of farm protest, Macune's path along the road of frontier isolation and obscurity had come to an end.

The origins of the Farmers' Alliance in Texas date to the formation of farmers' clubs starting after the Civil War to deal with local problems. The earliest associations sought to protect small farmers from land sharks who filed fraudulent land claims in hopes of either dispossessing the original landowner or forcing some type of legal compromise. Farmers also cooperated with local sheriffs in tracking down horse thieves and cattle rustlers. In September 1877, a small group of farmers in Lampasas County joined together as the "Knights of Reliance." Members, described as "comparatively poor," took a strong antimonopoly position. Recognizing the need to better understand the political economy, they urged preparation "for the day that is rapidly approaching when all the balance of labor's products become concentrated into the hands of a few, there to constitute a power that would enslave posterity."[2] Members soon renamed their new organization the Farmers' Alliance and adopted the secretive fraternal rituals of passwords and handshakes. Spreading into a number of neighboring counties, the organization became absorbed in the inflationary program of the Greenback Party and ultimately collapsed from political dissension in 1878.

A new Farmers' Alliance, however, soon reappeared in Parks County, Texas, in 1879. Avoiding the political bickering that had wrecked its predecessor, the new order obtained an official state charter in 1880 and quickly spread through the counties of central and northern Texas. By the end of 1885, the Alliance claimed to have 50,000 members and roughly 1,200 locals or suballiances in Texas. The rapid growth of the Farmers' Alliance was indicative of the worsening economic conditions that faced farmers not only in Texas but also throughout the South. Driven by desperation, farmers had opted to join a movement of protest against the high prices they paid for goods, the low prices they received for farm commodities, and the near-monopoly power that merchants exercised over money and credit.

The most pernicious mechanism working against the farmer was the crop lien system. Managed by rural "furnishing" merchants, the borrowing arrangement was oppressive not only to tenants but to landowning farmers as well, who were sinking into tenancy under its burden. Under the crop lien, the tenant mortgaged his crop to the furnishing merchant (banks were few in the South and reluctant to lend to landowners and unwilling to lend to tenants) as security against which he could borrow to obtain necessary supplies. The farmer pledged his crop, usually cotton, instead of his land because cotton was a marketable commodity, while land had very little market value. The system itself was viable because the merchant (the creditor) was rooted in the local community and could easily monitor the spending of borrowed capital as well as oversee the planting and cultivation of a crop. Loans were rarely transacted in cash. The furnishing merchant found it far more profitable to offer credit in the form of charges at his country store. In the process, he would make money on interest and on sales at his store. Taking advantage of this inescapable system (the farmer had to have credit or starve), the furnishing merchant gouged the helpless farmer by setting exorbitant interest rates. Where the common rate of interest might have been 6 percent, the imposed rate was frequently 20 percent and could in some cases actually reach 10 percent per month or 120 percent per year. Interest was charged for one year even though the loan itself ran only until harvest (usually nine months or less). The farmer was often required to repay his loan in monthly payments. As a result, the furnishing merchant constantly recouped his loaned capital while still earning interest on the full amount for an entire year.

Compounding the southern farmer's woes were the prices he was forced to pay on goods purchased at the country store. The crop lien system allowed the furnishing merchant to establish a two-tiered pricing system—"cash" and "credit." The customer who paid cash received goods at the normal retail price. Credit customers, however, were forced to pay a higher price. The amount of the markup for credit customers varied widely but was at least 25 percent above the retail cost and in many instances 40 to 100 percent higher. As one observer noted, "[T]hey charge from 25% to grand larceny."[3] In actuality, the credit price meant that the farmer paid double for his loan via interest and credit. Once the farmer entered into a lien agreement with one merchant, no other merchant would sell him anything on credit because the only security he had (his crop) had already been forfeited. Competition had been destroyed.

The furnishing merchant not only controlled interest rates, prices, and the nature of the crop sown but also dictated the marketing of the mortgaged crop. As a result, the farmer could not hold his crop for a better price. At the end of the year, the farmer was most likely told that he had not "paid out." Still in debt, his contract bound him to renew the lien on his next crop with the same merchant and under the same conditions. As one historian aptly summed up the situation,

> When one of these mortgages has been recorded against the southern farmer, he has usually passed into a state of helpless peonage. . . . With the surrender of this evidence of indebtedness he has also surrendered his freedom of action and his industrial autonomy. From this time until he has paid the last dollar of his indebtedness, he is subject to the constant oversight and direction of the merchant. Every mouthful of food that he purchases, every implement that he requires on the farm, his mules, cattle, the clothing for himself and family, the fertilizers for his land, must all be bought of the merchant who holds the crop lien, and in such amounts, as the latter is willing to allow.[4]

While this form of debt peonage was not inevitable, it loomed as the haunting specter of farm life in the rural South.

In response to worsening economic conditions, the leaders of the Farmers' Alliance focused their attention on developing new purchasing and marketing strategies to confront those problems. In an attempt to realize lower prices on retail goods, various county Alliances attempted to form trade agreements with local merchants. Under the trade agreement idea, a committee from the Alliance would meet with various local merchants to see who would offer the lowest retail prices in return for a pledge that the entire membership of the county Alliance would trade only with that merchant. The argument was simply that the willing merchant would benefit more from increased sales than he would suffer by lowering his prices. The trade agreement arrangement, however, soon exposed problems that ultimately killed it. Although the program had utility for many Alliance members who were able to make their purchases in cash, it did nothing to help the growing number of farmers who were forced to rely on credit. The arrangement also invoked disputes over pricing. Although the agreements stipulated a certain charge above the wholesale price, farmers were usually uninformed as to the exact wholesale price of a product. Charges of price manipulation led to demands to examine merchants' account books. When retailers refused to do so, trade agreements were terminated.

Another problem involved disruption to the existing retail system caused by these trade agreements. A successful purchasing arrangement with one merchant meant a severe drop in cash-paying customers for his competitors and could possibly force them out of business. Other merchants foresaw that eventuality and immediately took steps to prevent it. Typically, they would appeal to the wholesaler to exert pressure on the merchant cooperating with the Alliance. Wholesalers, who had a financial stake in the success of every retail store, were very protective of the existing retail arrangement. If the profits of other merchants were threatened, the wholesaler would refuse to supply credit to the merchant cooperating with the Alliance and pressure that merchant to terminate his trading agreement.

As disappointment mounted over the trade agreement idea, county Alliances rekindled the earlier Grange program of cooperative retail stores to circumvent the retail merchant and reduce the cost of supplies. But to raise the necessary capital to run the stores, the Alliance-run cooperatives were forced to sell shares of stock and promise shareholders at least modest dividends. Once in operation, however, the local cooperatives ran on a cash-only basis. As a result, they were of no more use to debt-ridden farmers than the trade agreements. For those who had cash, there was disappointment as well. Forced to pay dividends on stock, the prices at the Alliance stores were never as low as some farmers had hoped. Some stores, however, were successful, reported sales of from $5,000 to $36,000 a year, and claimed that goods at the Alliance stores were sold at 20 to 30 percent below normal cost. Such successes brought new members into the Alliance, but it once again generated a reaction from merchants. Threatened by their cooperative rivals, they undercut the cash prices at those stores (often raising the credit prices to make up for losses). Merchants again pressured wholesalers (with whom they had long-standing credit agreements) not to trade with the Alliance cooperatives.

In 1885, the Alliance, through a special purchasing agent, tried one other scheme to circumvent the merchant and wholesaler by purchasing farm implements and machinery in bulk quantities directly from the manufacturer. Manufacturers would fill large orders at discounted prices but only for cash. Once again, as most farmers lacked cash, they could not participate in any alternative-purchasing program on those terms. Even when goods were purchased at lower prices, they still had to be shipped over rail lines where high freight rates diminished any real savings. As with the trade agreement, farmers in the Alliance had consistently run up against entrenched market forces in retailing, wholesaling, and transportation.

While farmers struggled to find ways to break the hold that local merchants had over the purchasing system in the South, they also sought to find ways to increase the selling price of cotton. Under the existing cotton marketing system, cotton "factors" usually purchased cotton from small producers. Once they had amassed a sufficient quantity, they resold the cotton to a broker at one of the major cotton exchanges. In many instances, the cotton factors sent agents to small towns to purchase cotton from farmers in the area. They would often store the cotton in local warehouses while they sent along information on quality (grade), quantity, and price to the cotton factor in one of the larger cities. The factor would then negotiate a sale price with a broker at one of the major cotton exchanges and arrange for delivery of the cotton.

The system, which involved the movement of large quantities of cotton, worked against the small farmer by design. Unable to sell his small crop directly to a broker at an exchange, the farmer had to market his cotton crop to either a local merchant or a traveling buyer. In an attempt to enhance their selling position, small farmers adopted the tactic of "bulking" their cotton crops. In acting together to create a large, marketable quantity of cotton, farmers hoped to attract numerous buyers who would then bid competitively for the bulked crop. Unfortunately for the small farmer, the program did not work out as planned. Farmers found they still could not produce a sufficient number of bales to attract more than one buyer. In addition, farmers tied to the crop lien system could not bulk their cotton. Their entire crop had to be turned over to the merchant to cover their debts. In most cases, buyers, who did not wish to pay a higher price for raw cotton, were still able to purchase all the cotton they needed from individual farmers outside the Alliance. In a sense, the local nature of the bulking scheme severely limited its success. The cotton bulking strategy was doomed, as were the trade agreements and cooperative stores, unless a way could be found to bypass the merchant or the factor or to mobilize the cotton belt through the Alliance so that buyers could not find sufficient quantities of cotton from individual farmers.

When Macune accepted the leadership of the Farmers' Alliance after his riveting speech at the Waco convention in 1887, he also assumed the role of chief economic strategist of the organization. "He was," noted one historian, "a master of the art of escalation, responding to movement obstacles in most innovative ways."[5] Realizing that past efforts at economic cooperation had failed at the local and county levels, Macune proposed an ambitious statewide cooperative exchange that would both direct the marketing of the entire Alliance cotton crop and act as the central purchasing agency for all Alliance members in Texas. Because existing marketing monopolies had proven so powerful, he also urged that formal steps be taken to organize the entire cotton belt under the Alliance banner. Inspired by his ideas, members immediately approved a merger with the existing Louisiana Farmers' Union (the Alliance would eventually absorb the Agricultural Wheel of Arkansas as well), adopted a plan for grassroots organizing throughout the region, and agreed to accept the "National Farmers' Alliance and Cooperative Union of America" (changed to the "National Farmers' and Laborers' Union of America" in 1888 and finally to the "National Farmers' Alliance and Industrial Union" in 1889) as the new, formal name of their association. Still popularly referred to as the Southern Alliance, the revitalized association organized practically every southern state by the end of the year.

The Southern Alliance adopted specific positions in regards to race and gender. The racial policy of the association was that it should be a white-only order, but it left the task of enforcing that position to individual states. Although it imposed segregation in organization, the leaders of the Southern Alliance did stress the common problems of white and black farmers. Anticipating such exclusion, black farmers organized their own separate Colored Farmers' Alliance under the leadership of Richard Manning Humphrey, a white Baptist preacher and former missionary. White women, however, were eligible for membership in the Alliance, and, as historian C. Vann Woodward has noted, "it was through the Grange and Farmers' Alliance that [white] Southern women got their first real opportunity for direct participation in public life and politics."[6] It has been estimated that women comprised at least one-fourth of the national membership of the Alliance. Activist Annie Diggs of Kansas offered an explanation for the high level of female participation. To her, the traditional conception of the home as the "woman's sphere" was only partially correct. "The whole truth," said Diggs, "is that women should watch and work in all things which shape and mould the home, whether 'money,' 'land,' or 'transportation.' So now Alliance women look at politics and trace the swift relation to the home."[7]

As envisioned by Macune, the Alliance Exchange of Texas would rework the entire purchasing and marketing system. It would bypass both the wholesaler and the retail merchant and deal directly with the manufacturer. By purchasing in bulk without the added charges of middlemen, it was hoped that farmers would realize even greater savings than they had through their local cooperatives. The Exchange would employ county business agents who would gather cotton samples from crops brought to the local Alliance cotton yard by members. After weighing and grading, the samples would be sent to the Exchange, where they would be displayed for potential buyers. In a sense, the Exchange would assume the function of both cotton factor and broker, thereby enabling the hard-pressed farmer to realize a greater return for his toil.

For the Alliance to be successful, however, members would have to supply the initial start-up cost as large sums of money were necessary to underwrite purchasing contracts. Anticipating that 250,000 active members would pay a $2 assessment to defray such costs, the total capitalization of the Exchange was set at $500,000. When the city of Dallas offered a cash subsidy of $10,000 and a lot for a future building, the Alliance agreed to locate its headquarters there. Hopeful that members would readily respond with their assessments, the Exchange began operation in September 1887 and immediately began to concentrate on marketing that year's cotton crop.

Macune, as business manager of the Exchange, was well aware that previous Alliance strategies had not benefited the farmer tied to the crop lien system. To address that problem, he proposed a new joint-note program. Under the plan, members of the various local alliances who depended on the crop lien system would collectively estimate their yearly supply needs/costs. They would then write a joint note for the total amount and pledge cotton (as collateral) worth at least three times the amount of credit requested. The joint note would have to be approved both by the county business agent and by a special committee at the Exchange. That committee would then authorize Macune, as business manager, to make cash transactions. Under the program, there would be no "credit" pricing aside from a 1 percent interest charge on the extended credit. As one Alliance member remarked, the joint-note program created "the highest pitch of excitement in contemplation of abolishing the awful credit system which is a veritable millstone around the neck of the improvident farmer." The same observer noted that there was "the most hopeful and enthusiastic spirit possible to imagine, amounting to almost a universal conviction that financial salvation was come."[8]

It was hoped that Alliance members would meet their $2 assessments and that such contributions would be sufficient to cover all the necessary purchases made by the Exchange. By March 1888, however, the directors of the Exchange had approved advances of $128,000 in goods but had collected only $17,000. As a result, the Exchange was dangerously short of operating capital. To meet the crisis, the board of directors of the Exchange authorized using the joint notes as collateral with which to negotiate bank loans to continue purchasing supplies. Confident that they would be able to do so, the directors proceeded to order goods in large quantities and accrue even greater financial liabilities ($400,000 by the end of May). But when banks in Dallas, Houston, Fort Worth, Galveston, and New Orleans all refused to loan money on what they considered to be risky collateral, the directors of the Exchange realized that they did not have sufficient cash to pay their bills. As anxious creditors demanded payment, the Exchange teetered on the brink of disaster.

Embarrassed by their own financial naïveté and angry that the existing financial system had once again stymied their attempt at establishing a more equitable marketing and purchasing arrangement, the directors charged that bankers, wholesale merchants, and manufacturers had entered into a combine to crush the Exchange. To avoid abandoning their program, Macune and the other directors called for a renewed subscription campaign in which each member would be assessed an additional $2 to pay down the amount owed to creditors. The recapitalization effort garnered pledges of more than $200,000 by the end of July, but two months later only $58,000 had actually been collected. The explanation seemed to lie more with members' inability to pay rather than their unwillingness to do so, but the limited cash reserve and the uncooperative nature of powerful financial interests forced the directors of the Alliance to admit defeat. The Exchange discontinued its joint-note program in the fall of 1888. The Alliance Exchange continued to operate as a cash-purchasing operation until the end of the following year, when creditors finally foreclosed. Macune's dream of freeing farmers from the usurious credit system was at least temporarily dead.

Alliance members initially rallied behind Macune and the other directors of the Exchange. One typically supportive county Alliance resolution stated, "[W]e fully endorse the bold and worthy stand taken by the officers of the Exchange against the undermining efforts of the Dallas merchants and bankers. . . . [W]e . . . will bear hardship, suffer privations, make common stock of what we possess, weather the storm of oppression . . . , and gain an honorable victory, or starve in the attempt." Yet another county Alliance declared, "God forbid that their [*sic*] should be an Alliance man or woman in the state that should falter at this time and surrender in the hands of the task master. Three cheers for the State Exchange."[9] But such solidarity against the banking and business "task masters" did not last long. Soon newspaper articles began to appear charging directors of the Exchange with trying to hide their business inexperience and financial incompetence by inaccurately assigning blame. When a Committee of Five, appointed to investigate the operation of the Exchange, issued a report that condemned the business methods of the directors, these charges intensified. Macune bore the brunt of the assault, being explicitly or implicitly harangued as ambitious, scheming, and lacking sound business judgment. The charges were sufficiently demoralizing to compromise the recapitalization drive (to save the Exchange), cause a drop in Alliance membership in Texas from which the order would never fully recover, and forever tarnish the reputation of Macune.

While the Texas Exchange struggled as a business venture, dissidents within the larger Southern Alliance began to push more strongly for political action to bring about favorable legislation. Although priorities varied from state to state, they all seemed to echo the common theme that creditors were unfairly oppressing debtors. Solutions—demanding that railroads lower their rates, land monopolists dissolve their holdings, trusts be destroyed, interest rates be reduced, mortgage holders be protected, national banks be abolished, or more money be placed in circulation to keep pace with the increase in population, commerce, and industry—all required federal regulation.

Sensing the shift in thinking within the Southern Alliance and aware of the growing popularity of the idea of inflationary monetary reform, Macune told delegates at the organization's national convention in St. Louis in December 1889 that it was time to pressure the federal government to pass legislation to address the current farm crisis in a unique way. He proceeded to argue that low crop prices and economic hard times were the result of an insufficient national supply of money. Sobered by the failure of the Texas Exchange, Macune acknowledged that previous Alliance strategies had attempted to bring relief to the farmer without addressing the root cause of the current economic depression. That cause was an inadequate amount of currency in circulation. To Macune, it was time for the federal government to assume responsibility for adjusting the money supply so that economic prosperity could return to agrarian America. In a political culture that, with the passage of the Interstate Commerce Act in 1887, had begun to see the need for federal regulation and marveled at Edward Bellamy's best-selling utopian socialist novel, *Looking Backward* (1887), with its emphasis on the possibilities that might result if the government assumed a more positive role in economic life, maybe Macune's idea had merit.

What Macune had in mind was for the money supply to become flexible. It would expand during that time of the year when crops were harvested and then gradually contract after the harvesting/marketing season. He called his innovative plan to bring about this needed regulation the "subtreasury." The centerpiece of this idea was a commodity loan program that would democratize the marketing and financing of staple crops through low-cost federal loans secured by those crops. The program would create a flexible money supply and allow the farmer to escape the dreaded crop lien system at the same time. As envisioned by Macune, the federal government would construct warehouses in every county that annually produced farm commodities worth at least $500,000. Farmers could then store their nonperishable crops—wheat, corn, oats, barley, rye, tobacco, cotton, wool, or sugar—in these warehouses or subtreasuries and wait for higher prices. They would receive, as a loan for up to one year, negotiable treasury notes equal to 80 percent of the current local market value of their crop at the time of deposit in the warehouse. Farmers would be required to pay interest on their loans at the rate of 1 percent per year. Insurance would be provided at reasonable cost, while additional charges for weighing, grading, handling, and storage would be nominal.

The benefits of the program were self-evident. Inexpensive storage facilities would allow farmers to stagger the sale of their crops and avoid the problem of abnormally low prices brought on by the glut that naturally occurred at harvest time. Loan advances would allow debt-ridden farmers to become less dependent on usurious creditors. The infusion of cash would increase the amount of money in circulation at harvest time and work against deflation. When the farmer eventually terminated his loan by withdrawing (selling) his stored crop, the money would be returned to the government and withdrawn from circulation until the next harvesting season. The money supply would fluctuate as the cycle of farm production necessitated, and the decline in farm prices would be reversed. The plan, like the previous Exchange joint-note idea, promised to destroy the exploitative crop lien system. Farmers who had formerly been victims of exorbitant interest charges could now obtain loans at low rates of interest. The subtreasury plan offered economic salvation to tenant and small yeoman farmers, but this time the financial resources would come from the government and not a cash-strapped Alliance membership.

Macune's brilliant scheme did, however, pose a threat to a number of powerful interest groups—merchants and larger landowners who would lose revenues generated by the crop-lien system, speculators who would lose control over the sale of agricultural commodities, bankers who stood to lose their monopoly over borrowed capital, and, potentially, the Democratic Party, which stood to lose large numbers of political supporters and potentially political dominance in the South if it failed to embrace the radical Macune program or if disgusted farmers decided to create their own independent party.

To encourage support for the subtreasury, the Alliance increased its informational and lobbying efforts. To explain the details of the plan and to tout its merits, the Alliance sent scores of Alliance lecturers to remote rural communities to interact directly with local Alliancemen. To aid the overall campaign, the Alliance publishing house, headed by Macune, mailed out large quantities of pamphlets and reform literature. Equally important as a forum for explanation and exhortation was the pro-Alliance network of newspapers. Anchoring this system was the *National Economist*, the weekly newspaper of the Southern Alliance published in Washington, D.C. Founded in the summer of 1889 and edited by Macune (who had resigned as manager of the Alliance Exchange in the spring to assume this position), the newspaper quickly established a circulation of 100,000. Supporting the *National Economist* was the *Southern Mercury*, the organ of the Texas Alliance with 26,000 readers, and dozens of small town and county newspapers. In an attempt to carry this process one step further, the Alliance, at its December 1890 convention in Ocala, Florida, adopted a plan to coordinate hundreds of local newspapers. The vehicle created to accomplish this was the National Reform Press Association. With Macune again assuming the role as president, the association hoped to establish an alternative source for national news and increase grassroots understanding of the Alliance's reform agenda.

To intensify its lobbying efforts for passage of a subtreasury bill, the Alliance formed a legislative committee, also chaired by Macune. The committee successfully lobbied to have subtreasury bills introduced in the House and the Senate. They also circulated petitions among local Alliances demanding adoption of those measures and eventually generated nearly one million signatures. Macune personally testified before the Senate Agricultural Committee on behalf of the subtreasury program and arranged for other Alliance leaders to do so as well.

When it became obvious that Congress would not pass the bills, the Alliance urged its members to elect congressmen who would pledge themselves to support the plan. During the 1890 election, leaders of the Alliance urged voters to measure political candidates by whether they supported the subtreasury. Conversely, southern Democrats, who objected to the entrance of the Alliance into politics, used the provocative subtreasury plan as a means of discrediting the larger farmers' movement. Ironically, when southern Democrats refused to include the subtreasury in their various state party platforms, they accelerated the drift of the Alliance along the course of independent political action that would culminate in the formation of the Populist Party in 1892.

One other area in which the Alliance leadership in general, and Macune in particular, took a keen interest was education. "[T]he Alliance was," stated Macune, "founded on education. All it is and all it will ever be must emanate from that source." What Macune and others had in mind was to use education as a tool of social reform. They would instruct farmers and their families in the science of political economy and develop a self-conscious class of rural producers in the process. As editor of the *National Economist*, Macune played a central role in setting the educational agenda of the farmers' movement. His position was clear from the very first editorial in the *Economist*: "Questions of public policy," said Macune, "are not too complicated for the average common mind." The idea was to teach basic skills and then apply those skills to the producer environment that surrounded the farmer. To accomplish this, Macune styled the *Economist* as a political primer to be used at local Alliance meetings (which in most instances took place in local schoolhouses). The "curriculum" would draw on the problems confronting farmers every day, such as liens, mortgages, and interest charges on store accounts.[10]

On January 16, 1892, Macune began a series of instructional lessons in the *Economist* designed for use in the local Alliances. Each of the twenty lessons followed a pattern. An introductory lecture, given by a local instructor or Alliance lecturer and outlined by Macune ahead of time, was followed by blackboard exercises in mathematics or English composition. Through oral presentation and discussion, instructors tried to introduce their charges to principles and concepts relevant to their daily lives. As such, the exercises became important tools for political education. At the least the sessions taught basic mathematics and literacy, and at best they encouraged farmers, as producers, to develop logical arguments on current issues. With their emphasis on economic inequality and the moral superiority of producers over their capitalist exploiters, Macune's critics could easily label the lessons exercises in propaganda. But the sessions did teach one important concept central to the Alliance movement: farmers, possessed of a shared sense of purpose, should take control of their lives and initiate "direct political action to reorient the distribution of political power and economic rewards from the privileged class to the common man and woman."[11] In hoping to create a more democratic, producer-oriented political culture, the lesson Macune really hoped to teach was empowerment.

When the Populist Party entered the 1892 political campaign, Macune supported it editorially in the *National Economist*. However, by the late summer, Macune, who had never believed in third-party politics as a solution to the economic problems plaguing farmers, had concluded that the Populists would be badly defeated. As a result, he began to disassociate himself and the Alliance (via the *National Economist*) from the Populist Party. When he did so, his enemies began to charge that he had sold out to the Democrats. Such accusations took on new meaning when, just before the election, members of the Southern Alliance began receiving campaign literature in the mail (often arriving with issues of the *National Economist*). Accompanying the literature was a letter from J. F. Tillman of Tennessee, a member of the executive committee of the Alliance and director of the Alliance lecture bureau, that urged members to rejoin the Democratic Party. Macune denied any knowledge of Tillman's letter, and Tillman denied having consulted with Macune before mailing the correspondence, but many Alliancemen found Macune guilty by association. Although probably not complicit in the affair, Macune would have agreed with Tillman's proposal. As one historian has noted, "Faced with the choice between trying to preserve the Alliance in the South and participating in a long-range struggle to build a new party—a struggle that others were leading—Macune opted for the Alliance."[12]

Although the charges against him were never proven, Macune's credibility had been undermined. Defeated in his bid for election as president of the Alliance, he withdrew from the organization in 1892 and just as quietly disappeared. He practiced law in Cameron, Texas, for eight years and then became a traveling preacher for the Methodist Church. He continued to preach in small Texas towns until 1918. After that, he worked with his son, also a preacher, doing volunteer medical work among the poor. Macune died in 1940 at the age of eighty-nine.

The ironies surrounding Macune are numerous. It was his intellectual and practical progression through the various radical cooperative ventures that brought the Alliance to the point of independent political action. But as partisan politics became the only means left to solve the farmers' deepening economic problems, it placed the Alliance on a political course Macune regarded as futile. He helped create the mass movement that eventually took political form as Populism, but he never became a Populist. He possessed the insights of a radical innovator who could envision structurally changing the existing economic system in America, but he could never see beyond the established two-party system or relinquish his faith in Bourbon Democracy and its racially exclusive parameters. He alienated both the political radicals within the Alliance and the economic conservatives outside the Alliance. He was a man of principle, but he could never escape charges of being a manipulator and self-aggrandizer. In the end, his "political traditionalism, his economic radicalism, and his recurrent opportunism" combined to leave him isolated, unappreciated, and soon forgotten.[13]

Macune deserved much better. Like Henry George, he was one of the most imaginative economic theorists of his time and his subtreasury system, like the single tax, one of the boldest and most creative economic ideas put forward in nineteenth-century America. He should also be remembered as the chief organizer and economic thinker at the head of one of the great mass democratic reform movements in American history—the Farmers' Alliance, which by 1892 could claim two to three million members in forty-three states. As historian Lawrence Goodwyn has noted, "In practical as well as theoretical terms, Macune . . . made more sustained contributions, and a greater variety of contributions, to the theory and practice of mass democratic movement-building than any other single political activist of his time." Macune's legacy, however, ultimately might best be gauged in simple terms. Perhaps his most important contribution was the one he made in the lives of the people he desperately wanted to help. Through his speeches and his earnest economic arguments, his "reasoned appeals for justice brought confidence to intimidated people."[14]

NOTES

1. Lawrence Goodwyn, *Democratic Promise: The Populist Moment in America* (New York: Oxford University Press, 1976), 90.

2. Goodwyn, *Democratic Promise*, 33.

3. Michael Schwartz, *Radical Protest and Social Structure: The Southern Farmers' Alliance and Cotton Tenancy, 1880–1890* (Chicago: University of Chicago Press, 1988), 36.

4. C. Vann Woodward, *Origins of the New South, 1877–1913* (Baton Rouge: Louisiana State University Press, 1971), 181.

5. Donna A. Barnes, *Farmers in Rebellion: The Rise and Fall of the Southern Farmers' Alliance and People's Party in Texas* (Austin: University of Texas Press, 1984), 78.

6. Woodward, *Origins of the New South*, 195.

7. Robert C. McMath Jr., *American Populism: A Social History, 1877–1898* (New York: Hill and Wang, 1993), 126.

8. Barnes, *Farmers in Rebellion*, 82.

9. Barnes, *Farmers in Rebellion*, 85.

10. Theodore R. Mitchell, *Political Education in the Southern Farmers' Alliance, 1887–1900* (Madison: University of Wisconsin Press, 1987), 5, 94.

11. Mitchell, *Political Education in the Southern Farmers' Alliance*, 118.

12. Robert C. McMath Jr., *Populist Vanguard: A History of the Southern Farmers' Alliance* (Chapel Hill: University of North Carolina Press, 1975), 143.

13. Goodwyn, *Democratic Promise*, 562.

14. Lawrence Goodwyn, "Charles William Macune," in *American Reformers*, ed. Alden Whitman (New York: H. W. Wilson Co., 1985), 567, 569.

SOURCES

Barnes, Donna A. *Farmers in Rebellion: The Rise and Fall of the Southern Farmers Alliance and People's Party in Texas*. Austin: University of Texas Press, 1984.

Goodwyn, Lawrence. *Democratic Promise: The Populist Moment in America.* New York: Oxford University Press, 1976.

Hicks, John D. *The Populist Revolt: A History of the Farmers' Alliance and the People's Party.* Lincoln: University of Nebraska Press, 1961.

Macune, C. W. "The Farmers Alliance." Typed manuscript in C. W. Macune Papers, Center for American History, University of Texas, Austin.

McMath, Robert C., Jr. *American Populism: A Social History, 1877–1920.* New York: Hill and Wang, 1993.

———. *Populist Vanguard: A History of the Southern Farmers' Alliance.* Chapel Hill: University of North Carolina Press, 1975.

Mitchell, Theodore R. *Political Education in the Southern Farmers' Alliance, 1887–1900.* Madison: University of Wisconsin Press, 1987.

Saloutos, Theodore. *Farmer Movements in the South, 1865–1933.* Berkeley: University of California Press, 1960.

Schwartz, Michael. *Radical Protest and Social Structure: The Southern Farmers' Alliance and Cotton Tenancy, 1880–1890.* Chicago: University of Chicago Press, 1988.

Shannon, Fred A. "C. W. Macune and the Farmers' Alliance." *Current History* 28 (June 1955): 330–35.

Smith, Ralph A. " 'Macuneism,' or the Farmers of Texas in Business." *Journal of Southern History* 13 (May 1947): 220–44.

Whitman, Alden, ed. *American Reformers.* New York: H. W. Wilson Co., 1985.

Woodward, C. Vann. *Origins of the New South, 1877–1913.* Baton Rouge: Louisiana State University Press, 1971.

4

Ida B. Wells's Crusade against Racism

One method open to African Americans seeking racial advancement in the South during the decades following Reconstruction was black capitalism. In pursuit of that goal, a group of black residents in Memphis, Tennessee, opened a cooperative business venture, the People's Grocery, in 1889. President of the new joint stock venture was Thomas Moss, a close friend of Ida Wells. Located in a mixed neighborhood in the "Curve" district of the city, the new black-run enterprise opened in direct competition with an existing white-owned store operated by W. H. Barrett. With a loyal customer base rooted in the church and lodge associations in the black community and supported by some white customers as well, the People's Grocery quickly gained a competitive advantage. Having lost his business monopoly, Barrett was hostile to the new establishment.

Desperate for a way to eliminate his new competitors, Barrett attempted to have a grand jury indict Moss and the other directors of the People's Grocery for maintaining a public nuisance. Unsuccessful, Barrett's action did, however, trigger an angry meeting in the black community in which inflammatory threats were made against him. Hearing of the meeting, Barrett then convinced a judge of the Shelby County criminal court to issue arrest warrants for two of the speakers who were believed to frequent the black-run store. Aware that police officers would be sent to the People's Grocery, Barrett then spread a rumor that a white mob was preparing to raid the store. To guard against this possibility, the store's owners stationed armed guards to protect their property. On Saturday night, March 5, 1892, gunshots were heard from the back room of the People's Grocery. The guards had fired on nine armed white men who had approached the store in civilian clothes. Three deputies were wounded in the shoot-out. In response, the police arrested about a dozen suspects, including store president Thomas Moss.

The white press in the city further inflamed passions and exacerbated tensions by charging that the black shooters had been motivated by racial prejudice. Mob activity followed. Vandals looted the People's Grocery, and white "deputies" broke into black homes and arrested several dozen other alleged conspirators. Four days later, a group of whites entered the jail at around 3:00 A.M. and took three of the prisoners—Thomas Moss, Calvin McDowell, and Will Stewart. The three had no prior police records and claimed to have fired no shots during the melee at the store. All three were respected members of the black community, and all three held positions in the ownership and operation of the People's Grocery. The mob took the three victims about a mile north of the city and shot them. Their bodies were discovered the following morning in a field. One of the bodies was badly mutilated.

The black community was shocked and horrified by the brutal murders and demanded that the members of the lynch mob be apprehended, tried, and convicted. A grand jury met to hear testimony, but none of the witnesses said they could identify any of the participants. After two weeks of hearings, the grand jury failed to issue a single indictment. No one was ever tried for the murders.

Ida Wells was in Mississippi during the Memphis incident and did not return to the city until after the funerals. Close friends with the Moss family and a godmother to their daughter, Wells was outraged by what had happened. Venting her anger in an editorial, she commented,

> The city of Memphis has demonstrated that neither character nor standing avails the Negro if he dares to protect himself against the white man or become his rival. There is nothing we can do about the lynching now, as we are outnumbered and without arms. . . . There is therefore only one thing left we can do; save our money and leave a town which will neither protect our lives and property, nor give us a fair trial in the courts, but takes us out and murders us in cold blood when accused by white persons.[1]

Responding to the pleas of Wells and others, as many as 2,000 African Americans reportedly left the city, many as "exodusters" bound for Oklahoma Territory. Many who remained in Memphis voiced their anger by boycotting the city's newly opened streetcar line and pushing the company to the verge of bankruptcy.

The Memphis lynchings affected Wells on a deeply personal level and in doing so challenged her basic assumptions. She had been angered by the expanding specter of segregation and dismayed by the declining political power of African Americans since Reconstruction. But lynching was remote from her middle-class world. She found herself having unwittingly accepted the dominant cultural explanation for lynching in the South—that it was the crime of rape that led to lynching and that it was the unreasonable anger over that offense that caused the mob to justify the action of lynching the perpetrator. But the three men who had been brutally murdered in Memphis in 1892 had not committed any crime against white womanhood. "This is what," she remarked, "opened my eyes to what lynching really was. An excuse to get rid of Negroes who were acquiring wealth and property and thus keep the race terrorized and 'keep the nigger down.'"[2] Emboldened by her self-discovery and her soul inflamed by an indignity greater than segregation or disenfranchisement, Wells prepared to wage a lifelong crusade against lynching.

Ida Wells was born a slave in Holly Springs, Mississippi, in 1862. She was the oldest daughter of James Wells, a slave-born carpenter and mason hired out by his owner to a local contractor, and Elizabeth Warrenton, a cook. By all indications, Ida was greatly influenced by her parents. Both were strong role models with firmly established principles and commitments. Her mother was devoted to learning and religious teaching, while her father also valued education and took an active interest in local politics. When his employer tried to coerce him to vote the Democratic ticket during Reconstruction, James Wells chose to quit his job and move his family from the property rather than compromise his political independence. James Wells later became a local businessman, a Mason, and a member of the Board of Trustees of Shaw University (later Rust College), which was established by northern Methodist missionaries in 1866 and supported by the Freedmen's Bureau.

When Wells was sixteen years old, her parents and her youngest brother died in a yellow fever epidemic that struck western Tennessee (including Memphis) and northern Mississippi in 1878–1879. In an effort to keep the family together as a surrogate parent, Ida took a job as a teacher at a country school. During the week, she lived at the school while a family friend took care of the younger children. She returned on weekends to manage the family and assume a burdensome list of household chores, returning to school each Sunday evening. Struggling under the load of single "parent" and provider, Wells ultimately placed the older children in various apprenticeships or with relatives and moved to Memphis with her two younger sisters. She secured a teaching position in a rural Shelby County school at Woodstock and began to study for the examination that would eventually gain her an appointment in the Memphis public school system.

In September 1883, while commuting on the train to her teaching job outside of Memphis, Wells experienced the humiliation that came with segregation. The ability to purchase a first-class railway ticket carried with it an importance not overlooked by many African American women. The first-class coach was the "ladies" car. The inability to sit there labeled an individual unfit to assume the status of "lady." Unwilling to allow herself to be dehu-manized and defeminized, Wells made it her practice to purchase a first-class ticket each time she rode the Chesapeake, Ohio & Southwestern Railroad from her home in Memphis to her teaching position in Woodstock. On one of these trips, a conductor confronted Wells and told her she would have to move to one of the second-class cars. In defiance, Wells refused to surrender her seat. When the conductor grabbed her arm to remove her, Wells forcibly re-sisted. She did so by grabbing the back of her seat, bracing her feet on the seat in front of her, and biting the conductor on his hand. Other passengers came to the aid of the conductor and helped carry Wells out of the car. Rather than remain in the second-class car, Wells, disheveled and with her jacket torn, got off the train at the next stop to the humiliating cheers of the other white passengers.

Raised not to take such an affront lightly, Wells sued the railroad in civil court in May 1884 and won an award of $200 in damages. That same month, however, another conductor on the same rail line again denied Wells entry into the "ladies" car. She immediately filed a second suit against the railroad for as-sault (the conductor had shoved her) and discrimination. The judge, who dis-missed the assault charge, found again in Wells's favor and awarded her $500 in damages. Although not a legal victory for integration, the court ruled that the railroad had violated an 1881 "separate but equal" law by failing to provide al-ternate first-class passage after selling her a first-class ticket. To avoid the legal precedent of paying damages and admitting fault, the railroad offered to settle out of court, but Wells indignantly refused the offer. The railroad then filed an appeal, and the case finally reached the Tennessee Supreme Court in the spring of 1887. This time, the justices, presaging the U.S. Supreme Court ruling in *Plessy v. Ferguson* (1896) that would uphold the doctrine of "separate but equal," showed what flimsy threads legal guarantees of equality were in the late nineteenth century. Reversing the previous decisions, the court now ruled that the second-class accommodations were "alike in every aspect as to comfort, convenience, and safety" as to those in first class and held Wells liable for court costs. The decision fundamentally undermined Wells's faith in the rule of law and her belief that justice would prevail in legal questions involving race. Bit-terly disappointed, she remarked, "I feel . . . utterly discouraged, and just now if it were possible would gather my race in my arms and fly far away with them. O God is there no redress, no peace, no justice in this land for us?"[3] Ironically, given the chance to write about her encounters with the railroad in the local black press, Wells would begin to find a new career for herself as a journalist and a national platform for her crusade.

As a teacher in the public schools, Wells gained automatic membership into the black elite of Memphis and eventually an opportunity to develop her talents as a journalist. She eagerly joined the Lyceum, a literary society comprised mainly of schoolteachers that met every Friday to play music, read essays, and conduct debates. The Lyceum sponsored a newspaper, the *Evening Star*, which informed the membership on current events but did not circulate to the general public. By 1886, Wells had become "editor" of this paper and quickly gained notoriety. At the same time, she was asked to write a regular column for the *Living Way*, a religious weekly. Her articles, which she signed "Iola," were in the form of letters to readers and discussed current issues and problems of interest to them. The popularity of this column soon led to her national syndication in the African American press. It was during this same period that readers learned of her ordeal with the railroad and her legal struggles with the Jim Crow laws governing public transportation. Wells also began to attend and present papers at conventions of the Colored Press Association (later the African-American Press Association) and gained election as secretary of that body in 1889.

Wells's journalistic career took another step forward that same year when she was asked to become editor and part owner (along with J. L. Fleming and Reverend Taylor Nightingale) of the *Free Speech and Headlight*, a small Baptist weekly. Two years later, she and Fleming bought out Nightingale's interest in the paper and shortened the name to the *Free Speech*. As she moved more securely into journalism, her editorials began to center more on racial protest, and her style became bolder and more censorious. Typical of her new focus and style was an editorial she penned in 1891 in which she praised African Americans in Georgetown, Kentucky, who had responded to a local lynching by setting fire to the town. "Not until the Negro rises in his might and takes a hand in resenting such cold-blooded murders, if he has to burn up whole towns," she said, "will a halt be called in wholesale lynching."[4] Her condemnations targeted powerful groups as well. She criticized black elites for ignoring the problems of others in the black community because their wealth shielded them from many of the indignities of discrimination. She criticized the black clergy for failing to speak out strongly enough against segregation. She also assailed black political leaders for betraying their race to curry the favor of whites. When she wrote an article that criticized conditions within black schools and took the school board to task for not adequately supervising the training of new teachers, she was fired from her teaching position. Wells had become her own person, but in defiantly establishing her independence, she had compromised her earning capacity, curtailed any possible dialogue with southern whites, and greatly reduced her support base in the black community.

Wells had written editorials in the *Free Speech* attacking the practice of lynching even before the Memphis incident in 1892. As the topic began to

occupy more of her attention, she started to study newspaper accounts looking for alleged causes of lynchings. She soon discovered that rape was not
even charged in more than two-thirds of the cases. Of those actually charged
with rape, guilt was doubtful in many instances. But if rape was not the real
explanation for the increase in the number of lynchings (an average of 187
per year during the decade of the 1890s), then what was? Wells concluded
that the real cause was racial terrorism. White fears of Negro insurrection during slavery had given way to white fears of black rule during Reconstruction,
which, in turn, had been superseded by white fears of African American advancement after 1877. White store owners like W. H. Barrett did not want
competition from enterprising and educated black men. Legalized segregation and political disenfranchisement served as reminders that the black man
was still regarded as inferior. Lynching was a form of intimidation, while rape
served as the metaphor in the southern white mind for any challenge to white
supremacy.

As Wells began to grasp the underlying dynamic behind lynching (made
obvious by her research and the example of Thomas Moss and others in
Memphis), she became the most vocal critic of the "rape myth." Her most
pointed editorial to date on the topic of rape appeared in the May 21, 1892,
edition of the *Free Speech*. After recounting eight recent lynchings in
Arkansas, Alabama, Louisiana, and Georgia, she boldly proclaimed, "No-
body in this section [of the country] believes the old thread-bare lie that Negro men assault white women. If Southern white men are not careful they will
over-reach themselves and public sentiment will have a reaction; a conclusion
will then be reached which will be very damaging to the moral reputation of
their women."[5] The implication of what she was saying—that white women
often encouraged liaisons with black men—had the impact of an explosion.

Wells was attending an African American Methodist Church convention in
Philadelphia when her editorial appeared. The white press in Memphis initially assumed the column had been written by her business partner, J. L.
Fleming, and threatened him with retaliation. Fearing that he might be
lynched, Fleming fled the city for his own safety. A white mob ransacked the
offices of the *Free Speech* and destroyed the presses. As whites in Memphis
learned that the offending editorial had actually been written by Wells, rumors
soon began to circulate that should she ever return to Tennessee, she would
be killed. In a sense, Wells had been banished from the South. Accepting an
offer from T. Thomas Fortune, one of the best-known African American editors of the day, Wells agreed to become a writer for his nationally circulated
newspaper the *New York Age*. She exchanged the circulation list of the *Free
Speech* for a one-fourth interest in the *Age* and immediately began to write a
series on lynching. Her article on June 25, 1892, was most dramatic. Writing

under the byline "Exiled" and filling a seven-column newspaper page, she provided detailed statistics on lynchings and again attacked the myth that they were the direct result of rape. The exposé was such a forceful indictment of both the practice of lynching and its rationale that approximately 10,000 copies of that issue were distributed to the public. The article eventually became the basis for two famous pamphlets on lynching titled *Southern Horrors* (1892) and *A Red Record* (1895).

It was Wells's growing prominence as a journalist that launched her speaking career. Not long after her provocative article appeared in the *New York Age*, a group of African American women in that city, led by Victoria Earle Matthews, a journalist, and Maritha Lyons, a schoolteacher, organized a meeting to honor Wells. The celebration, which took place at Lyric Hall on October 5, 1892, was a great success. The meeting included not only the leading black women from New York City but also groups from Boston and Philadelphia. Her speech, which was well received in the press, triggered a flood of speaking requests and encouraged her to immediately undertake a speaking tour of eastern cities. While speaking in Washington, D.C., Wells had the opportunity to meet Frederick Douglass, at that time still the dominant black figure in America. Aware that the famous abolitionist had praised her articles on lynching, Wells asked him to write an introduction to her forthcoming pamphlet, *Southern Horrors: Lynch Law in All Its Phases*. Wells and Douglass quickly became friends and allies in the crusade against lynching.

While on another speaking tour to Washington, D.C., in March 1893 as a guest of Douglass, Wells received an invitation from Isabella Mayo, a Scottish author and reformer, and Catherine Impey, a British editor and activist who had already begun a crusade against the caste system in India, to come to Great Britain and help launch an antilynching/human rights campaign there. The two women had initially requested that Douglass come to speak, but he deferred to Wells as the one who had "the story to tell."[6] *Southern Horrors* had already appeared in print in London as *U.S. Atrocities* and accounts of lynchings in the United States had begun to enter the British press. In agreeing to an extended speaking tour, the first of two such engagements in the British Isles during the early 1890s, Wells hoped to draw her foreign listeners into the antilynching debate as Douglass had once done for the abolitionist cause and bring pressure to bear on those in her own country. As Wells stated during her tour,

> The pulpit and press of our own country remains silent on these continued outrages and the voice of my race thus tortured and outraged is stifled or ignored whenever it is lifted in America in demand for justice. It is to the religious and moral sentiment of Great Britain we now turn. These can arouse the public

sentiment of Americans so necessary for the enforcement of law. The moral agencies at work in Great Britain did much for the final overthrow of chattel slavery. They can in like manner pray, write, preach, talk and act against civil and industrial slavery; against the hanging, shooting and burning alive of a powerless race.[7]

The speaking tour accomplished a great deal. It brought about the creation of the British Anti-Lynching Society, a model of citizen activism that Wells hoped to replicate someday in the United States. Additionally, the British press provided extensive coverage of her speeches as well as news of prominent individuals and associations in England that had publicly endorsed the antilynching campaign. To make sure that Americans were informed as well, copies of her speeches and endorsements were mailed to the leading ministers and newspapers in this country. The southern press responded in kind, undermining Wells's credibility, attacking her character, questioning her statistics, and challenging her basic assertions regarding the rape myth and the existence of a racially biased legal system in the South that had made a mockery of the rule of law.

Beginning with the publication of her sensational editorial on May 21, 1892, through the publication of her two major pamphlets and her speaking tours in the United States and Great Britain, Wells continued to refine her thinking concerning the causes behind mob violence that resulted in lynching. As she did so, she never wavered from one central point: lynching was not merely a punishment for the crime of rape but also a conscious act of intimidation and oppression. The public justification for lynching as the defense of southern white womanhood was really a facade to conceal a racist agenda contrived by southern white men to maintain power. As Wells analyzed the public record on lynchings, she was able to show that blacks were being lynched for charges other than rape—for murder, burglary, arson, insolence toward whites, exercising the right to vote, speaking publicly for civil rights, or sometimes for no specific reason or charge at all. She discovered that even when rape was the charge, it was not always true. Wells used evidence of consensual relationships between white women and black men to confound the notion that white women could have no interest in African American men. She also pointed out that African American women were more likely to be raped by white men and that these assaults frequently went unacknowledged and unpunished. If lynching was a justifiable response to rape, then there was a double standard.

In dismissing the racist stereotype of black men raping white women in the South, Wells understood rape as the symbol in the white southern mind for all the racial "insults" to white male honor and manhood. The African American had become, in effect, the scapegoat for white frustration. As one historian aptly put it, "The 'false chivalry' of lynching cast [white] women as Christ-like symbols of racial purity and regional identity and translated every sign of black self-assertion into a metaphor for rape—black over white, a world turned upside down."[8] The real crime of the black race in the South follow-ing the Civil War was that they seemed to be acquiring the potential—socially, politically, and economically—to achieve equality and demonstrate racial progress. Black men were no longer compelled to be deferential. Fear-ing a loss of race control, white men sought to maintain power through ter-rorism and intimidation. They used the cultural explanation that lynching was a justifiable action in response to rape as a means to that end. "This cry [of rape] has had its effect," said Wells. "It has closed the heart, stifled the con-science, warped the judgment and hushed the voice of press and pulpit on the subject of lynch law throughout this 'land of liberty.'"[9] In reeducating Amer-icans about lynching, Wells hoped to show that such actions were offenses against American values and the universal concept of justice. To remain silent was to be complicit in the crime.

Wells's unwillingness to tolerate expediency at the expense of principle alienated her from most people she came in contact with, including other po-tential collaborators for reform. She quarreled with Frances Willard, president of the Women's Christian Temperance Union, accusing her of accepting the rape myth and for subordinating the question of black rights to win the back-ing of southern whites for prohibition. Similarly, she criticized Susan B. An-thony for accepting segregation in the South in order to gain broader support for woman suffrage. Her most significant public confrontation, however, arose from disagreements she had with Booker T. Washington. By the mid-1890s, Washington had gained notoriety for the success of his school, the Tuskegee Institute, and for his ability to raise money among white philan-thropists. Washington's teaching program at Tuskegee stressed black self-reliance and self-discipline and taught African American students skills in agriculture and the trades that would allow them to become economically in-dependent. In 1895, he emerged as the dominant black leader in America (Frederick Douglass died earlier that same year) after a speech at the Cotton States International Exposition in Atlanta, Georgia. Often referred to as the "Atlanta Compromise," Washington's address proscribed the basis for inter-racial cooperation in the South. He believed that African Americans should concentrate on industrial education and economic advancement and defer de-mands for social and political equality. If southern whites would enable black opportunity (provide jobs), Washington suggested that whites would be re-paid for their efforts with greater economic prosperity and racial harmony. In time, African American advancement in education (industrially defined) and overall contributions to economic growth would win white support for broadened civil rights.

That Wells and Washington would argue publicly concerning the proper course of action for black advancement was inevitable. Their temperaments and ideologies were too much in conflict. Wells was outspoken, uncompromising, and militantly confrontational. Washington, on the other hand, was soft spoken, accommodating, and conciliatory. Wells regarded lynching as a white contrivance designed to prevent black progress. Washington argued that black success would come through patient striving and white acceptance. Wells sought immediate equality as a fundamental right, while Washington tolerated inequality to foster economic uplift. Although Wells and Washington did share some common beliefs, such as the conviction that blacks should help themselves and strive for economic independence, there were still disabling differences. Washington viewed economic power as a reward achieved by conforming to the status quo, while Wells saw it as a weapon to be used against white control. She believed that southern blacks would be an "industrial factor" as a labor force in an industrializing South. In recognizing that reality, blacks could gain leverage. "To Northern capital and Afro-American labor the South owes its rehabilitation," she argued. "If labor is withdrawn capital will not remain. The Afro-American is thus the backbone of the South. A thorough knowledge and judicious exercise of this power in lynching localities could many times effect a bloodless revolution."[10] Like Washington, Wells reasoned that white elites held the key to social change. Unlike Washington, however, she was less concerned about courting their good graces than with redirecting their self-interest.

When William Monroe Trotter and W. E. B. DuBois, two "radicals" in the anti-Washington camp, joined efforts to form a new protest organization in 1905, Wells quickly joined it. Called the Niagara Movement, the association condemned segregation, disenfranchisement, and lynching and harshly criticized Washington's program of deferring immediate civil rights. Giving strength to this new body was a race riot that took place in Springfield, Illinois, in the summer of 1908. The riot had erupted when a white woman accused a well-known black man of trying to rape her. After two nights of mob violence, authorities were forced to call in the state militia to restore order. Several days after the rioting, the white woman confessed that the black man in question had not tried to assault her. Apparently, the incident involved a white man and was not a case of rape at all. Occurring in Abraham Lincoln's hometown and burial place, the riot showed that racially motivated white mob violence was not unique to the South. To many in the Niagara Movement, the Springfield race riot offered proof that accommodationism did not work.

One of those appalled by the violence in Springfield was William English Walling, a well-known settlement house worker, suffragist, labor leader, and socialist. After visiting Springfield in the aftermath of the riot, he concluded that a national organization was needed to fight racial oppression. His plea caught the attention of Mary White Ovington and Oswald Garrison Villard, each a descendant of white abolitionists. In 1909, Walling and his supporters issued "The Call" for like-minded individuals of both races to join in a national conference to discuss ways in which African American political and civil equality might be obtained. Issued on the one-hundredth anniversary of Lincoln's birth in 1909, the petition included the signatures of sixty activists, including Wells.

The conference, which eventually led to the creation of the National Association for the Advancement of Colored People (NAACP) in 1910, was a major disappointment for Wells. Asked to speak at the opening session of the conference, she presented an address, "Lynching: Our National Crime," in which she opened with three "facts":

> First: Lynching is color line murder.
> Second: Crime against women is the excuse, not the cause.
> Third: It is a national crime and requires a national remedy.[11]

To Wells, agitation to stop lynching would have to be backed up with an appeal to law, which would include federal antilynching legislation and a federal bureau to investigate and publicize the details of every lynching. "Federal protection of American citizenship," said Wells, "is the remedy for lynching."[12] Her speech, however, proved to be her only shining moment at the conference. Slighted at being omitted from the "Committee of Forty" that was selected to perfect the new organization, she walked out of the meeting. Although she was later added to the executive committee of the NAACP, she would never play a major role in the association. Offended and distrustful of the liberal white leadership that controlled the NAACP in its early days, she decided to retreat to her home base in Chicago and concentrate on forming local organizations that she could direct. Later, Mary White Ovington tried to explain the break in terms that had a ring of truth. "She [Ida Wells] was a great fighter," said Ovington, "but we knew she had to play a lone hand. And if you have too many players of lone hands in your organization, you soon have no game."[13] Ironically, the most powerful voice opposing lynching for over twenty years and a persistent advocate of a national association to combat racial discrimination and oppression was not among the active leaders of the NAACP.

Wells had taken a keen interest in creating local agencies to improve the lives of black people for a number of years. She became interested in the reformist activities of British women's civic groups while in Great Britain on her speaking tours. After returning to the United States in 1893, she encouraged African American women to do likewise. Wells's call came at a time when African American women were very receptive to such an idea. Because the two dominant agencies of influence in the black community—the Republican Party and the black church—were controlled by men, black women needed a forum to discuss issues important to them. Between 1893 and 1895, such groups began to multiply in major American cities. One of the earliest of these new civic agencies for black women was the Ida B. Wells Club in Chicago, founded in 1893, for which she served as president.

Wells became even more rooted as a Chicago activist and community organizer after 1895. That same year, she married Ferdinand L. Barnett, a lawyer, black rights activist, and founder and editor of the *Chicago Conservator*, the city's first black newspaper. She continued to be an active lecturer even after the birth of her first child in 1896 but began to reduce her speaking commitments after the arrival of her second child the following year. She remained very busy writing for the *Conservator*, working with her civic club, and teaching a Sunday school class for young men at the Grace Presbyterian Church. In 1910, she encouraged her students to start, under her supervision, the Negro Fellowship League (NFL) and actively engage themselves in social service. Although still an integrationist, Wells-Barnett began to see an increased need for new race-based programs of black self-help. The NFL established an African American settlement house in the Chicago ghetto. Funded largely by contributions from Victor F. Lawson, the owner/editor of the *Chicago Daily News*, the new center provided a meeting place and offered religious services. It also served as an employment bureau to assist the rapidly increasing number of black migrants from the South. Wells-Barnett increased her workload in 1913, when she accepted a patronage position as the first woman adult probation officer for the Chicago Municipal Court. She immediately began use her new post to draw attention to abuses in the criminal justice system. Concern for the poor treatment of black prisoners led the NFL to appoint "jail visitors" who would meet with inmates at the major correctional facilities.

Wells-Barnett's social activism included the cause of woman suffrage as well. When many white leaders in the National American Woman Suffrage Association continued to rely on expediency as their primary tactic and insist that gender interests should be placed above those of race or class, she publicly disagreed. She believed that suffrage achieved by condoning segregation would leave black women as disenfranchised as black men. Unwilling to participate in an organization that held such a double standard, Wells-Barnett founded the Alpha Suffrage Club in 1913, the first black woman suffrage association in Illinois.

As the United States entered the World War I era, events occurred that would allow Wells-Barnett to reclaim the national spotlight. Unfortunately—and unfairly—her participation in those events would earn her the label "race agitator" and serve to further marginalize her within the movement to achieve racial equality. With the outbreak of World War I, European immigration declined drastically. At the same time, war preparedness created an industrial boom and an even greater demand for workers. To fill this need, northern factory owners began to recruit black workers from the South. The resulting black exodus caused concern in the white-dominated labor movement and friction with white majorities in northern cities. When a race riot erupted in East St. Louis, Illinois, shortly after the United States entered the war, it signaled a widening racial rift in the country.

The result of economic competition between white and black workers and pent-up racial hostility, the East St. Louis riot caused the deaths of at least thirty-nine African Americans in July 1917. Outraged by the news of the violence, Wells-Barnett went to East St. Louis and quickly became appalled at not only the destruction caused by the white mobs but also the negligence and complicity of the local police and state militia. Her published account of the incident, *The East St. Louis Massacre, the Greatest Outrage of the Century*, helped persuade Congress to launch an investigation of the riot. But when she urged "Negroes everywhere to stand their ground and sell their lives as dearly as possible when attacked" and her husband advised blacks to "[g]et guns and put them in your homes," they alarmed federal authorities who accused the couple of stirring up "a great deal of racial antagonism."[14]

The implication that Wells-Barnett was a "subversive" took on an added dimension when she publicly supported black soldiers in Houston, Texas, who had been charged with mutiny and murder in the fall of 1917. Trouble had started when black soldiers of the Third Battalion of the Twenty-fourth Infantry became the targets of racial abuse by the city's white residents and police. The flare-up occurred when black soldiers, upset at the taunting and at the army's apparent indifference to existing segregation ordinances in the city, resorted to violence. On the night of August 23, 1917, about 100 soldiers engaged in a three-hour riot in which twenty people died. Court-martial convictions followed, and thirteen black soldiers were eventually hanged. Wells-Barnett saw the incident as another example of racial injustice and, in protest, began to distribute buttons with the words, "In Memorial MARTYRED NEGRO SOLDIERS." Her action brought two secret agents to her office who threatened her with arrest if she continued. When informed by the agents that other African Americans did not agree with her, Wells-Barnett responded, "I don't care. I'd rather go down in history as one lone Negro who dared to tell the government that it had done a dastardly thing than to save my skin by taking back what I have said. I would consider it an honor to spend whatever years are necessary in prison as the one member of the race who protested." One year later, W. H. Loving, an agent for the Military Intelligence Division, recalled the button incident in requesting that the government deny a passport application to Wells-Barnett, a "known race agitator."[15]

During the last decade of her life, Wells-Barnett became increasingly disillusioned. For a time, she was drawn to Marcus Garvey's Universal Negro Improvement Association. Although she never totally accepted the idea of black separatism, she did like Garvey's call for black self-help and economic independence. She was also impressed with the way in which Garvey was able to instill a new racial consciousness and racial unity among many African Americans. But as the postwar decade signaled increased racial prejudice as manifest in a reinvigorated Ku Klux Klan, Wells-Barnett became increasingly despondent. It was in such an atmosphere that she began work on her *Autobiography*, in many ways a defense of her life's work. She had, sadly, begun the project after a young woman admitted that she did not know why Wells-Barnett was important, a sobering reminder just how much her position as a spokesperson on racial issues had diminished. She was at work on the book when she became ill and died of uremic poisoning on March 25, 1931.

Wells-Barnett should be remembered as someone who was deeply affected by racial injustice. To fight against such injustice, she undertook a single-handed crusade to express and interpret the indignities, wrongs, and sufferings being inflicted on an oppressed race. Her stark depictions of the horrors of lynching and her fact-based discussion of that practice attracted public attention for the first time both here and abroad and began the slow, tortuous process toward public rejection of those crimes. She broke the silence. In militantly refusing to condone racial prejudice, Wells-Barnett often compromised her effectiveness as an organizational leader, but her determination kept the issue alive and forced others, white and black, to confront it. She possessed the personal courage of a Mose Wright, who stood up in court and identified a white man whom he accused of murdering his nephew Emmett Till; a Rosa Parks, who refused to give up her seat to a white man on a crowded, segregated inner-city bus in Montgomery, Alabama; or a Martin Luther King Jr., who used nonviolent protest to confront segregation in the South. She was, for her time, the racial conscience of the nation.

NOTES

1. Alfreda M. Duster, ed., *Crusade for Justice: The Autobiography of Ida B. Wells* (Chicago: University of Chicago Press, 1970), 52.

2. Duster, *Crusade for Justice*, 64.

3. Linda O. McMurray, *To Keep the Waters Troubled: The Life of Ida B. Wells* (New York: Oxford University Press, 1998), 29–30.

4. Thomas C. Holt, "The Lonely Warrior: Ida B. Wells-Barnett and the Struggle for Black Leadership," in *Black Leaders of the Twentieth Century*, ed. John Hope Franklin and August Meier (Urbana: University of Illinois Press, 1982), 42.

5. Jacqueline Jones Royster, ed., *Southern Horrors and Other Writings: The Anti-Lynching Campaign of Ida B. Wells, 1892–1900* (Boston: Bedford/St. Martin's Press, 1997), 1.

6. Duster, *Crusade for Justice*, 86.

7. McMurray, *To Keep the Waters Troubled*, 193.

8. Royster, *Southern Horrors and Other Writings*, 32.

9. Royster, *Southern Horrors and Other Writings*, 61.

10. Holt, "The Lonely Warrior," 45.

11. McMurray, *To Keep the Waters Troubled*, 280.

12. Patricia A. Schechter, *Ida B. Wells-Barnett and American Reform, 1880–1930* (Chapel Hill: University of North Carolina Press, 2001), 135.

13. McMurray, *To Keep the Waters Troubled*, 282.

14. McMurray, *To Keep the Waters Troubled*, 317.

15. McMurray, *To Keep the Waters Troubled*, 319, 320.

SOURCES

Duster, Alfreda M., ed. *Crusade for Justice: The Autobiography of Ida B. Wells.* Chicago: University of Chicago Press, 1970.

Holt, Thomas C. "The Lonely Warrior: Ida B. Wells-Barnett and the Struggle for Black Leadership." In *Black Leaders of the Twentieth Century*, ed. John Hope Franklin and August Meier. Urbana: University of Illinois Press, 1982.

McMurray, Linda O. *To Keep the Waters Troubled: The Life of Ida B. Wells.* New York: Oxford University Press, 1998.

Royster, Jacqueline Jones, ed. *Southern Horrors and Other Writings: The Anti-Lynching Campaign of Ida B. Wells, 1892–1900.* Boston: Bedford/St. Martin's Press, 1997.

Schechter, Patricia A. *Ida B. Wells-Barnett and American Reform, 1880–1930.* Chapel Hill: University of North Carolina Press, 2001.

Tucker, David M. "Miss Ida B. Wells and Memphis Lynching." *Phylon* 32 (Summer 1971): 112–22.

5

Walter Rauschenbusch and the Social Gospel

In 1910, muckraking journalist Ray Stannard Baker issued *The Spiritual Unrest*, a collection of his articles that had originally appeared in the *American* magazine. Baker was looking to assess the state of spirituality in America. He sensed that the Protestant Church was in a period of decline, and he wanted to know why that was happening and what attempts were being made to restore vitality and meaning to organized religion. Baker's concern was actually a growing public concern. America's Protestant churches were losing much of their authority. Citizens in increasing numbers were beginning to have doubts about the relevancy of old theological tenets and about the role of the church in turn-of-the-century urban-industrial America. Instead of providing a Christian critique of society, it seemed to many that the church had stagnated. Having become aligned with conservative or reactionary forces, churches and church leaders seemed unwilling to change or challenge the status quo. They held to the old assumption that religion had relevance only in questions of personal or individual morality. Very much influenced by the Gilded Age's emphasis on social Darwinism, church officials remained confident that laissez-faire capitalism would solve economic problems even in the face of mounting evidence to the contrary. Declining church membership among the working class offered a further indication that Protestant churches were alarmingly out of step with burgeoning urban populations. Feeling increasingly oppressed by the socioeconomic conditions surrounding them, city dwellers chafed at the complacent outlook of the church and its seeming refusal to consider reform proposals aimed at ameliorating those conditions. They wanted sermons that were relevant to their everyday existence and practical help that promised to improve the quality of their lives.

As Baker talked with Protestant clergymen to gain information for his articles, he asked them to name a recent book or individual who had done the most to challenge the existing intellectual parameters of the Protestant Church. The seemingly unanimous response was *Christianity and the Social Crisis* (1907), written by a relatively obscure professor of church history at the Rochester Theological Seminary by the name of Walter Rauschenbusch. The book, which would eventually sell over 50,000 copies through several reprint editions, was popular in part because of its timeliness. It confronted the problem of "spiritual unrest" through a detailed and expanded criticism of the Protestant Church. It also offered the promise of spiritual peace by providing a radical prescription for what it meant to live as a true Christian in a capitalistic society. It was perhaps the clearest expression to date of the rise within American Protestantism of a new "social gospel," the effort to mold faith into a tool of social reform. But who was this new prophet who had been thrust to prominence on the strength of this influential treatise?

Walter Rauschenbusch was born in Rochester, New York, in 1861, the only son of August Rauschenbusch and Caroline Rhomp. His father, a first-generation German immigrant and theologian, was the sixth in an unbroken succession of evangelical German ministers dating back to the seventeenth century. Growing up, Walter had no doubt that he would follow in his father's footsteps. Heeding his father's advice as to the value of the German system of education, young Rauschenbusch spent several years as a youth studying in that country. It was perhaps through his contact with German educators that he obtained the relativistic perspective that would later free him intellectually from the more deterministic thinking of the classical economists. After graduating from the Gymnasium at Gutersloh, Germany, with honors in 1883, he finished his formal education at the University of Rochester (A.B., 1884) and the Rochester Theological Seminary (B.D., 1886), where his father was a professor. He was immediately ordained as a minister in the German Baptist Church.

As he prepared to begin his new career, Rauschenbusch had no doubt that his purpose in life was to encourage each parishioner in his church to seek personal salvation. He firmly believed that the supreme achievement of religion was to instill in man the love of God. Had he accepted a position in a rural church, he probably would have given free rein to his enthusiasm as a twenty-five-year-old evangelist. Instead, Rauschenbusch took a post at the Second German Baptist Church in a depressed section of New York City on West 54th Street near Tenth Avenue only a couple of blocks from the infamous Hell's Kitchen. Surrounded by crowded tenements, factories, and

Walter Rauschenbusch, circa 1916. Library of Congress, Prints & Photographs Division.

sweatshops and comprised of a small poverty-stricken congregation of 125 immigrant working-class worshippers, the task of rejuvenating the church was a formidable one indeed. He accepted a salary of $600 that he had to pinch and scrimp to live on. His own economic hardship made it easier for him to sympathize with those around him, but he could not help but feel at sea in a strange environment. In New York, an individual "feels the waves of human life all around," he said, "as it really is, not as it ought to be according to the decretum absolutum of an old theology."[1]

Rauschenbusch quickly found that his initial assumption regarding his mission as a minister was out of step with congregants who were living lives of desperation bordering on destitution. He remembered seeing "good men go into disreputable lines of employment and respectable widows consent to live with men who would support them and their children. One could hear human virtue cracking and crumbling all around."[2] When conditions worsened during the depression of the 1890s, Rauschenbusch later remarked that he could never forget "the procession of men out of work, out of clothes, out of shoes, and out of hope. They wore down our threshold and they wore away our hearts."[3] As he became more and more absorbed with his surroundings, he increasingly found the old evangelism that had been preached to him—to save their souls and his—too inadequate, too indifferent to the problems facing those trapped in urban squalor. As he wearied of telling his congregation that God would be good to them in the next life, he began to wonder about their rights in this life.

As Rauschenbusch struggled to adjust to the appalling waste of human life that seemed to mock him in his tenement district, he began to question the efficacy of capitalism as a humane economic system. Helping him formulate answers to his questions were two pioneering economists: Henry George and Richard Ely. In October 1886, the year Rauschenbusch arrived in New York City, Henry George had launched his campaign to become mayor of New York City. George understood the economic hardship that confronted wage earners daily. In his mind, this "industrial slavery" occurred when men abridged "the eternal laws of the universe." George believed that God had intended land to be used for the benefit of all the people, but unjustly some individuals had been allowed to monopolize the land and accrue unearned wealth to themselves and poverty to others. George's idea of placing a single tax on land being held for speculation was seen as a means to broaden economic opportunity, create employment, raise wages, and lower rents. It had a tremendous impact on Rauschenbusch. "I owe my own first awakening to the world of social problems," he said, "to the agitation of Henry George in 1886."[4]

The economic ramifications of what George was saying—that poverty was not inevitable or necessarily the result of personal failure and that it could be eliminated—fascinated Rauschenbusch. He was also stirred by George's almost religious vision of what society could become: "With want destroyed; with greed changed to noble passions; with the fraternity that is born of equality taking the place of the jealousy and fear that now array men against each other . . . who shall measure the heights to which our civilization may soar?"[5] In recounting the George campaign, Rauschenbusch remembered hearing Father Edward McGlynn, an ardent George supporter, speak at Cooper Union and recite the words, "Thy Kingdom come! Thy will be done on earth." "As the great audience realized for the first time the social significance of the holy words," said Rauschenbusch, "it lifted them off their seats with a shout of joy."[6] He must have been among those who stood, for to him as well the words gave Jesus' prayer an entirely new social meaning.

A second influence on Rauschenbusch at this time was Richard Ely, a professor of political economy at Johns Hopkins University. While studying in Germany, Ely had become influenced by German academic economists who challenged the established claims of conservative English economists that immutable natural laws determined who succeeded and who failed in life. Instead, they argued that individuals could modify the existing economic order and ensure that no one's material well-being would be denied. Through his writing, teaching, public lectures, and position as a founder of the new American Economic Association in 1885, Ely argued that there was a moral component to economics and such a thing as proper social relations. However, society could realize these ideals only in a healthy economic climate. Ely believed that such environments could be quickly improved by state intervention. This might manifest itself as municipal ownership of natural monopolies in utilities such as gas and water and by allowing workers greater freedom to bargain in their own behalf through organizations like trade unions.

More than Henry George, Ely believed that churches should take an active role in bringing about social and economic reform. Convinced that laissez-faire capitalism was incompatible with Christianity, Ely was receptive to the ideas of F. D. Maurice and other earlier English Christians that came to be known as Christian socialism. Generally, Christian socialists criticized both the individualistic and the competitive nature of industrial capitalism that they believed worked to widen the gap between rich and poor and the Protestant Church that supported such a system. Instead, they envisioned a cooperative commonwealth that benefited everyone and a Protestant Church that preached a true social gospel. In a paper that Rauschenbusch heard presented at a meeting of Baptist ministers in 1888, Ely argued that the church had forgotten the true gospel, which included a passion for social justice, and had come to focus solely on the "one-sided half gospel" of individual salvation.

"The Gospel of Christ," said Ely, "is both individual and social. It proclaims individual and social regeneration, individual and social salvation." And as Ely encouraged Christians to become activists, he reminded them, "It is as truly a religious work to pass good laws, as it is to preach sermons; as holy a work to lead a crusade against filth, vice, and disease in slums of cities, and to seek the abolition of the disgraceful tenement-houses of American cities, as it is to send missionaries to the heathen."[7] The ideas of George and Ely had taken hold of Rauschenbusch, and he began to recommend books written by them to other German Baptists searching to better understand their social mission.

Inspired by the writings of George and Ely, Rauschenbusch began to expand his reading to further explore the "social question." As he intensified his interest in the relationship of religion to the urban working class, he became convinced that he needed to embrace some form of socialism. In 1889, after attending Baptist meetings in Boston, Rauschenbusch became acquainted with the Society of Christian Socialists established in that city only a few months earlier by William Dwight Porter Bliss, an Episcopal priest. Christian socialists distanced themselves from the more doctrinaire Marxists who advocated class conflict by arguing that the socialist goal of the cooperative commonwealth was "embraced in the aim of Christianity."[8] Concerned about the plight of workers and the need for a meaningful Christian response to the exploitation that accompanied industrial capitalism, Rauschenbusch was ready to enlist in their ranks.

In November of that same year, Rauschenbusch joined with three other Baptist clergymen to begin publication of a newspaper titled *For the Right*. The aim of the publication was to discuss labor problems from the perspective of Christian socialism. The editors hoped to articulate "the needs, the aspirations, the longings of the tens of thousands of wage-earners who are sighing for better things; and to point out, if possible, not only the wrongs that men suffer, but the methods by which these wrongs may be removed." During the next year and a half, Rauschenbusch wrote twenty-one articles for the newspaper in which he took the moderate position that workers should pursue gradual, nonviolent means to bring about economic improvement through organization, publicity, dialogue with their employers, and use of the ballot box. Specific ideas endorsed by Rauschenbusch included the eight-hour day, the single tax, municipal ownership of utilities, and ballot reform. *For the Right* struggled along until March 1891, but meager subscriptions and mounting debts ultimately killed the venture. Affluent Christians apparently found the editorial stance too "radical," while workers eager for tangible solutions thought it too "Christian." For Rauschenbusch, however, the experience was invigorating. The opportunity to share ideas with other like-minded Christian dissenters and to experiment with one method of agitation had given him the freedom to begin to formulate his own theological basis for a course of action that would encourage Christians to become more socially conscious. Rauschenbusch's first steps into the arena of social reform had convinced him that it was no longer adequate to wait for the church to change the lives of individuals and to hope that those individuals might then correct social wrongs. Instead, the church had to confront "the wrongs of human society and the unjust laws of the community to bring about righteousness."[9]

In 1891, Rauschenbusch shocked his congregation by announcing that he was resigning from his position and going abroad for a year of study before beginning a career as a writer. His decision was motivated by his deepening desire to have more free time to continue to reformulate his theology but also by the realization that his physical condition had compromised his duties as a minister. Rauschenbusch was experiencing almost total deafness. He first became aware of the condition in 1885, but by 1890 his condition had worsened to the point that he could hear only what was spoken directly to him and very near to him. To his surprise, however, the officials at his church offered him a one-year sabbatical with pay and agreed to hire an assistant minister if he needed help when he returned. Finding the proposed arrangement agreeable, he left for Europe eager to begin a period of uninterrupted thought and reflection.

Rauschenbusch first traveled to London, where he spent some time learning about British organizations that were working to ease the burden of poverty. He attended a conference at Toynbee Hall, a settlement house in the impoverished Whitechapel section of East London. The hall, which had such a moving effect on American Jane Addams, had been established a few years before as a memorial to Arnold Toynbee, a noted Oxford scholar who spent a good deal of time among London's poor prior to his death in 1883. The dozen or so settlement workers who lived at the hall provided various outreach programs to assist the impoverished residents of the area. He also became especially interested in the efforts of the Salvation Army. Under the direction of its founder, General William Booth, the Army recruited working-class men and women to preach the gospel in depressed urban areas. Booth believed that poverty stifled the acceptance of Christianity and felt that if the Salvation Army could help the poor escape poverty, it could help them realize a conversion experience. But after visiting food depots and shelters and listening to the advocates of social uplift, Rauschenbusch concluded that such efforts were inadequate because they addressed only the symptoms of poverty, not the causes. He did, however, respond enthusiastically to socialist speakers preaching their philosophy to working-class crowds in Hyde Park. One speaker who especially impressed him was John Burns, a prominent labor union leader. "Burns," said Rauschenbusch, "is the man who for weeks got up every morning at four, harangued the starving dockers, infused courage into them, persuaded them not to use violence, and then went off to his shop to earn his living."[10] It was that type of personal commitment wedded to direct action aimed at changing the system that appealed to Rauschenbusch's sense of activism.

It was in Germany, however, that Rauschenbusch began to crystallize his thinking and industriously started work on a book-length manuscript with the working title "Revolutionary Christianity." The fundamental point raised in the hastily completed 450-page rough draft (it would not appear in print as a substantially revised book for another sixteen years) was the failure of the modern church to correctly understand Christianity. In his mind, what had been forgotten was the revolutionary nature of Christianity and that the community created by Jesus was radically different from the one people had grown accustomed to in the late nineteenth century. As a result, the church had erred. It concentrated on a message that pandered to an individual's selfish quest for salvation, allowed itself to be controlled by wealth, neglected individuals on the bottom rungs of society, and offered no direction to those who sought the social regeneration of society. To Rauschenbusch, the church had to rediscover the authentic gospel and be reformed by it.

The key to Rauschenbusch's critique of organized religion and his hope for its redemption was the message of Jesus: live in conformity with the divine will. The coming of the Kingdom of God on Earth, he argued, was the center of Jesus' teaching. Jesus started the kingdom and embodied the righteousness of it in his own life. Christians were, thereby, empowered to do as Jesus had done: to recreate the Kingdom of God on Earth. Rauschenbusch's conclusion was a major step in both his theological development and the way he envisioned his own ministry. "It responded," he said, "to all the old and all the new elements of my religious life. The saving of the lost, the teaching of the young, the pastoral care of the poor and frail, the quickening of starved intellects, the study of the Bible . . . political reform, the reorganization of the industrial system . . . it was all covered by the one aim of the reign of God on earth."[11]

After returning to the United States in late December 1891, Rauschenbusch redoubled his efforts to articulate a Christian vision that could transform society. At a national Baptist convention in Philadelphia in May 1892, he seized the opportunity to proclaim his vision before a national audience of his peers. "The whole aim of Christ," he declared, "is embraced in the words 'the Kingdom of God.'" "In that ideal," he argued, "is embraced the sanctification of all life, the regeneration of humanity, and the reformation of all social institutions." A young pastor of a Baptist church in a tenement section of Philadelphia by the name of Samuel Zane Batten heard the speech and was roused to action. Meeting with Rauschenbusch and four other prominent Baptist ministers, he proposed the creation of a new group committed to the common pursuit of the Kingdom of God and that they meet periodically to exchange ideas and share their efforts to that end. At two other meetings during 1892, the group adopted a name for their association and a statement of purpose. As they declared in their original charter, "The spirit of God is moving men in our generation toward a better understanding of the idea of the Kingdom of God on earth. Obeying the thought of our master, and trusting in the power and guidance of the Spirit, we form ourselves into a Brotherhood of the Kingdom, in order to reestablish this idea in the thought of the church, and to assist in its practical realization in the world."[12]

The members of the Brotherhood presented papers and published collections of their essays that involved critical studies of the Scriptures and the need for Christian unity but also secular topics, such as improving municipal government and designing legislation to protect the rights of workers. Over time, the Brotherhood expanded its ranks with the addition of new members including women and non-Baptists. They also established contact with sympathizers in England, France, and Germany and invited papers from American friends of the Brotherhood such as Henry George, Richard Ely, Josiah Strong, W. D. P. Bliss, Washington Gladden, and Jacob Riis. There was at that time no other group of American Christians who regularly addressed such a thorough agenda of religious and social reform.

In the first of several pamphlets he wrote for the Brotherhood, Rauschenbusch attempted to summarize the extent of the problem facing Christians who were trying to understand the true message and meaning of the church. As one historian put it, "It was as though he were nailing theses to the door of Christendom."[13] According to Rauschenbusch,

Because the Kingdom of God has been dropped as the primary and comprehensive aim of Christianity, and personal salvation has been substituted for it, therefore men seek to save their own souls and are selfishly indifferent to the evangelization of the world.

Because the individualistic conception of personal salvation has pushed out of sight the collective idea of a Kingdom of God on earth, Christian men seek for the salvation of individuals and are comparatively indifferent to the spread of the spirit of Christ in the political, industrial, social, scientific and artistic life of humanity, and have left these as the undisturbed possession of the spirit of the world.

Because the Kingdom of God has been understood as a state to be inherited in a future life rather than as something to be realized here and now, therefore Christians have been contented with a low plane of life here and have postponed holiness to the future.

> Because the Kingdom of God has been confined within the church, therefore
> the church has been regarded as an end instead of a means, and men have
> thought they were building up the Kingdom when they were only cementing a
> strong church organization.[14]

He was certain that once Christians had realized that the church had mis-
understood Jesus' teachings about the Kingdom, they could correct the wrong
by seeking to make God's will a reality in this life as, in their mind, it was in
heaven.

In 1893, Rauschenbusch married Pauline Rother, a German-language
teacher from Milwaukee, Wisconsin, whom he had met while attending a
German Baptist convention in that city several years earlier. In doing so, he
unwittingly gained a valuable helpmate as well as a soul mate. Pauline immediately took an active interest in his work. She helped with his daily duties
as a pastor and often called on church members with him. Much of Rauschenbusch's ability to overcome his hearing handicap and become a successful
public speaker was due to her assistance as his "hearing ear." She often traveled with him and would write shorthand summaries of questions he could
not hear so that he could respond to his audiences directly. Pauline truly
believed her husband had a calling as a reformer and once wrote to him, "I
delight in the influence for good that you carry wherever you go."[15]

In 1897, the president of the Rochester Theological Seminary asked
Rauschenbusch to become professor of theology in the German department at
that institution. Although he was reluctant to leave the congregation he had
served for eleven years, he saw the offer as a great opportunity. He truly believed that German Baptists were leaders in "radical Christianity" doing "out-
post duty" for the larger Christian movement. By training future ministers to
shape the direction of the church, he believed he could do more than he could
as a pastor of a single church. He decided it was the right move to make.
Shifting to the English department in 1902 to become professor of church
history to accommodate his research and writing, he would remain on the
faculty for the rest of his life.

As Rauschenbusch settled into his new career as a teacher and a scholar, he
quickly learned that the city of Rochester suffered from most of the same
problems that he had encountered in New York City: crowded and dilapidated
working-class housing, inadequate recreational facilities for children, industrial pollution, and powerful businessmen who placed their own economic advancement above the welfare of the public. To confront these common urban
dilemmas, Rauschenbusch allied himself with the city's bipartisan Good
Government clubs under the leadership of businessman Joseph Alling and
others who were either pastors or lay leaders of local churches. He soon found

himself as one of Rochester's civic reform leaders, fighting to obtain lower gas and electric rates and improved service for consumers, pleading for the creation of public "swimming baths" on the Genesee River that would be open during the summer, campaigning for local-option liquor laws, making suggestions for improving public school curriculum, and heading a Young Men's Christian Association (YMCA) muckraking-style investigation of social problems in the city.

One of the reasons for involving himself with other church-based reform groups was to use those existing organizations as the means to address what he increasingly perceived as the primary problem facing Christians everywhere: how to narrow the gap between organized Christianity and the growing numbers of working-class people who were increasingly estranged from it. Rauschenbusch believed that the church's message, shaped by the mind-set of an earlier era and controlled by the upper classes, needed to be reformulated to become relevant once again to the working class.

Seeking to end this estrangement, Rauschenbusch joined with Paul Moore Strayer, a Presbyterian minister and member of the city's Central Labor Council, to create a new civic forum. Under Strayer and Rauschenbusch's leadership, a group of ministers agreed to host Sunday-night programs in a large downtown theater that workers would be invited to attend. In addition to the usual hymns and prayers, there would be speakers on contemporary topics and feedback from the audience. Launched on November 1, 1908, the endeavor was a great success. Attendance for the first five months exceeded 30,000. Many idle workers found employment through contacts made at these meetings and perhaps discovered a new appreciation for Christianity, while ministers developed pastoral ties among individuals with no formal religious or church affiliation. Rauschenbusch, who relished the opportunity to establish a dialogue with workers, found that "audiences were . . . profoundly interested in strong, vital, earnest discussions that got to the marrow of the social questions of life," and he regarded the Sunday programs as a triumph of participatory democracy.[16] City ordinances allowing for Sunday movies eventually began to undercut attendance until distractions related to the deepening world war finally forced the termination of the program in 1916.

Despite Rauschenbusch's reputation as a Baptist theologian and his notoriety as an emerging civic reform leader in Rochester, it was the publication of *Christianity and the Social Crisis* in 1907 that thrust him into national prominence as the leader of the social gospel movement. The manuscript, hastily completed in Germany sixteen years before under the working title "Revolutionary Christianity," had sat idly while he waited for the inspiration to revise it. "Three times I started," he said, "and each time I was compelled to stop in the middle on account of work. When I went back to my book, I found each time that I had outgrown my book, so I discarded all three."[17] Finally, over two summer vacations in 1905 and 1906, he had the manuscript ready to submit for publication. Anxiety apparently plagued the entire revision process, as Rauschenbusch later recalled feeling that he was writing a "dangerous" book whose radical ideas were likely to generate anger and resentment and perhaps even jeopardize his academic position. Unsure as to how critics would review his book, he left almost immediately after its publication for a six-month sabbatical in Germany.

The thrust of the book was a plea for Christians to begin the formidable task of creating a new social order. Using biblical and historical data, Rauschenbusch sought to challenge existing understandings of Jesus, both the man and his mission. In drawing on ten years of experience as a professor of church history, he critically reexamined the Old and New Testaments and the primitive church in searching for their true meaning. As one historian has noted, however, he was selective. "He largely disregarded the legalistic sections of the Old Testament, all Gospels but Luke's, all periods of Jesus' life except that in which He was most sanguine about winning an immediate victory on earth, all the pre-millennialism of the early Church. He concentrated on a single message from the prophets, Jesus, the early saints: that men must strive for social justice."[18] He wanted Christians to recover Jesus' true social purpose: to continue the mission of the early prophets of Israel who sought to elevate the collective life of their people along the path of justice as willed by God and refashion a new conception of what it meant to be human.

Recovery of this social mission with its attendant sense of social responsibility would allow civilization to avert impending catastrophe. Rauschenbusch believed that industrialized society had become dominated by an economic system that victimized everyone it touched. Workers received less than they deserved for their labor and suffered diminished health and dignity in the process. Capitalists, on the other hand, appropriated more than they deserved and suffered the loss of those qualities that made life human. The division between rich and poor had widened to the point where class war was a distinct possibility. The best hope of avoiding this catastrophe, he believed, was for the church to recapture its moral vision and undertake to lead a new social mission. "It is," he said, "either a revival of social religion or the deluge."[19]

In arguing that positive action could avert the impending social crisis, Rauschenbusch targeted the professional and business class that made up such a large part of Protestant church membership. He wanted them to experience a spiritual regeneration that would awaken them to the sobering realization that they were complicit in society's sins and inspire them to undertake a new commitment to social reform. Protestant ministers would lead by proclaiming Jesus' gospel of the Kingdom of God on Earth, while the regenerated churchgoer would seek to further the idea of the Kingdom in daily life by advancing more humane ways of thinking and behaving. As was characteristic of the social gospel movement, Rauschenbusch was attempting to redefine Christian obligation in a way that would transform individuals and institutions.

The book was a major success. When Rauschenbusch returned after his sabbatical, he was famous. A banquet held in his honor in New York City on his return was only the beginning of his celebrity. Assuming the role of an evangelist, he traveled the country speaking before churches, university groups, the YMCA, theological schools, and summer conferences and forums. In a nine-month period during 1908–1909, he gave thirteen sermons, forty-one lectures and papers, and thirty-five addresses. Even President Theodore Roosevelt sought him out for a personal conversation at the White House. The popularity of *Christianity and the Social Crisis* convinced Rauschenbusch to agree to publish a sequel focusing on the same historical and theological themes to be called "The Church and the Kingdom." That book was never written because his own intellectual interests were increasingly drawn toward practical questions that had been raised by audiences during his speaking engagements. Having been persuaded of the need to rework the social order, listeners wanted to be told what practical steps they could take to bring about such a transformation. Rauschenbusch attempted to address those questions during two series of lectures he gave at the Pacific Theological Seminary in Berkeley, California, in 1910 and at Ohio Wesleyan University in 1911. He then agreed to publish those lectures in revised form as the follow-up to *Christianity and the Social Crisis.*

The finished book, published as *Christianizing the Social Order* in 1912, provided a sharper critique of capitalism and offered a variety of practical goals for those eager to reform the system. Rauschenbusch thought that industrial capitalism was the root of all the evils confronting society. As such, he assailed competition as a form of survival of the fittest and argued that as a principle it denied fraternity. He accused middlemen of being irresponsibly selfish and doing harm to society through sinful practices such a food adulteration, short weighing, and false advertising. He attacked the profit motive, at least where it rested on monopoly privilege, as "tribute collected by power from the helpless." In short, Rauschenbusch found industrial capitalism to be "a mammonistic organization with which Christianity can never be content." The solution was deductively simple. A new society must replace jungle law with moral law. "Christianizing the social order," he argued, "means bringing it into harmony with the ethical convictions which we identify with Christ. . . . The fundamental step is the establishment of social justice by the abolition of unjust privilege."[20] For this to happen, however, citizens must see the state as a positive force for promoting the welfare of the larger community. It would be through state action that unearned income could be taxed, monopolies dissolved, corporations regulated, natural resources (minerals, forests, and water) protected, natural monopolies (gas, electric light and power, and water) municipally owned, aid for the needy provided, protective labor legislation enacted, and labor's right to organize, bargain collectively, and strike guaranteed.

Rauschenbusch's optimistic hope for a better world could not survive the hatred and disruption that came with World War I. In January 1914, the impending war provoked him to prophesy that if the world went to war, it would "absorb the attention of the people, consume their capacity for moral enthusiasm, and set free such forces of greed, debauchery and demoralization that all our religious aspirations would be cut down like young wheat in a hailstorm." The prospect saddened him greatly. After the war started, Rauschenbusch appeared to defend Germany by accusing the national press of a pro-British bias and (in words similar to the socialist analysis of the war as an economic struggle) assailing American munitions manufacturers who seemed determined to push the United States into the war for profit. His frank public comments unleashed a "hailstorm" of xenophobic anger and turned friends and parishioners against him. Rauschenbusch soon found himself isolated in his own community. He found some solace in joining the Fellowship of Reconciliation, a group of fellow dissenters who opposed the war on religious grounds. Inspired by the group's pacifism, he told a friend that it was "an electric shock to get together with people more radical than I am, that take the Sermon on the Mount seriously."[21] As loneliness increasingly took hold of him, doctors diagnosed that he had cancer. Knowing that he had only a short time to live, he attempted to clear the air of animosity. "I leave my love," he said, "to those friends whose souls have never grown dark against me. I forgive the others, and hate no man."[22] He died on July 25, 1918.

Rauschenbusch's place in the history of American reform is an important one. Like his contemporaries Lester Frank Ward and Henry George, he challenged entrenched conservative dogmas and offered a social philosophy that held out the potential of an obtainable positive alternative. He crafted the right message at the right moment and changed the thinking of American Christianity in the process. The Progressive Era of self-criticism and active reform was gathering momentum. It was a time when people were developing an expanded sense of economic, social, and political possibilities. Most individuals regarded the adoption of such reforms as protective labor and consumer legislation, governmental regulation of corporations, conservation, and extensions to popular democracy (initiative, referendum, and recall) as positive advances. In arguing that society could act more responsibly and more humanely, Rauschenbusch tapped into that reform spirit and offered a biblical basis for it. Fifty-three years after the publication of *Christianity and the Social Crisis*, the Reverend Martin Luther King Jr. remembered that the book had left "an indelible imprint" on his thinking. "Of course there were points," said King, "at which I differed with Rauschenbusch. I felt that he had fallen victim to the nineteenth-century 'cult of inevitable progress,' which led him to an unwarranted optimism concerning human nature. . . . But in spite of these shortcomings Rauschenbusch gave to American Protestantism a sense of social responsibility that it should never lose."[23]

NOTES

1. Paul M. Minus, *Walter Rauschenbusch: American Reformer* (New York: Macmillan, 1988), 51–52.

2. Walter Rauschenbusch, *Christianity and the Social Crisis*, ed. Robert D. Cross (New York: Harper and Row, 1964), xii.

3. Ralph Henry Gabriel, *The Course of Democratic Thought* (Westport, Conn.: Greenwood Press, 1986), 274.

4. Dores Robinson Sharpe, *Walter Rauschenbusch* (New York: Macmillan, 1942), 61.

5. William M. Ramsey, *Four Modern Prophets* (Atlanta: John Knox Press, 1986), 13.

6. Minus, *Walter Rauschenbusch*, 62.

7. Minus, *Walter Rauschenbusch*, 63–64.

8. Minus, *Walter Rauschenbusch*, 65.

9. Minus, *Walter Rauschenbusch*, 66, 68.

10. Minus, *Walter Rauschenbusch*, 74.

11. Robert T. Handy, ed., *The Social Gospel in America* (New York: Oxford University Press, 1966), 256.

12. Minus, *Walter Rauschenbusch*, 84, 86.

13. Minus, *Walter Rauschenbusch*, 88.

14. Minus, *Walter Rauschenbusch*, 88–89.

15. Minus, *Walter Rauschenbusch*, 94.

16. Minus, *Walter Rauschenbusch*, 129.

17. G. Bromley Oxnam, *Personalities in Social Reform* (New York: Abingdon-Cokesbury Press, 1950), 72.

18. Rauschenbusch, *Christianity and the Social Crisis*, xiv.

19. Minus, *Walter Rauschenbusch*, 160.

20. Gabriel, *The Course of Democratic Thought*, 275–76.

21. Minus, *Walter Rauschenbusch*, 177, 182.

22. Oxnam, *Personalities in Social Reform*, 82.

23. Handy, *The Social Gospel in America*, 259.

SOURCES

Baker, Ray Stannard. *The Spiritual Unrest*. New York: Frederick A. Stokes Co., 1910.

Gabriel, Ralph Henry. *The Course of American Democratic Thought*. Westport, Conn.: Greenwood Press, 1986.

Handy, Robert T., ed. *The Social Gospel in America, 1870–1920*. New York: Oxford University Press, 1966.

Hopkins, Charles Howard. *The Rise of the Social Gospel in American Protestantism, 1865–1915*. New Haven, Conn.: Yale University Press, 1967.

Minus, Paul M. *Walter Rauschenbusch: American Reformer*. New York: Macmillan, 1988.

Oxnam, G. Bromley. *Personalities in Social Reform*. New York: Abingdon-Cokesbury Press, 1950.

Ramsay, William M. *Four Modern Prophets*. Atlanta: John Knox Press, 1986.

Rauschenbusch, Walter. *Christianity and the Social Crisis*. Edited by Robert D. Cross. New York: Harper and Row, 1964.

Sharpe, Dores Robinson. *Walter Rauschenbusch*. New York: Macmillan, 1942.

6

Jane Addams and the Settlement House Idea

Women coming of age in late nineteenth-century America witnessed not only tremendous advances in industry and technology but also fundamental changes in the roles of women in a modernizing society. Earlier in the century, the culture had defined women as nurturers, relegating them to the private sphere and denying them access to public life. It was not until the founding of Vassar (1861), Smith (1872), Wellesley (1875), and Bryn Mawr (1886) and the gradual trend toward coeducational instruction at universities like Cornell, Harvard, and a number of state universities that college education became a reality for many women. For the most part, those women who attended college in the 1870s and 1880s approached the experience with a sense of exhilaration and mission. They now had the opportunity to decide what their role in life would be, to realize new career opportunities, and to make a mark on society. However, this transition from the traditional definition of womanhood to a more expanded role for women was not without its tensions. The key, for many, was in finding some sort of accommodation. Jane Addams certainly fit the new self-conscious feminist mold. "[W]e are not restless and anxious for things beyond us," she stated in a college address, "we simply claim the highest privileges of our times, and avail ourselves of its best opportunities." However, she was also reluctant to make a clean break with the past, noting that the special function of the new educated woman was to "retain the old ideal of womanhood—the Saxon 'lady' whose mission it was to give bread unto her household. So we have planned to be 'bread-givers' throughout our lives, believing that in honor alone is happiness, and that the only true and honorable life is one filled with good works and honest toil."[1] Her longing for a life of independent thought and action and her ingrained sense of true womanhood would eventually lead her to fame as America's best-known social reformer.

Jane Addams was born in 1860 in Cedarville, Illinois, a small town in the northern part of the state near the Wisconsin border. Her father, John Huy Addams, epitomized the nineteenth-century self-made man. Attracted to the sparsely settled area as a land of limitless opportunities, he purchased a sawmill and a gristmill on Cedar Creek about six miles north of Freeport and set to work to build both a prosperous business and a prospering community. He invested in land, railroads, and banks and soon became president of both a bank and a life insurance company. As a town leader, he also helped organize Cedarville's first church, school, and subscription library. Joining the newly created Republican Party in 1854, he won election that same year as a state senator. During a sixteen-year career in the state legislature, he established a reputation for uncompromising honesty. John Addams had a strong belief in hard work and maintained an equally resolute faith in God. He taught his daughter the value of ambition and purpose in life and celebrated hard work and achievement as ideas strongly rooted in the Protestant ethic. He valued education for women but believed that women should be schooled to become better wives and mothers, not career-oriented professionals. This contradiction between ambition and accomplishment on the one hand and acceptance of the traditional domestic role for women on the other would trouble Jane Addams for years.

Jane's stepmother, Anna Haldeman Addams (her birth mother died from complications related to childbirth when Jane was two years old), was a disciplinarian, and relations between mother and daughter were often confrontational. She also accepted the traditional belief that a woman's sphere was the home and reinforced the perplexity that Jane felt concerning the proper role for women. Anna Addams regarded herself as an aristocrat and an intellectual. A talented musician and avid reader, she consciously strove to make her home a center of culture. In the regulated cultural environment of the Addams household, Jane acquired poise and self-assurance. She also developed a sense of social status and a lifelong affinity with an elite social class that would later allow her to use that identity to gain access to and support from wealthy patrons for her many social projects.

Jane Addams's college years were extremely important to both her personal development and her final choice of a career. She had wanted to enter Smith College, a model of the new educational opportunities open to women, but her father insisted that she stay closer to home and attend Rockford Female Seminary, of which he was a trustee. He was undoubtedly comfortable with the mission of the college, which was to combine domestic training with religious and cultural instruction to promote piety, purity, and the submissive

Jane Addams, circa 1914. Library of Congress, Prints & Photographs Division.

role of women. To Anna Sill, Rockford's founder, the goal was to "elevate and purify and adorn the home and to teach the great Christian lesson, that the true end of life is . . . to give oneself fully and worthily for the good of others."[2] Students were strongly encouraged by Sill to become Christian missionaries after graduation. Despite its religious emphasis and traditional outlook, college allowed Addams to enter into a world divorced from her immediate family. She quickly developed a sense of solidarity with other bright, outward-looking women. As a group, they talked, argued, discussed, and debated. Allowed the freedom to express herself in public as both a writer and a speaker, the previously quiet and introspective Addams quickly became a campus leader and someone other young women looked to for guidance.

Her notebooks from her Rockford years reveal a strong drive and ambition to succeed, to become someone. She served as president of the Literary Society, wrote essays for the *Rockford Seminary Magazine*, and eagerly took the opportunity to voice her opinions at various school debates and assemblies. Her speeches reveal someone who was trying to break from the traditional woman's role. At a junior exhibition, she remarked that changes in women's education had allowed women to move from accomplishments in the "arts of pleasing" to the development of their "intellectual force" and their "capacities for direct labor." Less religiously devout than her teachers or her parents might have wished, Addams sought to accommodate religion with her developing worldview. "You long for a beautiful faith, an experience," she wrote to Ellen Gates Starr, a close friend she had met during her first year at Rockford. "I only feel that I need religion in a practical sense, that if I could fix myself with my relations to God and the universe . . . I could use my faculties and energy so much better and could do almost anything."[3] When she graduated at the head of her class in 1881, she seemed determined and poised to do something important as a "new" woman.

The hopefulness that characterized Addams's college years quickly turned to disillusionment and despair immediately after college. Only a month after graduation from Rockford, her father died suddenly from acute appendicitis. Despite the blow, Addams pressed forward with plans to enroll at the Women's Medical College in Philadelphia. Classes, however, proved uninspiring. She lost interest and became increasingly despondent and, finally, physically ill. By February, she was forced to discontinue her studies and seek medical treatment for what was diagnosed as a form of nervous exhaustion. When rest did not alleviate her depression, she concluded that an aggravating back problem was a contributing cause and agreed to undergo back surgery. The operation left her bedridden for another six months. Recovery at home under her stepmother's supervision led to additional bouts of mental anguish, depression, and soul-searching. She felt totally adrift. For the next seven years, her life would be filled with uncertainty about her future and doubts about her capabilities.

In an attempt to give some meaning to her life, Addams agreed to her stepmother's suggestion to follow the Victorian stereotype and take a grand cultural tour of Europe. Along with a small entourage of friends and relatives, she made two extended trips to Europe between 1883 and 1888. She toured England and the continent, took language lessons, attended concerts and operas, and visited art galleries and museums. It did not take long, however, for Jane to begin to regard as devoid of meaning the pursuit of culture as an end in itself. "You doubt," she told a friend, "whether any good is accomplished in placing yourself as a mere spectator to the rest of the world." On another occasion, she noted, "[Y]ou gain a great deal of showy knowledge, but after all it is not the kind that satisfyieth [*sic*]." She was obviously becoming impatient with a life that lacked purpose. "I have constantly lost confidence in myself," she wrote on another occasion, "and have gained nothing and improved in nothing."[4]

One positive outcome of Addams's visits to Europe was a growing interest in Christian social reform movements then under way in England. During her second tour of Europe in 1888, Addams decided to pursue that interest and, in June of that year, attended the International Conference of Protestant Missions in London. While there, she visited People's Palace, an institute with meeting rooms, club rooms, and workshops for the working class. She also read two of Walter Besant's novels—*The Children of Gibeon* and *All Sorts and Conditions of Men*. The books presented a similar look at the miserable conditions that characterized urban slum life. In each, the major character discovers the harsh lives of tenement dwellers in London's East End. Deeply affected, they abandoned a life of ease to go live among the poor to help awaken a "new sense of pleasure," a "craving for things of which as yet they knew nothing."[5] It would not be surprising to imagine Addams being emotionally affected by what she read and inspired by the noble examples of Besant's fictional heroines.

The culmination of Addams's growing interest in the mission side of London came when she accepted an invitation to visit Toynbee Hall, a settlement house located in one of the poorest sections of the city. The settlement was largely the work of Samuel Barnett, a young curate in a London parish, and his wife, Henrietta. Together with some friends at Balliol College in Oxford, they came up with the idea of establishing a secular institution that would serve the poor inhabitants of the city's East End. Their aim was to bring people together across denominational lines through Christian ethics and to soften class distinctions by "sharing what the British poet Matthew Arnold once called 'the best that has been said and thought in the world.'"[6]

The Toynbee settlement was an assemblage of university-educated young men who chose to live among the poor but to conduct their recreation, club and social life, and intellectual activities in the same style they would if they lived exclusively in their own class-stratified circle. Some of the young men had regular jobs, others did service work in the East End, but all participated in some sort of community service—offering classes and lectures, providing meeting rooms for labor organizations and sponsoring clubs, giving art or music lessons, or joining with local residents to discuss topics such as housing, sanitation, and education. Addams was fascinated by the idea. "It is so free from 'professional doing good,'" she said, "so unaffectedly sincere and so productive of good results in its classes and libraries . . . that it seems perfectly ideal."[7] "The essence Jane was able to extract from Toynbee Hall," noted one historian, "was not its paternalistic assumptions . . . nor its democratic ideals. . . . What she grasped there . . . was an enduring faith in every individual's capacity to live by Christian ethics and to parlay those ethics, collectively, into the active creation of a civil society that dignified labor, culture, and religious diversity."[8] Toynbee Hall also offered a model that could provide Addams with a sense of purpose and an outlet for the type of "direct labor" that could give meaning to her life. It offered the opportunity to fulfill "woman's noblest mission" of honest toil and good works by sharing her education and knowledge of art and literature with the poor while, at the same time, living her life the way she would want to live it. Her model would have religious underpinnings, but it would be a secular religion rooted in social action and social service. Committed to the Toynbee idea, she decided, along with close friend Ellen Gates Starr, to establish a settlement in a poor immigrant section of Chicago.

The Addams–Starr settlement house experiment in Chicago would not be America's first. Others of her generation were also deeply influenced by British social movements. Experiencing a similar awakening of their social conscience, they too wanted to address problems related to urban poverty. Stanton Coit, a young Amherst graduate who went on to obtain a Ph.D. from the University of Berlin, visited Toynbee Hall in 1886. On returning to the United States, he founded the Neighborhood Guild in New York City. Vida Scudder and other young women from Smith College also shared the Toynbee Hall experience and the literary works of Walter Besant and John Ruskin (whose *Unto This Last* became something of a Bible to idealistic social reformers) and wanted to replicate the idea in this country. They organized the College Settlement Association in 1887 and would open a settlement in New York just a week before the Addams–Starr venture in Chicago.

Addams and Starr approached their goal with enthusiasm. They visited existing Chicago missions in the most depressed sections of the city that provided kindergartens, libraries, and lectures for the poor and signed up for classes in industrial arts. Mindful that financial assistance would be necessary to keep their experiment afloat, they made a conscious effort to meet and gain the support of Chicago's religious leaders, its prestigious Woman's Club, and prominent philanthropists. They met new friends who gave them tours of the

Bohemian district of the city to learn more about the various ethnic groups and even investigated an anarchist Sunday school where they observed "some young men trying to teach free thought without any religion or politics" to 200 children in a hall in back of a saloon.[9] They presented their ideas to the local branch of the Association of Collegiate Alumnae and talked to graduates of Smith, Vassar, and Wellesley who, like Addams herself, lacked creative outlets for their intellect and energies or ways to utilize their college training and who might want to genuinely help those mired in poverty.

The two young women also realized that they needed a place to settle. They were looking for a house to rent that was large enough to hold classes or lectures and with enough room to house those who they expected would join them and yet still small enough to be homelike. They finally discovered a dilapidated, run-down house on Halsted Street in a largely Italian neighborhood. Charles J. Hull, a wealthy Chicago businessman, had originally constructed the old brownstone mansion in 1856 on the outskirts of the city. The house had survived the fire of 1871 but had eventually been engulfed by the city's rapidly expanding immigrant population. Addams and Starr moved into their new home on September 18, 1889. Their venture would be forever known as Hull House.

As Hull House began to define its mission in the community, the resulting social and professional interaction provided an educational function for Addams as well. Before moving to Halsted Street, she knew something of the poor housing, inadequate sanitation, and overcrowded conditions that characterized urban life, but she soon learned firsthand the stark realities behind those abstractions. "One is so overpowered by the misery and narrow lives of so large a number of city people," she noted, "that the wonder is that conscientious people can let it alone."[10] The human misery she observed caused her to reexamine the era's basic assumptions concerning poverty. She was becoming part of the reform Darwinian crusade that insisted that poverty was caused not by heredity but by an environment that limited opportunity. Contact with residents of the emerging urban ghettos convinced Addams that those in the middle and upper classes had much to learn about the complexities of the lives of the poor, the foreign born, and the working class before they started preaching to them.

When Addams and Starr opened Hull House, they had the Toynbee model as a general guide but had no set plan for activities and were "without preconceived social theories or economic views."[11] They knew only that they wanted to share their knowledge of literature and art and open their house for clubs, classes, lectures, and receptions. They did, however, possess a very pragmatic view of their endeavor. When neighborhood women came and brought their children, Addams and Starr realized that they needed to create a playground and start a kindergarten and nursery. As they became aware of the large number of children and young adults forced to work to supplement family incomes, they began a boy's club and a club for young working women. They offered classes on basic homemaking skills such as cooking and sewing, English-language training, and more vocationally oriented instruction in areas such as woodworking, pottery, and telegraphy. To encourage social interaction, they held special German and Italian evenings. Fortunately, volunteers offered to help with money, time, and useful talents of their own. Hull House quickly became a center of activity in the community.

Also working to alter the direction of the original Toynbee-inspired idea over the years were the women who came to Hull House for extended periods and added new perspectives and viewpoints on social and economic problems. Two of these remarkable women were Mary Kenney O'Sullivan and Florence Kelley. Mary Kenney had grown up in Hannibal, Missouri, where she had dropped out of school after fourth grade to start work as an apprentice dressmaker to help support her invalid mother. After changing careers to bookbinding and printing, she moved to Chicago, where she became an active leader in the labor movement. Politicized by her own experience with working conditions, she began to organize the first female bookbinders' union in Chicago. After Addams invited her union to hold its meetings in the settlement and offered to work with her to improve conditions for workers, Kenney decided to stay. Through Mary Kenney, Addams met other working women, learned about the labor movement, and obtained a new perspective on the working class. The two women started a boarding cooperative for working girls that became known as the Jane Club. Even after becoming an organizer for the American Federation of Labor, Kenney continued to work with residents to lobby for the state's first factory law and eventually became a deputy state factory inspector. She broadened Addams's labor awareness and "helped her move from a position of wanting to comfort the poor—to one of a determination to eliminate poverty."[12]

Florence Kelley also caused Addams to broaden her social reform initiatives. As the daughter of a Philadelphia judge and congressman, she grew up in an upper-class environment. After college study at Cornell University and graduate work at the University of Zurich, she converted to socialism and married a Polish-Russian doctor. Moving to New York, she joined the Socialist Labor Party, began to write articles on the abuses of child labor, and offered lectures at the College Settlement in New York City. Divorced with three children when she moved to Hull House, Kelley had a background much different from Addams's. Following her growing interest in labor issues, she gained an appointment as a special agent for the Illinois State Bureau of Labor Statistics to investigate the sweatshop trade in Chicago in 1892. Her

commitment as a social investigator and her enthusiasm as an agitator for reform affected Addams in much the same way as had Kenny. It was Kenny and
Kelley who made Hull House a center for social reform and not merely a
place to study art and listen to lectures. They pushed Addams from philanthropy to reform.

During the 1890s, Addams became increasingly active in numerous campaigns to improve the human condition in an urban-industrial environment.
Provoked by the stench of uncollected garbage and encouraged by evidence
that cleaner streets reduced the overall death rate, she campaigned for more
effective garbage collection and even served as garbage collector for her
ward. She helped organize a community improvement association to pressure
city government to pave the streets and to build public baths, parks, and playgrounds. She also took the lead in forming consumer cooperatives as a means
of securing lower prices for coal and better-quality milk and joined the lobbying effort that saw the first juvenile court established in the United States
in 1899.

As Addams expanded her reform interests, she found herself sharing common concerns with those who would become the country's first sociologists
as well as a growing number of proponents of the social gospel. In 1895, the
Thomas Y. Crowell Company published *Hull House Maps and Papers*, a
house-to-house social investigation of the area surrounding the settlement to
determine the nationality and income of the residents. A collaborative venture
on the part of the residents of Hull House, the study was an outgrowth of
Florence Kelley's earlier investigation of the sweatshop trade in Chicago.
Modeling their work after Charles Booth's *Labour and Life of the People of
London*—the first systematic analysis of a poor section of a major city—the
residents at Hull House sought to duplicate the feat for an American metrop-
olis. The study contributed to the newly emerging field of urban sociology
and encouraged Addams and others to make Hull House a laboratory where
college instructors and graduate students could combine research and social
work. When Albion Small began publication of the *American Journal of Sociology* in 1895, he reaffirmed the link between abstract thought and practical action by including an article by Addams in one of the first issues and regularly featured other essayists who had done their research at Hull House.

The work of Addams and other residents at Hull House also attracted the
attention of social gospelers. One of the most prominent of this group, George
Herron, lectured at the settlement and, much like Walter Rauschenbusch, argued that modern capitalism and traditional Christianity were incompatible.
Seeing the need for a new social ethic, he, like Addams, called for a new
sense of community responsibility that would replace the selfish individualism spawned by competitive capitalism. William T. Stead, another noted

social gospeler, also visited Hull House. He worked with Addams and other Chicago reformers in a campaign to end the flourishing prostitution business in the city. In his famous book, *If Christ Came to Chicago* (1894), Stead, like Addams, appealed to the conscience of the city in portraying Jesus as a settlement house worker seeking to redeem society from evil.

The most shocking event of the decade—and the one that did more than anything else to influence Addams's intellectual evolution on the topic of labor—was the Pullman Strike, which began at George M. Pullman's model factory town just a few miles outside of Chicago. She knew Pullman personally and served on a six-member committee appointed by the Chicago Civic Federation that worked unsuccessfully to arbitrate the strike. The confrontation, at first between Pullman and his workers and then later between other railroad owners (organized as the General Managers Association) and Eugene V. Debs's American Railway Union, disturbed Addams as an example of growing class bitterness. Trying to make some sense out of the impasse that eventually resulted in violence and the use of federal troops to suppress the strike, she wrote "A Modern Lear." The essay compared Pullman to Shakespeare's King Lear, who earned nothing but ingratitude for his dictatorial benevolence. To Addams, it was another example of a capitalist who valued commercial considerations above social welfare. Although she placed blame on both sides of the strike, it was Pullman's selfish impulse that took the brunt of her scorn. But even her mild condemnation of such a prominent capitalist was enough to make publication of her essay difficult (at least four prominent journals turned it down) and suggested the delicate position that Addams and other settlement house workers occupied. To those who knew her, however, her position on the strike was not surprising. As previously mentioned, she had made Hull House a center for union activity. She truly believed that unions offered the best immediate means to protect the rights of workers and adjust the capitalistic system toward a more equitable outcome. Eventually, the state would have to assume a more positive role in rectifying labor problems. She realized that the government would ultimately have to protect the weak (the industrial worker) by imposing restraints on the strong (the factory owner). Toward that end, she lobbied to get the Illinois legislature to enact legislation regulating child labor and establishing a maximum eight-hour law for working women.

Radicalized by the Pullman Strike, Addams began to listen more closely to the arguments of the socialists who aspired to a utopia of mutual cooperation that they called the cooperative commonwealth. To facilitate the exchange of ideas, she allowed Hull House to become a forum for radical social theorists. There had been a Working People's Social Science Club at the settlement since 1890 to encourage discussion of various ways for reorganizing society.

Marxist doctrine received a good deal of attention, as did the single tax theories of Henry George and the utopian socialist ideas of Edward Bellamy. Motivated by the intellectual consideration of alternatives to capitalism, Addams traveled to Russia in 1896 to study the life and thought of Count Leo Tolstoy. Tolstoy, who had renounced a comfortable existence to live communally with poor peasants in a rural village, was something of an icon to many anticapitalist and antimaterialist idealists of the time. When she finally met the famous writer, he criticized her bourgeois dress (asking if she found her attire to be a barrier between herself and those she wished to help) and scolded her for earning an income from her family's Illinois farm as an absentee landlord instead of tilling the soil herself. After a short experiment in which she attempted to spend two hours a day making bread in the Hull House kitchen to answer Tolstoy's call to share in the common labor of the world, she concluded that his model was "more logical than life warrants." "[T]he demand of actual and pressing human wants," she concluded, could not be "pushed aside . . . while I saved my soul by . . . baking bread."[13] Addams was committed to the reform model of seeking positive change within a capitalistic context.

In the early years of Hull House, Addams avoided partisan politics primarily because she thought it might limit her influence and alienate individuals who provided support for her social programs. She soon found, however, that she could not live in political isolation. Alderman Johnny Powers, a powerful political boss, represented Hull House, located in Chicago's nineteenth ward. Addams, who had clashed with Powers over the garbage removal issue and later over her request for a new public school in the ward, finally decided to work for his defeat. Residents at the settlement led campaigns to unseat him in 1896 and again in 1898 but were soundly defeated both times. In the process, Addams came to understand something of the nature of boss politics and the basis of his popularity. She learned that the boss's hold on ward politics rested on loyalty, on the bond he established with largely immigrant voters who regarded him as a friend and neighbor. That friendship revolved around a crude form of welfare. The boss dispensed jobs, burial money, bail money, buckets of free coal, wedding presents, and free Christmas turkeys. With the exception of settlement workers and social gospelers, he was the slum dwellers' only friend. They thanked him with their votes and thereby secured his political position. He then used that position to award franchises and contracts and determine how city monies would be spent. Contrary to the feelings of many, Addams realized that the immigrants were not supporting the boss because they were ignorant or venal and understood that the corruption that surrounded the boss was not motivated primarily by personal greed. In a general way, she understood what muckraker Lincoln Steffens would soon articulate in sensational detail—that corruption was a system and that the goal was power.

Convinced that the boss lacked a genuine concern for the poor and that his actions addressed only the symptoms of poverty and not the causes, Addams worked on several levels to undermine his influence. In January 1898, she published an essay, "Why the Ward Boss Rules," in the *International Journal of Ethics* in which she described the forces at work in municipal politics. Reprinted in the *Outlook*, the *Review of Reviews*, and *Public Opinion* and summarized in many newspapers, the insightful article gained her national attention. She also sought to address the problem of boss politics by supporting "good government" reformers who she hoped would address the causes of urban poverty and the wastefulness that characterized city government. To facilitate that process, she invited nationally known municipal reformers like mayors Samuel "Golden Rule" Jones of Toledo and Hazen Pingree of Detroit to speak at Hull House. She also tried to maximize the limited political role open to women in the late nineteenth and early twentieth centuries by becoming a leader of the Chicago Civic Federation and the Municipal Voters League, both of which worked with Mayor Carter Harrison in an effort to break the multilayered system of political corruption in Chicago.

As Addams became more actively involved in reform issues, her attention eventually turned to woman suffrage. More interested in a woman's right to an education and to having the opportunity for a more creative role outside the home during her early years at Hull House, she tended to avoid the suffrage debate. In the late 1890s, however, she chose to confront the issue more directly. Her observations of the modern city had shown her that women were involved in what has been termed municipal housekeeping—experiencing daily concerns about sanitation, crowding, and health. To her, that involvement made women eminently qualified to be voters. She also believed that women possessed unique qualities of empathy and intuition that made them natural participants in movements for urban reform. Unlike many supporters of woman suffrage who wanted to limit the vote to more educated middle- and upper-class women, Addams argued that immigrant and working-class women would vote intelligently and that they needed to vote to protect themselves from exploitation and to improve the quality of their lives. Her ideas regarding women as potential voters reflected her broader optimistic faith in the essential worthiness of every individual regardless of social or economic background. As a humanist, she truly believed that every citizen had the right and also the capacity to participate in making social policy. Progress would result from a planned, cooperative attack on social problems, not from the millstone of competition as championed by social Darwinists like Herbert Spencer or William Graham Sumner.

As the pace of reform quickened during the Progressive Era, so too did Addams's work for suffrage. She joined the National American Woman Suffrage Association (NAWSA) in 1906 and began to lecture frequently before women's clubs, college students, and the public, arguing for women's right to take a more active role in government. She became a vice president of NAWSA in 1911 and led an aggressive suffrage campaign in Illinois to win the vote for women in all elections. She testified before legislative committees and vigorously lobbied congressmen in an unsuccessful effort. In 1912, she spoke at NAWSA's national meeting in Philadelphia and headed a group that traveled to Washington, D.C., to testify before Congress in support of a national suffrage amendment. In her desire to further the cause of women and achieve woman suffrage, she also joined the Progressive Party and the campaign to elect Theodore Roosevelt president in 1912.

Addams usually tried to avoid partisan politics if she thought it might alienate her supporters, but Roosevelt's Bull Moose campaign in 1912 convinced her to make an exception. One major attraction was the former president's pledge to support woman suffrage. Roosevelt had been a late convert to the pro-suffrage position, but Addams believed he was now dedicated to working for a national suffrage amendment. The new party, however, was about more than the vote for women. It supported the idea of graduated income and inheritance taxes; workmen's compensation for industrial accidents; prohibition of child labor; regulation of women's hours, wages, and working conditions; government-sponsored health, old age, and unemployment insurance; and stronger corporate regulation. Addams underscored the reasons behind her new political commitment in her speech seconding the nomination of Roosevelt at the Progressive Party convention. "A great party has pledged itself to the protection of children, to the care of the aged, to the relief of overworked girls, to the safeguarding of burdened men," she stated. "Committed to these human undertakings, it is inevitable that such a party should appeal to women." Caught up in the emotional moment of a moral crusade that had convention delegates singing "Onward, Christian Soldiers" and the "Battle Hymn of the Republic," she decided to compromise on principles and stand behind a platform that also pledged to support militarism (increased defense spending for battleships) and ignored the issue of Negro rights. The latter position must have been galling for Addams, who had signed the original "call" for a national discussion of racial issues and was one of the original founders of the National Association for the Advancement of Colored People in 1910. For her and other reformers, the opportunity to help craft the national agenda on social issues was just too promising. "Measures of industrial amelioration, demands for social justice, long discussed by small groups in charity conferences and economic associations," she said, "are at last thrust into the stern arena of political action."[14] But the new millennium was not to be. Roosevelt lost. After his defeat, Addams stayed with the Progressive Party for a while but slowly withdrew. Ironically, when President Woodrow Wilson began to incorporate many of Roosevelt's ideas into his program during his reelection campaign in 1916, she switched her allegiance to him despite his continued reluctance to support the cause of woman suffrage.

The outbreak of World War I shocked Addams. She saw it as an irrational rejection of the human intelligence that she believed shaped human progress. It would divert the nation's attention, as she and many other reformers believed the Spanish-American War of 1898 and the ensuing public debate over imperialism had done, from much-needed social, political, and economic reforms. The war also confounded the tendencies she thought were operating to render it obsolete. Her own observations of social interaction in the Hull House district of Chicago convinced her that its mixture of various ethnic groups offered a model for international understanding and peaceful coexistence. It was all part of a process by which the inhabitants of cosmopolitan cities had begun to create a new internationalism that would replace old national identifications and make war a thing of the past.

Addams took a lead role in numerous efforts to limit the war's destructiveness. She joined Carrie Chapman Catt, president of the NAWSA, in founding the Woman's Peace Party in 1915. Its original platform called for a permanent neutral commission of international mediators to end the current war and stop future wars before they started. In linking the peace movement with the suffrage movement, the platform also demanded that women, as "half of humanity," be consulted on matters of war and peace. Addams also presided over the first congress of the Women's International League for Peace and Freedom at The Hague, Netherlands, in 1915. The resolutions adopted at the conference included a call for liberal peace terms, the establishment of a permanent international court and permanent international peace conference, no transfer of territory without the consent of the people involved, and the representation of women in both national and international political life. Addams toured the belligerent countries of England, Belgium, Germany, Austria, Hungary, Italy, Switzerland, and France after the conference to promote the platform but found leaders reluctant to take a stand for peace if it might weaken their bargaining positions with their enemies.

When Addams returned to the United States in July 1915, she found herself on the defensive. Labeled a pacifist and discovering herself out of step with a growing pro-Allied sentiment in the country, she soon began to experience rebuke, ridicule, and abuse for her beliefs. After America entered the war in April 1917, she discovered that, as a pacifist, she had become grouped with many German Americans, liberal intellectuals, and radicals who also opposed the war. She was labeled a traitor. As the Creel Commission whipped patriotism into intolerance with anti-German propaganda, she found herself listed as a subversive. Superpatriots from the American Protective League watched Hull House, and Addams learned that she was being kept under surveillance by the Department of Justice. To find some breathing space amidst the vilification, she decided to try to be useful during the crisis by volunteering to work in Herbert Hoover's Food Administration. In that capacity, she traveled the country encouraging food conservation and worked to facilitate the distribution of food to the victims of war overseas. Even in this effort, however, she again called attention to herself by suggesting, unlike most Americans, that such humanitarian assistance should include starving Germans as well.

Although disheartened by the war and the failed peace efforts, Addams resumed her work for international peace immediately after the armistice and continued her crusade throughout the decade of the 1920s. She was selected to head the Women's International League for Peace and Freedom. She supported President Woodrow Wilson's fourteen-point program for peace, condemned the final Treaty of Versailles as punitive and designed to increase the chance of future war, and joined President Wilson's unsuccessful campaign to salvage an American commitment to the League of Nations. Through numerous writings, she sought to analyze why Americans were unwilling to accept a policy of cooperative internationalism that she believed was essential to any permanent peace. Her conclusion was that a postwar wave of self-righteousness had deluded Americans into thinking that they could best serve the cause of world peace by concentrating on their own interests. In her mind, America's indifferent attitude to the spirit of the Washington Conference on naval disarmament of 1921–1922, its less-than-sincere participation in the Kellogg-Briand Pact of 1928 to outlaw war, and its refusal to compromise more willingly on the issue of war debts and reparations only underscored her hypothesis. Ironically, her tireless efforts in behalf of international peace that had cost her legions of admirers won her the Nobel Peace Prize in 1931. Living long enough to see Franklin Roosevelt begin to use the power of the federal government to create the types of programs she had been advocating for decades to achieve social justice, Addams died of cancer in 1935 at the age of seventy-four.

Addams wanted Americans to change the way they looked at their society and, in the process, gain a new understanding of the meaning of democracy. She believed that society (individuals and the state) needed to assume a more positive role in securing for all members of the human community a basic level of health, welfare, and education so that they might be able to become active participants (equal citizens) in a democratic social order. She understood that democracy was compromised when any group was excluded. She agreed with Lester Frank Ward that society needed to replace the dominant ethic of self-interest (individualism) with a new social ethic and a realization of mutuality. Addams understood, firsthand, how Jacob Riis's "the other half" lived and gained a sense of kinship with that largely immigrant population. She, like Riis, wanted others to see things from their perspective and, it was hoped, learn to respect the dignity of every individual. It was this deep, perhaps naive faith in humanity that made her such an ardent pacifist. She truly believed that war devitalized democracy.

In a sense, Addams asked Americans to examine the larger processes—industrialization, urbanization, and immigration—affecting society at the time and to develop scientific responses to the social consequences of those developments. To further that process, she turned Hull House into an experimental laboratory in social reform. It served as a cultural center, a social service center that trained a new generation of women activists and social reformers who were redefining their own role as participating citizens, a university, and "almost" a church. Like Walter Rauschenbusch, Addams wanted to see a moral improvement in society, but her religion was more a secular one that willingly embraced the techniques of the new social sciences to usher in social change. As part of her progressive educational philosophy, she believed that knowledge should be used to change the environment and bring about social justice in social relations and an improved quality of life. In addressing the social consequences of economic change, Addams also contributed a great deal toward the progressive goal of redefining the role of the state in helping to regulate economic relations and foster social responsibility.

NOTES

1. Victoria Bissell Brown, *The Education of Jane Addams* (Philadelphia: University of Pennsylvania Press, 2004), 69–70.

2. Gioia Diliberto, *A Useful Woman: The Early Life of Jane Addams* (New York: Scribner, 1999), 62.

3. Diliberto, *A Useful Woman*, 67, 73.

4. Allen F. Davis, *American Heroine: The Life and Legend of Jane Addams* (Chicago: Ivan R. Dee, 1973), 36–37.

5. Davis, *American Heroine*, 50.

6. Brown, *The Education of Jane Addams*, 200.

7. Davis, *American Heroine*, 49.

8. Brown, *The Education of Jane Addams*, 205.

9. Davis, *American Heroine*, 55.

10. Davis, *American Heroine*, 71.

11. Davis, *American Heroine*, 67.

12. Davis, *American Heroine*, 79.

13. John C. Farrell, *Beloved Lady: A History of Jane Addams' Ideas on Reform and Peace* (Baltimore: The Johns Hopkins University Press, 1965), 142 and fn. 6.

14. Davis, *American Heroine*, 189.

SOURCES

Addams, Jane. *Twenty Years at Hull House*. Edited by Victoria Bissell Brown. Boston: Bedford/St. Martin's, 1999.

Brown, Victoria Bissell. *The Education of Jane Addams*. Philadelphia: University of Pennsylvania Press, 2004.

Davis, Allen F. *American Heroine: The Life and Legend of Jane Addams*. Chicago: Ivan R. Dee, 1973.

Diliberto, Gioia. *A Useful Woman: The Early Life of Jane Addams*. New York: Scribner, 1999.

Farrell, John C. *Beloved Lady: A History of Jane Addams' Ideas on Reform and Peace*. Baltimore: The Johns Hopkins University Press, 1965.

Lasch, Christopher ed. *The Social Thought of Jane Addams*. Indianapolis: Bobbs-Merrill, 1965.

Levine, David. *Jane Addams and the Liberal Tradition*. Madison: State Historical Society of Wisconsin, 1971.

7

Florence Kelley's Quest for Humane Labor Legislation

The rapid rise of industrialization, urbanization, and immigration during the late nineteenth century created a litany of worsening social problems. Factory work, in all its permutations, commonly meant long hours of low-paid labor and unsafe or unsanitary working conditions. Just as important, the growth of the cities compounded the densification of both the living and the working environment, while the influx of ever-increasing numbers of new laborers continued to depress already low wages and intensify the competition for jobs. The implications of these changes were a growing concern to an increasing number of working-class Americans. More and more willing to take steps to ameliorate their conditions, they eagerly sought membership in industrial or trade associations, experimented with cooperative alternatives to capitalism, and engaged in demonstrations and strikes to improve their circumstances.

Excluded from almost every discussion of labor problems and possible remedies for those problems, however, was the industrial exploitation of women and children. Except for a few upper-class associations engaged in charitable relief, there were no welfare organizations in the major industrial cities. Trade unions did exist, but they were small, relatively powerless, open only to skilled workers, and generally excluded women. When unions, such as the struggling American Federation of Labor, focused on the question of women or child laborers, they did so because they thought such employment threatened the wages of men. The argument that the economic needs of women were being exploited, that children were being denied the rights of childhood and that their health, welfare, and education were being impaired by their labor in industry, or that the human dignity of women and children who were forced to work in deplorable sweatshop environments was being disregarded had few active and committed advocates. One of those lone crusaders, however, was Florence Kelley.

Florence Kelley was born September 12, 1859, in Philadelphia, the third of eight children of William and Caroline (Bonsall) Kelley. William Kelley began his professional career as a judge in Philadelphia and then went on to gain election to the U.S. House of Representatives, where he served as a Republican member of Congress for almost thirty years. Nicknamed "Pig Iron" Kelley, he was known as a strong defender of protective tariffs for American industries. But he had also been a staunch abolitionist, strongly supported woman suffrage throughout his political career, and nurtured the development of an active social conscience in his daughter. He encouraged her, as a teenager, to read extensively from his own private library and avidly shared his political experiences with her in conversations at home and in correspondence when he was away in Washington. His letters often included copies of his congressional speeches. Grateful for the companionship, advice, and encouragement, Florence later remarked, "To his influence . . . I owe everything that I have ever been able to learn to do."[1]

William Kelley also took his young, impressionable daughter on various industrial sightseeing trips as a congressman. One memorable visit was to a steel mill to view the new Bessemer process of making steel. But while everyone else gazed intently at the giant furnaces and marveled at the new technology, Florence noticed the "presence and activity of boys smaller than myself—and I was barely twelve years old—carrying heavy pails of water and tin dippers, from which the men drank eagerly." Florence remembered being shocked. "The attention of all present was so concentrated on this industrial novelty that the little boys were no more important than so many grains of sand in the molds. For me, however, they were a living horror, and so remained." Just as disturbing was a similar visit to a glass factory. She remembered that each blower had a "dog," as the young boys were called, whose job was to take "the blower's mold the instant the bottle or tumbler was removed from it, scrape it and replace it perfectly smooth and clean for the next bottle or tumbler which the blower was already shaping in his pipe." The impression was the same—"the utter unimportance of children compared with products."[2]

Florence Kelley's mother, a descendant of botanist John Bartram, added her own influences to Florence's upbringing through her adopted parents and their siblings. Raised as the adopted daughter of Quakers Isaac and Elizabeth Pugh of Germantown, Pennsylvania, who had been close friends of her parents, the Pugh family added Quaker beliefs and principles to the Kelley household and enabled Florence to experience an extended family environment that stressed reformist ideas. Especially influential in heightening Florence's awareness of female empowerment and "the radical potential within women's activism" was great-aunt Sarah Pugh. Devoting her life to reform causes that included abolitionism and woman suffrage, she served as president of the Philadelphia Female Anti-Slavery Society for twenty-eight years between 1838 and 1870. The story has it that when Florence learned that her great-aunt never used sugar and wore linen instead of cotton underwear, she inquired why. Sarah Pugh reminded young Florence that cotton and sugar were grown by slaves and replied, "I decided many years ago never to use either and to bring these facts to the attention of my friends." Although the term *boycott* did not enter common discourse until the 1880s, preferential purchasing was well known to abolitionists a generation earlier. Proponents of the idea organized the National Requited Labor Association in 1838 to promote the need to abstain from the products of slave labor, and Sarah Pugh served on the executive committee of the society. Years later, when the issue of individual responsibility focused on the question of whether consumers should purchase items that had been produced in factory environments that exploited women, Florence would remember Sarah Pugh and her instructive comments.[3]

Caroline Kelley's life influenced her daughter in one other way—through its grief and suffering. Representative of the high rate of infant mortality during the nineteenth century (as late as 1870 almost one-third of all children in Philadelphia died before they reached the age of ten), five of Caroline's eight children died either in infancy or in early childhood. As a result, Florence remembered that her mother developed a "permanent terror of impending loss" and exhibited "a settled, gentle melancholy which she could only partly disguise."[4] In recalling the impact that these personal losses had on the family many years later, Florence commented,

> All this grief, this anguish of frustrated hope, occurred, not on the plains as a hardship of pioneer life, not in the Great American Desert where physicians were out of reach, but within four miles of Independence Hall, in one of the great and famous cities of the Nineteenth Century. These tenderly cherished young lives were sacrificed not to the will of God, as mothers were taught throughout the long history of the race, but as we know now, to the prevailing ignorance of the hygiene of infancy . . . from infections now universally recognized as preventable.[5]

One of Florence Kelley's reform efforts during the Progressive Era would be to help organize the U.S. Children's Bureau to lobby for the enactment of federal legislation to provide federal infant and maternity aid to states as part of a new national policy.

As a child, Florence Kelley attended school only in brief stints (she remembered her longest uninterrupted attendance as only five or six months). Susceptible to infection and her mother's fear of losing her only surviving daughter, she was often kept at home. In spite of these setbacks, she continued to read voraciously on her own. With an excellent memory and some tough cramming, she passed the examinations required for entry into Cornell University in 1876 at the age of sixteen (with conditional requirements in Greek, Latin, and mathematics to be completed during her freshman year). Like Jane Addams, Kelley had joined the first generation of college-educated women, and she understood the importance of that step. "Entering college," she said, "was for me almost a sacramental experience."[6] The time spent at Cornell would offer her the opportunity to learn the tools of social analysis that would help her later. At the end of her junior year, however, another severe illness (later diagnosed as diphtheria) forced her to drop out of school for the next two and a half years. Living in Washington, D.C., for part of that period, Kelley studied law with her father and read extensively on her own at the Library of Congress on the legal treatment of poor children, illegitimate children, and wage-earning children and divorce cases involving child custody. This reading became the foundation for her senior thesis, "On Some Changes in the Legal Status of Children since Blackstone," and allowed her to graduate from Cornell in June 1882 with a bachelor's degree in literature.

Her thesis, which was later published in the *International Review*, drew on both her father's view of an active state as the guarantor of social justice and her great-aunt's broadened perspective of the role of women in civic society and their ability to shape public policy. Her argument in the thesis was that the tendency in statute law since the time of Sir William Blackstone was to increase protections for children and make them more and more wards of the state. Diminished in this process was the degree of paternal authority. Kelley argued that children, in general, benefited from compulsory education and child labor and custody laws that regarded the interest of the child as more important than that of the father. In the process, the child had come to be regarded, in the eyes of the law, as "an individual with a distinctive legal status" and not merely "an appendage" of the "absolute ownership of the father." Importantly, by advocating the interest of children in contrast to the tradition of male patriarchal authority, Kelley examined the law from a new perspective. And as the authority of the state expanded in this regard, women stood to become empowered as officials, experts, or affected parties. Kelley used her examination of the law to argue for "the superiority of the moral over the legal qualifications of the home in securing the child's welfare." As this new emphasis on the welfare of the child took hold, "recognition of the child's need of legal power in the mother" would be enhanced as well. "For me," she later remarked, "it [the thesis] was of incalculable importance." It forced her to examine her own legal identity as a woman and permanently welded her sympathies to those of less fortunate women and children.[7]

College, however, offered women like Addams and Kelley only limited opportunities in choosing a career. After receiving her degree, Kelley applied to the graduate school of the University of Pennsylvania to study advanced Greek (her ultimate objective was law school) but was turned down because of her sex. Looking to engage herself intellectually in some other pursuit, she decided to start an evening school for working women in rooms made available by the New Century Club of Philadelphia and operating under the title the "Working Women's Guild." Founded in 1877, the organizers endeavored "to create an organized centre of thought and action among women, for the protection of their interests and the promotion of science, literature and art."[8] This new school offered instruction in a number of subjects of interest to mill hands, domestic servants, dressmakers, and shopgirls. Kelley taught history.

The experience at the Guild, which offered Kelley her first real personal contact with working girls, was a positive one and led to another publication in the *International Review* titled "Need Our Working Women Despair?" Concerned about the health and welfare of working women, Kelley offered an assortment of suggestions aimed at reducing exploitation experienced by working women that included protecting women from industrial hazards, creating associations for the legal protection of working women, raising female wages based on equality of pay (an idea previously suggested by the Knights of Labor), and extending voting rights so that women could use the franchise to obtain legislation for shorter hours, fair wages, and better (safer and more healthful) working conditions. Her development as a teacher, however, was cut short when her parents asked her, on short notice, to accompany her older brother to Europe, where he had been ordered by doctors to recover from a severe illness. But one opportunity lost was another gained. While staying in France, Florence chanced to meet an old college friend who told her that the University of Zurich in Switzerland was willing to award graduate degrees to women.

During the summer of 1883, after her brother's recovery and before deciding if she should attend the University of Zurich, Florence toured the industrial centers of the British Isles. Like her earlier encounters with the American factory system, she saw things that shocked her. In South Wales, she saw women and girls working at the mouths of coal pits loading and hauling cars filled with coal. In conditions that rivaled the American sweatshop, she observed women cottage workers in the Midland counties of the English "Black Country" (given the name because coal mining and other related industries had ravaged the countryside) sweating as nail makers and chain makers. "There was no limit to the hours of work when the unhappy women had material and the order had to be rushed," she said. "The owners kept the wages at the lowest conceivable notch by lengthening the lists of workers and pitting them against each other. We were told by one woman after another that the uniform answer of the bringer of the raw material to the complaints of the worker was: 'If you don't want this work, there's plenty as does.'"[9] The trip once again raised the question of the need for protective labor legislation and seemed to heighten Kelley's sense of class consciousness in opposition to unregulated capitalism. That September, she decided to enter the University of Zurich.

The University of Zurich, in 1883, had become a hotbed of radical ideas and a refuge for young intellectuals fleeing repressive regimes in Europe. The students seemed to have one cause that united them: socialism. The socialist press, driven out of Germany, had relocated to Zurich, and leaders of the movement frequently came to the city to speak. Kelley aptly summed up her state of mind at the time: "Coming to Zurich, the content of my mind was tinder awaiting a match." She remembered being filled with so much excitement on attending her first socialist meeting that "I grasped the sides of my chair and held them firmly." Caught up in the intellectual fervor and the exciting exchange of ideas, she readily embraced socialism as the solution to those "baffling, human problems" that she found inherent in the capitalist system. Through socialism, the means of production would be owned and controlled by society as a whole, and the energies released by industrialization would be used to benefit everyone rather than the privileged few. Caught up in the excitement, Kelley ventured into a hasty marriage with Lazare Wischnewetzky, a young Polish-Jewish-Russian medical student who shared her enthusiasm for socialist ideas.[10]

While her husband pursued his medical studies, Florence continued to take classes (she would never complete her degree) and began the formidable task of translating into English Friedrich Engels's study *The Condition of the Working Classes in England*, written in German and published in 1845. At the same time, she began an ongoing correspondence with Engels, whom she regarded as a mentor. Engels had used the reports of doctors, factory inspectors, and poor law and sanitary monitors to describe in stark detail the misery and suffering that befell working-class families (men, women, and children) trapped in a vicious cycle of extremely long hours at starvation wages that characterized the factory system. It was through this study that Karl Marx developed his analysis of the development of working-class consciousness and the inevitability of social revolution.

In 1886, the Wischnewetzkys returned to America with their first son, made plans for Lazare to establish a medical practice, and joined the Socialist Labor Party (SLP) in hopes of continuing their political involvement as doctrinaire socialists. For the next five years, they lived in New York and added to their family another son and daughter. But the marriage soon began to go bad. Lazare's medical practice struggled. When debts mounted, Florence was forced to borrow money from friends and family members. At the same time, ideological differences with the leadership of the SLP led to their expulsion from the party. Constantly unable to make ends meet, their relationship grew more acrimonious. When Lazare became physically abusive, Florence sought a divorce. Unable to file for divorce on grounds of nonsupport in New York, she moved to Illinois (where divorce law was more liberal), filed for divorce, eventually received custody of her three children, and resumed her maiden name.

At the time of her arrival in Chicago in 1891, Kelley was penniless and jobless, but she had gained a reputation for scholarly activity in the field of child labor. Her interest in the topic had been renewed while reading the official British investigations and reports on factory conditions in England as she worked on Engels's translation. In contrast to the detailed record keeping in England, the various state bureaus of labor statistics in the United States provided almost no useful information in their publications on what was happening to children in industry. Kelley pointed out these glaring inadequacies in numerous published letters to newspaper editors and called for competent investigation. Her criticisms gained notice, and in June 1889, she was invited to read a paper on child labor at the Annual Convention of Commissioners of State Bureaus of Labor Statistics. Here she again underscored the inadequacy of existing statistics and called for detailed regional investigations of typical industries, such as silk manufacturing in the East, mining in the Midwest and West, and textiles in the South, that heavily employed children. The next year she published an article on the inadequacy of protective labor laws for children that had resulted in childhood becoming an object of exploitation. Her argument was a humane one—that children should be guaranteed leisure and an education—rather than the practical one made by organized labor and state bureaus—that the jobs of adult men needed protection. The question to Kelley was one of children's rights rather than family economy. Although her constructive comments on the issue of child labor were gaining her recognition, Kelley still needed a position to support herself and her three children. Sometime between Christmas 1891 and New Year's 1892, she decided to go to work at Hull House.

Kelley fit right in with the women at the settlement and relished the opportunity to be able to make a positive contribution to the field of social welfare. Her friend Alice Hamilton aptly summed up her own experience at Hull House in terms that would have been shared by Kelley. "To me the life there

satisfied every longing—for companionship, for the excitement of new experiences, for constant intellectual stimulation and for the sense of being caught
up in a big movement which enlisted my enthusiastic loyalty."[11] With the help
of Jane Addams, Kelley soon found her niche in settlement house work that
related to working women. It is perhaps not readily known that settlement
houses like Hull House were the first centers for social research and hands-
on fieldwork in urban America. Sensing a need for further study of that environment, Kelley proposed, in 1892, that the Illinois Bureau of Labor Statistics make a formal investigation of the sweating trade in Chicago. Her
proposal was accepted, and she was hired by the bureau as a special agent.
Aware of Kelley's growing reputation as an authority on child labor, Carroll
D. Wright, the U.S. commissioner for commerce and labor, also appointed
Kelley to conduct an investigation of Chicago as one of sixteen designated
cities to be part of a federal inquiry into urban slums.

Under her supervision, a one-square-mile area around Hull House was targeted for study, a section of the city that encompassed people of eighteen different nationalities and included filth and crowding on a scale that Kelley had
not seen except in Naples, Italy, and on the east side of New York City. Her
investigations showed sweatshops to be ill-ventilated dens (often underground) where workers labored at excessive speeds operating fatiguing foot-
powered sewing machines. Employed at this work were men and women but
also young boys and girls. Kelley noted that the effects of the speeding machines could be seen in the waxy color of their faces and found young people
between the ages of fifteen and twenty who were temporarily disabled by exhaustion. Such debilitating work wore out even young workers and limited
their earning power to just a few years. Their poverty resided in their wages
as well. Kelley encountered one girl who worked fifteen hours a day, seven
days a week, and earned only $18. In numerous instances she found little girls
working at finishing knee pants and sewing on buttons for literally no pay.
They were said to be "learning the trade." Her findings showed that tenement
work ("finishing" work done at home as an extension of the sweatshop system) was universal and forced all members of the family into service. Kelley
noted that children were drawn into the work to "pull out basting threads, sew
on buttons, paste boxes and labels, [and] strip tobacco."[12]

The information gained in Kelley's investigations ultimately became part
of a book, *Hull House Maps and Papers*, designed to be. like Charles Booth's
earlier study *Labor and Life of the People of London*, the first systematic
study of a poor section of a major city. The project, a collaborative one that
involved many Hull House residents, attempted to create a social portrait of
Chicago's Nineteenth Ward based on the nationality and income of the inhabitants of every household. It was the first attempt to analyze a working-

class neighborhood in an American city, and most of the credit for the study belongs to Kelley. In recognizing her contribution, Jane Addams remarked, "[She] galvanized us all into more intelligent interest in the industrial conditions around us."[13]

Public interest had been so aroused by the investigations that the Illinois legislature was forced to consider corrective legislation. As a preliminary step, it appointed a joint committee to make its own fact-finding foray into Chicago's slums. Kelley and Hull House colleague Mary Kenney took the lead in personally guiding the committee through the tenements, sweatshops, and factories as they collected data. As a result of that highly publicized report, the legislature passed the Illinois Factory Act of 1893, the state's first such statute. The law included many groundbreaking provisions: a standard eight-hour workday for women, girls, and children, with fourteen the minimum age that a child might be employed in any branch of manufacturing; the creation of a state factory inspection department with powers to confiscate and destroy garments manufactured in homes where contagious diseases were found; and the requirement that owners of sweatshops maintain lists of the names and addresses of contractors and workers.

The new law did not include all the provisions that Kelley had recommended, such as requiring the use of labels identifying where garments were made, requiring mechanical power in sweatshops, and requiring more rigid inspection (the weak link in any regulatory law). On this last point, Kelley regarded the law as the key to social improvement. "Mere enactments are idle in the face of a menace like this," she said. "The delinquent must be confronted not only with the law on the statute book but the law-officer at his door." Her sweatshop proposals indicate how Kelley's thinking had evolved. She now had a sharper vision on how governmental authority could be extended to economic issues for the benefit of working people. For Kelley, the state could be the agency that would challenge established laissez-faire thinking, place "human relations" above "market relations," and become, as one historian has put it, "a moral arbiter of social justice."[14]

It was up to newly elected Governor John Peter Altgeld to appoint the first state factory inspector. He initially offered the position to noted Chicago reformer Henry Demarest Lloyd, but he was busy writing *Wealth against Commonwealth* (1894), a classic study of monopolies and their control of the railroads that many regard as the first example of investigative journalism that would become known as muckraking. When Lloyd declined the offer, he recommended Kelley. Following Lloyd's advice, Altgeld appointed Kelley to become the chief inspector of factories for Illinois in July 1893, the first woman to hold such a position. With a staff that included an assistant inspector and ten deputy inspectors (six men and four women) and a meager budget of

$28,000, Kelley was determined to expand the state's responsibility for social welfare.

As factory inspector, Kelley struggled against parental resistance as well as the capitalist system and the bureaucratic structure that supported it at every step, especially in the area of child labor. She fought parents who evaded the child labor provisions of the law by dishonestly claiming that they were dependent on their child's income or who falsely signed age affidavits that should have excluded their children from work. She warred with the Chicago Board of Education for not enforcing the Compulsory Education Act to keep children at school. She battled manufacturers who knowingly employed underage children and required them to work as butchers on the killing floors of slaughterhouses or as "blower dogs" in glass factories where they fetched and carried for adult glassblowers. Notorious in the latter case was the Illinois Glass Company in Alton. The firm employed over 700 boys under age sixteen, many of whom had been "recruited" by greedy "guardians" from orphan asylums in nearby St. Louis, Missouri. Chronically sick, often injured (severe burns), forced to do night work, and denied adequate schooling (illiterate), they were often prevented from being able to support themselves later in life. As Kelley saw it, they had been ruined "in body and mind before they entered upon the long adolescence known to happier children."[15] The unsafe factory conditions, especially for children, prompted Kelley to argue (unsuccessfully) for increased authority to inspect machinery and require safeguards and also to be able to prosecute for injuries (parental release forms exempted companies from prosecution). When she attempted to enforce the penalty provisions of the law, the Cook County district attorney claimed that his office was too overworked to deal with the cases in a timely manner.

Kelley also found it difficult to enforce the provisions of the law against sweatshop work and encountered legal roadblocks as well. With nearly 15,000 garment workers employed in the trade and garments going out to countless rooms of home finishers in tenement houses, the task of inspection was virtually impossible. Exasperation with the sweatshop dilemma forced her to boldly advocate legislation prohibiting manufacturers from sending goods to be finished in homes. More frustrating than inadequate enforcement of the law, however, was the court's reaction to it. In 1895, the Illinois Supreme Court in *Ritchie v. People* declared a portion of the Illinois Factory Act invalid. The specific challenge was to the section of the law providing an eight-hour day for women and girls employed in factories. The court found that the law violated the "freedom of contract" of workers under the Fourteenth Amendment. As long as the court could claim that there was "no reasonable ground, at least none which has been made manifest to us in the argument of counsel for fixing eight hours in one day as the limit," then

Kelley and other state factory inspectors were stymied. Despite the publication of four annual reports that were described as "[s]o moving and human . . . so full of indignant satire, so honest in their relentless description of conditions as they really existed, with no attempt to cover up or conceal the evils with which the state must deal," she lost her job when her term expired in 1897. The incoming governor had decided to appoint a man to replace her who had previously been employed by the Illinois Glass Company.[16]

For the next two years, Kelley resumed her work at Hull House and spent a good deal of time lecturing and writing articles on labor-related topics that viewed the state as the key to bringing about systematic social improvements. She also found a new outlet for her activism in working to organize purchasers' leagues to protect working women and children. During the 1890s, the production of consumer goods and their merchandising and marketing launched a new consumer culture. Ingeniously, reformers in several states began to think about ways of channeling that new consumer consciousness into political action. Soon, various consumers' leagues started to form in cities such as New York City (1891), Brooklyn (1896), Philadelphia (1896), Boston (1897), and Chicago (1897). These early leagues drew on the antislavery traditions of abolitionists like Kelley's great-aunt Sarah Pugh who had refused to use sugar and cotton because they were products that had been created with slave labor. The idea, in its modern form, was to convince consumers not to purchase the goods of free laborers if those goods had been produced in factories or shops that exploited women and children. What Kelley and others pushed for was the creation of a "white list" of employers who met a standard (on wages, hours, working conditions, management–employee relations, and child labor) established by the leagues. Following the practice of organized labor of placing union labels on goods produced in union shops, Kelley and others also proposed that consumers' labels be handed out to trade union shops that also met consumer league requirements.

Discussion of this general idea, as well as the obvious need for united action, led to the creation of the National Consumers' League (NCL) in New York City in 1898 with John Graham Brooks, a writer, lecturer, and Unitarian pastor, as president. The objective of the new body was simple: to organize consumer pressure (via the boycott) to ensure improved working conditions, especially for working women. President Brooks saw the issue in simple terms. "This is the economic truth," he stated. "To buy a sweated garment is to have someone work for you under sweated conditions as definitely as if she were in your own employ."[17] The following year, Brooks asked Kelley to become general secretary of the NCL. In accepting the position, which she would hold until 1932, Kelley believed she had assumed leadership of a potentially powerful agency for social change. She moved to New York City,

exchanged her lodgings at Hull House for similar ones at Henry Street Settlement, and began to develop a professional alliance with headmistress Lillian Wald that was much like her previous relationship with Jane Addams.
Wald was nationally known for her work in the field of public health and
for her efforts to utilize trained nurses as field agents to teach hygiene to
working-class immigrant families in the ghetto. Under Kelley's leadership,
the NCL spread rapidly with the organization of over sixty branches in twenty
states during its first five years.

In 1907, Kelley and the NCL played an integral role in the case of *Muller
v. Oregon* (1908) in which the U.S. Supreme Court rendered a landmark decision regarding the constitutionality of maximum-hours laws for women.
The case began in Oregon when Curt Muller, the owner of a laundry, was
fined for violating that state's ten-hour law for women employed in factories
and laundries. Muller's attorneys argued that his right to freely enter into a
contractual relationship with an employee had been abridged. He lost his appeal to the Oregon Supreme Court but had decided to carry his appeal to the
Supreme Court. In October 1907, the Consumers' League of Oregon alerted
Kelley and the national headquarters that such legal action was imminent.
Fearing that not only the Oregon law but nineteen other state laws regulating
the working day for women would be overturned and the protective scope of
a state's police power permanently compromised by an adverse federal decision, Kelley procured, with the State of Oregon's consent, the services of
noted attorney Louis Brandeis.

Brandeis thought he could win the case if he could establish, as the Illinois
Supreme Court had previously asserted, a "reasonable" connection between
the law and the public health, safety, or welfare proposed to be secured by it.
He agreed to argue the case if the NCL would gather the statistical information needed to make his argument. What Brandeis wanted was everything that
had been published on the topic of industry and its relation to women's hours
of labor—the reports of factory inspectors, physicians, boards of health, trade
unions, economists, and social workers both in this country and abroad. Using that material, Brandeis prepared his now famous "Brief" and successfully
argued that factory work was dangerous to the health, safety, and morals of
women and that Oregon's ten-hour law was a valid use of the state's police
powers. Brandeis utilized the same kind of sociological information that Kelley had been compiling for most of her professional life to overturn the
Supreme Court's broad definition of the right to freedom of contract under the
due process clause of the Fourteenth Amendment as it applied to the hours
that women worked. The acceptance of the use of sociological data as a
means of legal argumentation and the U.S. Supreme Court's decision that the
meaning given to law should evolve in relation to social needs revived the en-

tire field of protective labor legislation. It also assured a place for the NCL as a potent political force for the enactment of further labor legislation for women and children.

While attending the first International Meeting of Consumers' Leagues in Geneva, Switzerland, in 1908, Kelley learned that both England and Australia had established boards to set minimum wages in sweated industries. Although the laws in those countries were not gender specific, Kelley thought the establishment of a legal minimum wage was especially applicable in the United States, where girls and women did not have the protection of unions. As she saw it, "Society itself must build the floor beneath their feet." She presented the idea at the annual meeting of the NCL in 1909 and convinced the delegates to recommend that state and local leagues study the topic with an eye to a possible legislative campaign in 1910. Kelley believed that a legal minimum wage was the best method yet put forward to fight poverty rooted in substandard wages. She also saw it as a necessary complement to shorter-hours legislation. Here she shared the fear of many that if hours were reduced and hourly wages were not adjusted, then workers would be, as she put it, "unable by honest work to live in health and frugal decency."[18]

The first substantial progress toward actual minimum-wage legislation began in 1911, when the Massachusetts legislature established a commission of inquiry on the subject and began a study of wages in candy factories, laundries, department stores, and textile factories. Finding wages in those industries to be far below minimum living costs, the commission recommended a bill calling for the creation of wage boards in the various industries. The legislature, however, was reluctant to move forward. Then, in the spring of 1912, the state was rocked by the great textile strike at Lawrence, triggered by low wages. The strike focused public attention on the issue and hastened passage of a minimum-wage law in June of that year. In doing so, it brought the minimum-wage idea into the realm of practical politics. The Massachusetts law was not without its defects. In setting wage levels, wage boards were required to consider not only the cost of living but also the "financial condition of the industry," a factor that served to limit wage minimums. The law also lacked enforcement powers. Employers who refused to pay the minimum did not face punishment. They confronted only the potential loss of business that might result from having the company name published in the newspaper as a noncompliant.

Despite its qualified start in Massachusetts, the minimum-wage idea caught on, and the following year eight additional states passed minimum-wage laws without the defects of the initial statute. After 1913, however, the minimum-wage movement slowed. World War I deflected attention, rising wages temporarily muted the substandard-living argument, the Red Scare created a negative climate for the enactment of any labor legislation, and doubts concerning the constitutionality of minimum-wage laws deterred further progress. Soon those doubts became reality. After a series of unsuccessful challenges to state minimum-wage laws (the NCL again helped prepare the legal brief in each case), the Supreme Court, in the case of *Adkins v. Children's Hospital* (1923), again invoked the Fourteenth Amendment to rule that wage restrictions could not be reconciled with freedom of contract. The battle for minimum-wage legislation had reached a legal impasse that would last for another fifteen years.

Another area in which Kelley continued to take a keen interest was in raising child labor standards. Prohibiting child labor had been one of the basic requirements to receive the first Consumers' League label, but Kelley realized that the campaign would have to include other interested groups. To facilitate the advance of the idea, Kelley assumed the leadership of a number of committees—the Child Labor Committee of the National American Woman Suffrage Association and the National Congress of Mothers—and was a member of a similar committee of the General Federation of Women's Clubs. She also spoke for and wrote articles on the subject to keep people abreast of the facts, help them assess the inadequacy of certain state laws, and encourage them to undertake additional action at the state level on a sound basis. In 1902, on action initiated by Kelley and Lillian Wald, the New York settlement houses appointed the New York Child Labor Committee and employed an investigator. One of the early successes to come out of the committee's work was the passage of a law requiring documented "proof of age" certification (parental affidavits of age were no longer acceptable) before a child could go to work. Realizing the imposition that the new law might place on families who did not have a proper birth certificate, the New York committee employed a worker to help obtain such evidence. Kelley also supported the idea of "scholarships." Under this program, monetary grants would be made to families who were genuinely dependent on the wages of their child so that the child could remain in school.

Even though child labor laws that restricted the age at which a child might be employed and regulated the number of hours that he or she might work had been enacted in some form in thirty-eight states by 1912, the requirements were not uniform and were often substandard and weakly enforced. Frustrated by this uneven development, Kelley started to campaign for federal legislation that would mandate a fourteen-year minimum for employment of children. Bills were introduced in Congress every year from 1906 to 1916, but resistance, primarily from southern states where textile manufacturers depended heavily on the employment of children, proved strong. Finally, in 1916, Congress passed the Keating-Owen Act, which prohibited the shipment of products in interstate commerce that had been made in factories that employed children under the age of fourteen or that permitted children between the ages of fourteen and sixteen to work more than eight hours a day. But Kelley's dream of a federal child labor law had only a brief statute life. In 1918, the Supreme Court, in the case of *Hammer v. Dagenhart*, declared the Keating-Owen Act unconstitutional. Fearing that the courts would forever stymie protective labor legislation for children, Kelley spent the last fourteen years of her life in an unsuccessful campaign for a federal amendment that would authorize congressional action in the field of child labor.

Kelley's death in 1932 prevented her from experiencing the satisfaction that would have come from the enactment of New Deal reform measures affecting women and children. The Social Security Act of 1935 included provisions for federal funding to poor families with dependent children, while the Fair Labor Standards Act of 1938 established maximum hours (an eight-hour day) and minimum-wage standards for both men and women. The 1938 law also prohibited children under the age of sixteen from working in industries engaged in interstate commerce and outlawed hazardous work for persons under eighteen years of age. Kelley's connection to these accomplishments was later remembered by Frances Perkins, secretary of labor under Franklin Roosevelt, in a magazine article published in 1954. "[Florence Kelley] effected basic changes in American life," she said, "by her brilliant analysis of the need of social advance, by her selfless dedication, by her grueling research and her reliance on facts, and by her courage and sense of personal responsibility. . . . Much of the humane social legislation we have in America today is the direct result of her life and labor."[19]

In raising the consciousness of the American public to the injustices created by unrestrained industrial expansion, Kelley, more than anyone else, underscored the need for the state to broaden its responsibility for human welfare. In making her case, she argued from both an economic and a moral perspective. Hours of labor, especially for women and children, were too long, wages were too low, and conditions, especially in the sweatshops, were deplorable. But it was also wrong to exploit the economic needs of women workers and to rob children of their childhoods. Kelley thought that workers had the right to a sustainable wage and to a workday and a work environment that did not threaten their health, safety, or morals and that the government (state and federal) should assume a greater responsibility for guaranteeing those rights. Through her fact-finding surveys at Hull House, her reports as Illinois state factory inspector, and her direction of the lobbying efforts of the NCL, Kelley exerted enormous influence in educating the public and winning early judicial victories like *Muller v. Oregon*. She also showed that in-depth investigation, factual reporting, and specific recommendations could lead to remedial legislation and that such legislation could bring about social change.

Not everyone, however, then or now, agreed with Kelley's view of protective labor legislation. Over time, a growing number of women have come to feel that the original decision in *Muller v. Oregon* actually harmed women more than it helped and that it actually slowed the advance toward gender equality. In looking back on *Muller*, they have been offended by both Brandeis's argument and the Supreme Court's written decision that treated all women as mothers or potential mothers. They argued that the language of the Court actually degraded women by treating the differences between female and male workers as evidence that women were inferior. In their mind, the decision embedded the principle of female difference in constitutional law—that women, as a class, could be treated differently and that such a special "protective" classification actually perpetuated their dependency and subordination.

Many working women were especially upset. Organizations like the Women's League of Equal Opportunity (1915) and the Equal Rights Association (1917) urged that protective labor laws be abolished because they disadvantaged women economically. Maximum-hour laws, for instance, often denied women employment (after the *Muller* decision, Muller fired his women workers and hired men), overtime pay, and promotion. Other protective restrictions, such as those that placed bans on night work, excluded women from certain occupations, or placed limits on weights that women could lift, could have similar negative results. (As white-collar workers began to outnumber blue-collar in the workforce in the decades following World War II, this same argument would be expanded and the suggestion made that women with administrative, professional, or executive experience be exempted from all maximum-hours legislation.) During the 1920s, Alice Paul and supporters of an Equal Rights Amendment added their voice to the charge that gender-specific protective laws denied women complete equality. Such statutes, they argued, defined women as weak and dependent, made them (along with children) wards of the state, limited women to low-paying jobs, compromised their earning capacity (denied them promotion), and prevented them from competing with men for jobs and advancement.

Although such arguments receded as the government assumed a greater role in guaranteeing rights for working men and women during the Great Depression, they resurfaced again during the 1960s as the feminist movement gained momentum. Finally, in 1964, Congress intervened. Title VII of the 1964 Civil Rights Act prohibited discrimination in employment on the basis of race, color, religion, national origin, or sex. No longer could women be placed in classifications that deprived them of opportunity. By the early 1970s, a combination of federal guidelines, state action, and court decisions appeared to have reversed fifty years of gender-specific protective legislation.

Focusing on the general debate through the lens of *Muller v. Oregon*, one historian noted the irony. The decision was, she said, "both a step forward on the road to modern labor standards and a step backward away from sexual equality."[20] Trying to avoid the trap of viewing the past through the prism of the present, this same historian also noted that reformers like Kelley faced powerful adversaries—a recalcitrant labor movement and the entrenched doctrine of freedom of contract—and that these formidable obstacles narrowed their options and molded their strategies.

NOTES

1. Josephine Goldmark, *Impatient Crusader: Florence Kelley's Life Story* (Urbana: University of Illinois Press, 1953), 6.
2. Kathryn Kish Sklar, *Florence Kelley and the Nation's Work: The Rise of Women's Political Culture, 1830–1900* (New Haven, Conn.: Yale University Press, 1995), 45–46.
3. Sklar, *Florence Kelley and the Nation's Work*, 15, 22.
4. Sklar, *Florence Kelley and the Nation's Work*, 28.
5. Goldmark, *Impatient Crusader*, 8.
6. Goldmark, *Impatient Crusader*, 11.
7. Sklar, *Florence Kelley and the Nation's Work*, 63–64.
8. Dorothy Rose Blumberg, *Florence Kelley: The Making of a Social Pioneer* (New York: Augustus M. Kelley, 1966), 30 fn. 17.
9. Goldmark, *Impatient Crusader*, 15.
10. Sklar, *Florence Kelly and the Nation's Work*, 86.
11. Goldmark, *Impatient Crusader*, 25–26.
12. Goldmark, *Impatient Crusader*, 33.
13. Sklar, *Florence Kelley and the Nation's Work*, 216.
14. Sklar, *Florence Kelley and the Nation's Work*, 216, 233, 236.
15. Sklar, *Florence Kelley and the Nation's Work*, 280.
16. Goldmark, *Impatient Crusader*, 37, 46.
17. Goldmark, *Impatient Crusader*, 53.
18. Goldmark, *Impatient Crusader*, 135, 169.
19. Frances Perkins, "My Recollections of Florence Kelley," *Social Science Review* 28 (March 1954): 19.
20. Nancy Woloch, *Muller v. Oregon: A Brief History with Documents* (Boston: Bedford/St. Martin's, 1996), 4.

SOURCES

Blumberg, Dorothy Rose. *Florence Kelley: The Making of a Social Pioneer*. New York: Augustus M. Kelley, 1966.

Goldmark, Josephine. *Impatient Crusader: Florence Kelley's Life Story*. Urbana: University of Illinois Press, 1953.

Kelley, Florence. *Notes of Sixty Years: The Autobiography of Florence Kelley*. Edited and introduced by Kathryn Kish Sklar. Chicago: Charles H. Kerr, 1986.

———. "Testimony on the Sweating System." Document 10 in *Women and Social Movements in the United States, 1600–2000*. http://womhist.binghamton.edu/factory/doc10.htm.

Perkins, Frances. "My Recollections of Florence Kelley." *Social Science Review* 28 (March 1954): 12–19.

Sklar, Kathryn Kish. *Florence Kelley and the Nation's Work: The Rise of Women's Political Culture, 1830–1900*. New Haven, Conn.: Yale University Press, 1995.

Stebner, Eleanor J. *The Women of Hull House: A Study in Spirituality, Vocation, and Friendship*. Albany: State University of New York Press, 1997.

Woloch, Nancy. *Muller v. Oregon: A Brief History with Documents*. Boston: Bedford/St. Martin's, 1996.

8

Louis Brandeis, the Law, and Social Change

During the late nineteenth century, conservative jurists viewed the law as static. They believed that the legal interpretation of the law was to be found in the Constitution and should be rigidly applied. Regarding the Constitution as a topic beyond political discussion, they considered the idea of modifying the strict constitutional interpretation of the law to accommodate economic and social reform as heresy. Instead, conservative legalists steadfastly applied the law to support the philosophy of laissez-faire and protect the rights of property and the freedom of contract. Laws, state or federal, that sought to protect workers, guarantee human rights, or promote the social welfare were simply deemed unconstitutional.

Among the first to challenge the "absolute truths of conservative law" was Oliver Wendell Holmes Jr. In his influential book *The Common Law* (1881), he argued that the "life of the law" had been "experience" and not "logic." "The felt necessities of the time," he said, "have had a good deal more to do than the syllogism in determining the rules by which men should be governed. The law embodies the story of a nation's development through many centuries, and it cannot be dealt with as if it contained only the axioms and corollaries of a book of mathematics."[1] Inspired by Holmes, progressive lawyers and legal scholars began to chip away at the assumption that the principles of law should be unchanging. They argued that fundamental legal principles and basic legal tenets could be preserved while allowing modifications to the manner in which they were applied. Central to their thinking was the idea that revolutionary changes in society required that the law evolve to keep pace with the times. Louis Brandeis, a young Boston attorney, aptly summarized the position of the dissenters:

Courts [have] continued to ignore newly arisen social needs. They [have] applied complacently eighteenth-century conceptions of the liberty of the individual and of the sacredness of private property. Early nineteenth-century scientific half-truths like "The survival of the fittest," which, translated into practice, meant "The devil take the hindmost," were erected by judicial sanction into a moral law. Where statutes giving expression to the new social spirit were clearly constitutional, judges, imbued with the spirit of individualism, often construed them away. Where any doubts as to the constitutionality of such statutes could find lodgment, courts all too frequently declared the acts void. . . . The law has everywhere a tendency to lag behind the facts of life.[2]

It would be up to Brandeis and other reform-minded lawyers in the late nineteenth and early twentieth centuries to break the traditional hold on legal thinking and work to harmonize the law with the needs of the community.

Louis Brandeis was born in Louisville, Kentucky, on November 13, 1856, the youngest child of Adolph Brandeis and Frederika (Dembitz) Brandeis. Both parents had migrated to America from Prague as part of extended families fleeing the reactionary atmosphere in central Europe following the German revolutionary movements of 1848. As "Forty-Eighters," the Brandeis and Dembitz families came to this country with a commitment to democracy as an ideal, a strong sense of cultural tradition, and a love of learning, music, and the arts. Frederika Brandeis encouraged the literary interests of all four of her children. Taking advantage of commercial opportunities in Louisville, Adolph Brandeis soon developed a successful grain and produce business. During the Civil War, the business furnished supplies to the Union army, and the family prospered. Anticipating the depression of 1873, Adolph Brandeis closed his business and took his family on an extended trip through Europe while he waited for economic conditions to improve. While in Europe, fifteen-year-old Louis enrolled in the Annen-Realschule in Dresden. During two years of study there, he learned to think methodically and inductively and realized that by using knowledge already acquired, he could develop new ideas. On graduation, the faculty awarded him a prize "for diligence and good conduct." The time spent in Germany convinced Brandeis that he wanted to study law. After returning to the United States in 1875, he entered Harvard Law School. During two years of regular study and one year of postgraduate work, he impressed everyone with his knowledge of the law and his ability to think in a logical manner.

After graduating from law school, Brandeis accepted an offer from classmate Samuel D. Warren to open a private law practice in Boston in 1879. Warren, who had graduated second in his Harvard law class behind Brandeis, came from a prominent New England family that owned paper mills. The Warrens were members of Boston's social elite, often referred to as "Boston's

Brahmins." Scions of the state's Puritan heritage, they possessed both a strong sense of social superiority and an ingrained sense of noblesse oblige. With Warren's social connections and his own proven abilities, Brandeis gained entry into this elite, Protestant-based society. That membership, however, was always qualified because Brandeis was a Jew. A subtle anti-Semitism among Boston's elite class served to isolate Brandeis socially and professionally.

Massachusetts had a tradition of social responsibility—in child labor legislation, women's suffrage, penal reform, and public education—that placed it ahead of most other states. But Massachusetts, like other states at the time, had its share of problems. Valuable municipal franchises and important grants of rights-of-way desired by railroads and other utility companies were often available to the highest bidder in the legislature. Bills that aimed at restricting or curtailing such concessions could be defeated for a price as well. Here again, Brandeis, as a Jew, faced a dilemma. Sympathy with the local Brahmin sense of responsibility placed him in sync with that group, but his willingness to challenge publicly the hypocrisy of members of that group in court (especially during his crusade against the New Haven Railroad) would intensify the anti-Semitic bias toward him. It would subject him to further social ostracism, gain him a reputation as a radical, and, ultimately, endanger his nomination to the Supreme Court of the United States.

Initially, Brandeis practiced commercial law, and his clients were mainly prominent businessmen. He could have been extremely successful as a business attorney, but he wanted the freedom to select his own clients and choose his own legal questions. He was also aware of the stigma attached to many corporate lawyers who had become little more than "guns for hire" and that many attorneys had abused the public's trust. "Instead of holding a position of independence, between the wealthy and the people, prepared to curb the excesses of either," said Brandeis, "able lawyers [had], to a large extent, allowed themselves to become adjuncts of great corporations and [had] neglected the obligation to use their powers for the protection of the people."[3] The way around this predicament for Brandeis was to develop a twofold view of his role as a lawyer. He would continue to be a legal adviser to the economically powerful, but he would also be a "people's lawyer" who felt a moral obligation to work (usually for no commission) in the public arena seeking practical solutions to the problems plaguing urban, industrial America.

During the late nineteenth and early twentieth centuries, the rapid physical expansion of America's cities necessitated the granting of municipal franchises. These contracts, in essence quasi-public monopolies, were lucrative prizes awarded to corporations to provide essential municipal services such as gas, water, or public transportation. It was not surprising that such

municipal corporations would seek to obtain the most advantageous and profitable contracts possible. The manner in which those corporations obtained
those contracts, however, raised questions about whether legislative bodies
were acting in the public interest and, in many cities, triggered citizen
campaigns to replace private ownership of utilities with public ownership. In
Boston, Brandeis offered his own remedy to what was becoming a common
urban problem.

Brandeis's battle over public franchises began in 1897, when the Boston
Elevated Railway Company was about to obtain a charter from the state legislature that would give it exclusive rights over certain routes and protect it
from having to reduce its five-cent fare for twenty-five years. When Brandeis
learned the details of the new agreement, he thought the interests of the public were being trampled. The contract, he argued, in language in keeping with
the Bay State's reform heritage, was "at odds with the established policy of
the Commonwealth and would, if enacted, sacrifice the interests of the public to that of a single corporation."[4] But Brandeis had protested too late in the
game, and the legislature awarded the franchise. Only a few years later, however, when the City of Boston started construction of a subway under the
downtown business district, the issue reappeared. When completed, suburban
commuters could transfer to the planned subway and take the most direct
route to the hub of the city. Brandeis and others saw the subway as the crucial link in the transportation system and believed it offered the city leverage
in their dealings with the Boston Elevated. As long as the city maintained
ownership of the subway (which it would build) and leased it on short and
reasonable terms to the railway company to operate, the city could control the
corporate monopoly that the legislature had created in 1897.

In 1901, Brandeis joined some of Boston's most civic-minded businessmen
to organize the Public Franchise League and used the new organization to
spearhead a major publicity campaign that included letters to the editors of
the city's major newspapers, petitions from labor and civic groups, and mes-
sages to the legislature protesting the corporation's proposal. Despite these
efforts, the Brandeis-led group could not stop the legislature from granting a
franchise that would have allowed the Boston Elevated a free and uncon-
trolled use of the new line for fifty years. Only a veto by Governor Murray
Crane, a League sympathizer, blocked what Brandeis regarded as a franchise
giveaway.

The following year, the railway company again attempted to secure an extended franchise and again came close to success. This time, however, after
Brandeis publicly refuted the company's claim that it was losing money, the
legislature passed the measure sponsored by the Public Franchise League.
The city would build the line and then lease it to the Boston Elevated for

twenty-five years at an annual rate of 4.5 percent of cost and reserve the right to terminate the lease at the end of the twenty-five-year period. In the end, both the company and the public, through a referendum, agreed to the plan. To Brandeis, the issue was simple. A public service corporation had "responsibilities." As he noted in testimony before the legislative committee, "[T]he Elevated Railway Company, or any company that serves us as transporters of passengers, is the servant and not the master of the public."[5] The interests of the community had to be protected.

Brandeis's concern for the public welfare in municipal issues was tested again in the debate over the proposed consolidation of Boston's gas companies. The city's gas business was a competitive one with eight different companies in the business as suppliers. But despite its competitive nature, service was substandard and rates a public concern, conditions resulting from poor planning, inefficient operation, and the cost of paying off public officials to maintain those high rates and maximize profits. But change was at hand. In 1903, the Boston Board of Gas and Electric Light Commissioners asked the legislature to allow the eight companies to merge their interests into one company and base the stock of the new concern on the fair market value of the combined properties. With little public opposition, the legislature approved the general plan. All that remained was for the city's utility commission to value the combined properties. When the new Boston Consolidated Gas Company requested that the capitalization be set at $24 million, consumer advocates cried foul. Under law, gas rates would have to be set at a rate that would guarantee the company a fair return on the value of its property. But an inflated valuation of the property would allow the company to charge the public rates that did not fairly reflect actual capital investments.

Opponents (including many members of the Public Franchise League) contested the $24 million figure and claimed that the real assessed value of the new company was closer to $15 million. To protect consumers, they argued that gas rates should be no higher than eighty cents per thousand cubic feet (twenty cents less than the current rate). Brandeis, always a capitalist rather than a socialist in public utility matters, understood the issue of fair valuation and that the gas company, as a public utility, had to provide quality service at a fair price. But he also felt that the $15 million figure did not accurately reflect the true replacement value of the property and that stockholders were entitled to a fair return on their investment. Brandeis wanted justice for both parties. His unique solution, the sliding scale, would cost him the support of his allies in the Public Franchise League who cared only for lower rates based on lower valuation.

Originated in London, the creative sliding scale idea offered a way to curb corporate abuse in the public utility field by pegging the rates charged by a company to the efficiency of its operation. If profits increased, the company could increase the dividends it paid to its stockholders only if it also reduced the rates it charged to its consumers. After talks with James L. Richards, the open-minded head of the Consolidated Gas Company, Brandeis and Richards were able to reach a workable agreement. The company would accept the $15 million amount as its capital value, agree to a regular 7 percent dividend, and promise to sell gas at ninety cents per thousand cubic feet (a 10 percent reduction from current rates). For every additional 1 percent increase in profits, the company would reduce gas rates by five cents per thousand cubic feet. The legislature eventually approved the sliding scale plan, and the governor signed the measure in May 1906. Over the next eighteen months, improved management pushed the company's dividend to 9 percent, while gas rates fell to eighty cents. The solution reflected Brandeis's overall thinking as well as his willingness to do what he thought was right and fair regardless of criticism. Both interests, public and private, gained fair treatment, and the plan encouraged economy and efficiency. In addition, the arrangement avoided public ownership, which Brandeis considered less efficient and vulnerable to political pressures. In fact, Brandeis regarded his victory as one more for good government than for lower gas rates. "The officers and employees of the gas company," he said, "now devote themselves strictly to the business of making and distributing gas, instead of dissipating their abilities, as heretofore, in lobbying and political intrigue."[6]

In 1905, Brandeis became engaged in a lengthy legal battle with the New York, New Haven and Hartford Railroad. The corporation, controlled by J. P. Morgan interests, had been an attractive financial investment for many banks and investors in New England for years. Although Massachusetts law prohibited railroads from holding "directly or indirectly" stock in other corporations, the New Haven had invested in street railways and steamship companies and controlled nearly one-third of the shares of the Boston and Maine Railroad (B & M), the other major rail line in the region. Fearful of being engulfed by a giant holding company, B & M shareholders retained Brandeis as legal counsel. Although defenders of the New Haven Railroad argued that a merger with the B & M would provide a more integrated and efficient transportation system, Brandeis saw only the potential harmful effects that monopolistic control of transportation would have on shippers, consumers, and rail competition in general.

During the legislative session of 1907, Brandeis worked with lawmakers to have a bill introduced that required the New Haven to divest its B & M holdings. This action marked the beginning of Brandeis's public opposition to large corporations that he believed threatened the community by placing themselves beyond the control of state legislatures and seizing the power to dictate transportation rates to an entire region. "No system of regulation can safely be substituted for the operation of individual liberty as expressed in competition," he said. "Human nature is such that monopolies, however well intentioned, and however well regulated, inevitably become . . . oppressive, arbitrary, unprogressive, and inefficient."[7] Although Brandeis's measure failed to win approval, he managed to delay a vote on the proposed merger for another year.

In the meantime, the New Haven issued its annual financial report. Brandeis's own in-depth examination of that report convinced him that, contrary to public perceptions and official statements from company president Charles Mellon attesting to its economic soundness, the New Haven Railroad was using deceptive accounting procedures to cover up huge financial losses. Certain of his findings, Brandeis published a pamphlet in which he charged the directors of the New Haven with financial misconduct by paying dividends out of earnings that did not exist. The company had paid high dividends but had done so by making drastic cuts in maintenance and repairs and by digging into its financial reserves. In reality, the B & M was in much better financial condition than the New Haven and the proposed merger really a scheme to garner B & M assets to cover New Haven losses.

Brandeis's pamphlet triggered a series of actions and reactions. First, the Massachusetts Supreme Court ordered the New Haven to sell its trolley lines. Then the Massachusetts House of Representatives passed a measure requiring the New Haven to sell its B & M stock within two years. Ostensibly complying with the wishes of the legislature, the New Haven then sold off its B & M stock to John Billard, an out-of-state resident and, in reality, a dummy buyer. The directors of the New Haven then convinced Governor Eben Draper to issue a message to the legislature requesting that it allow a new railroad incorporated under the laws of the Commonwealth of Massachusetts to repurchase the B & M. Urged on by lobbyists for the New Haven Railroad, the legislature proceeded to charter this new corporation to act as a holding company for the stocks and bonds of the B & M. With legislative authorization completed, Billard immediately sold back his stock to the new company, an entity that was, in reality, wholly owned by the New Haven Railroad. Merger had finally been achieved.

Outmaneuvered by the New Haven's use of political influence and legal subterfuge, Brandeis decided to take his case to Washington, D.C., where Senator Robert M. La Follette helped him attack the New Haven from a national forum. Those charges triggered an Interstate Commerce Commission investigation of the New Haven, and subsequent hearings confirmed all of Brandeis's charges. The Billard deal had been fraudulent. The profits of the New Haven had been fictitious. And the company had been paying dividends out of capital resources and borrowed money. To save money, the company had compromised on repairs and maintenance, neglect that had actually caused an increase in accidents. As a result of the investigation, New Haven stock collapsed, the president of the company resigned, and although the company stayed in business, it was never again the blue-chip stock it had been. Brandeis had won a legal battle against monopoly, but the real significance of the New Haven case, which had dragged on for nearly ten years, was that it signaled the beginning of Brandeis's war against corporate power. His emerging philosophy on the evils inherent in "bigness" would soon catch the eye of Woodrow Wilson, who would, as Democratic candidate for president in 1912, incorporate much of Brandeis's thinking into the progressive political program that became known as the "New Freedom."

As Brandeis became increasingly aware of the social problems that resulted from the rise of industrial capitalism, he became more and more concerned over the reluctance of legal thinking generally to accommodate the new conditions of modern American life—to remain relevant to contemporary social and economic needs. Nowhere was this inconsistency more glaring than in the field of protective labor legislation. It was in this area, as one historian has noted, that "judges, in ignorance of modern industrial life, had erected their own economic prejudices into impassable legal barriers, and made these part and parcel of the Constitution itself."[8]

Prior to 1908, legal challenges to established working conditions had made little headway. The sticking point was the Fourteenth Amendment to the Constitution prohibiting a state from depriving citizens of "life, liberty, or property without due process of law." The Supreme Court had gone on to define "liberty" in the due process clause as liberty of contract and found this principle violated when the government interfered with the employee–employer relationship. The assumption was that an individual had not only the freedom to sell his labor but also the power, as an individual, to negotiate a fair bargain with his employer. State-imposed limitations on workers' hours were thus regarded as violations of this liberty unless a state could demonstrate that such limitation was necessary under its police power to protect the health or safety of the general public. In a case handed down by the Illinois Supreme Court in 1895, the court had ruled an eight-hour law for women engaged in manufacturing to be unconstitutional and made a point to note that it saw no "reasonable connection" between the law and "the public health, safety or welfare proposed to be secured by it."[9] In a similar decision in *Lochner v. New York* (1905), the U.S. Supreme Court overturned a ten-hour law for bakers, finding the law an unreasonable interference with the right of the individual to his personal liberty and an unwarranted use (counsel had not demonstrated that the law was necessary to protect the health of the workers) of the state's police powers.

In 1907, Florence Kelley and Josephine Goldmark of the National Consumers' League learned that a 1903 Oregon law prohibiting the employment of women in factories, mechanical establishments, and laundries for more than ten hours a day was to be challenged before the Supreme Court. Joe Haselbock, the supervisor of the Grand Laundry in Portland, violated the law in September 1905 by requiring one of his workers, Mrs. Elmer Gotcher, to work more than ten hours. Curt Muller, the owner of the laundry, was found guilty of the misdemeanor and fined $10. In challenging the constitutionality of the law, Muller claimed that his right to freedom of contract under the due process clause of the Fourteenth Amendment had been violated. This line of reasoning was, however, open to challenge. The preindustrial assumption that both parties to a contract were free and equal negotiators was no longer valid in modern industrial society. Kelley, who had worked as chief factory inspector for the State of Illinois, knew what conditions in factories were like — poor lighting and heat, inadequate ventilation, and unbearably long hours at meager wages. To her, the "liberty of contract" defense was merely a legal smoke screen used by employers to justify the exploitation of working men and women. Fearful that the Oregon law would be overturned, Kelley and Goldmark asked Brandeis if he would take part in the case. Brandeis accepted but insisted that Oregon agree to make him its official counsel so that he could determine the line of argument to be followed and be able to present the case before the court in both its written and its oral form. He then made plans for a very innovative defense — a short legal argument supported by extensive economic and sociological data gathered by the National Consumers' League underscoring the negative effects of long hours and pointing out the possible benefits that might result from their limitation.

In his now famous 104-page legal brief, in which only two pages dealt with abstract logic and prior legal precedents, Brandeis presumed that existing law acknowledged that the right to purchase or sell labor was part of the "liberty" protected by the Constitution and that such liberty was subject to such reasonable restraints as a state might impose, in exercise of its police power, to protect the health, safety, morals, or general welfare of the public. The question at issue, he argued, was whether Oregon's maximum-hour law was a necessary restraint. Did a woman's anatomical and physiological differences and her lack of physical strength in relation to men require restricting her duration of work? The answer to that question, said Brandeis, could not be answered by legal logic, only by facts. Armed with data from hundreds of reports (both domestic and foreign) of factory inspectors, physicians, experts in hygiene, and special industrial commissions that had been gathered for his use by the National Consumers' League, Brandeis submitted over 100 pages of factual material to prove that long hours of work were dangerous to the health, safety, and morals of women. In a unanimous decision, the Supreme Court overrode the contention of Muller's lawyers that the freedom of women workers to bargain with their employers was impaired by the Oregon statute and affirmed the state's ten-hour law. A "woman's physical structure, and the [maternal] functions she performs in consequence thereof," said the Court, "justify special legislation restricting or qualifying the conditions under which she should be permitted to toil."[10]

The decision in *Muller v. Oregon* revived the entire field of protective labor legislation, and over the next eight years, forty-one states enacted laws for working women. The decision also opened the way for future restrictions on hours for men, on working conditions, and even on minimum-wage levels. In a broader sense, however, the Supreme Court changed. In accepting Brandeis's sociological brief, the Court allowed a new means of legal argumentation and accepted the position that the meaning given to the law should evolve in relation to social need. The decision, in effect, sanctioned what came to be known as "sociological jurisprudence"—presenting factual data to establish the need for social legislation.

Brandeis's growing reputation as a defender of the public interest also drew him into one of the most publicized debates over environmental policy to occur during the Progressive Era. A defining aspect of Theodore Roosevelt's presidency was his commitment to conservation. As an avid sportsman and naturalist, he appreciated wilderness and became concerned about the consequences of the unchecked commercial development of America's natural resources. Working in close cooperation with chief forester Gifford Pinchot, Roosevelt sought to limit private development on public lands. Using his executive powers, Roosevelt removed millions of acres of undeveloped government land and placed them in Pinchot's national forest system. When William Howard Taft succeeded Roosevelt as president, he promised to continue his predecessor's conservation policy. Conservationists, however, were skeptical. They feared a reversal of environmental policy when Taft selected as his secretary of interior Richard A. Ballinger, a lawyer who had represented private corporations in suits involving public lands. Their fears became heightened in August 1909, when Secretary Ballinger reopened for sale valuable coal lands (the Cunningham claims) in Alaska that Roosevelt had previously withdrawn from sale or development.

Ballinger's action alarmed Louis R. Glavis, a young Seattle field agent in the General Land Office of the Department of the Interior, who suspected that Ballinger might be involved in a conspiracy to assist the Morgan-Guggenheim mining syndicate in gaining control of Alaskan coal fields (the Cunningham claims). When Glavis confronted Ballinger, the secretary dismissed his charge as unfounded. Glavis, on the advice of Gifford Pinchot,

then sent his report to President Taft. After conferring with Ballinger and ostensibly reviewing additional material presented to him by Attorney General
George W. Wickersham, Taft rejected the charges and told Ballinger to fire
Glavis for insubordination. Outraged by his dismissal, Glavis took his report
to Norman Hapgood, an editor at *Collier's* magazine, who published it in
muckraking style under the title "The Whitewashing of Ballinger?" The cover
of the magazine featured a picture of Ballinger in the grasp of a clutched hand
and posed the question: "Are the Guggenheim's in charge of the Department
of the Interior?" The expose caused a sensation and triggered a demand for a
special congressional investigation of the charges. When Pinchot sent a letter
to the committee attacking the firing of Glavis and suggesting that the issue
went beyond the issue of conservation and raised questions about honest,
democratic government, Taft discharged him from his position as chief
forester. Realizing that *Collier's* might be sued for libel and that Glavis and
Pinchot would also need to be represented by legal counsel, *Collier's* retained
Brandeis as attorney.

As was his style, Brandeis quickly set out to become an expert on the case
before him. By the time the committee began its hearings, he had acquired a
thorough knowledge of the workings of the Interior Department, public land
law, and conservation policy. The Republican-controlled hearings started
slowly, and Brandeis had to constantly argue for permission to access documents and to cross-examine witnesses. Almost from the beginning, however,
Brandeis sensed that something was amiss with the president's exoneration of
Ballinger. Had Taft presented his statement clearing Ballinger before or after
having taken the time to read the summary of relevant documents prepared by
Attorney General Wickersham? The issue, in effect, had become not whether
Ballinger was innocent or Glavis guilty but whether the Taft administration
had lied to the American people to cover up official wrongdoing. While
searching for an answer to that question, Brandeis discovered, through cross-
examination, that politics had been a major factor in Interior Department ap-
pointments and that a number of key positions had been given to individuals
who had prior business dealings with the very interests they were now obli-
gated to regulate. In what could have been seen only as conflict of interest,
testimony revealed that Ballinger had previously done legal work for the
Guggenheims on the Cunningham claims.

Although stymied in his quest for additional documents that might prove his
suspicions, Brandeis got the break he needed. Frederick M. Kerby, a young
stenographer in the Interior Department, agreed to provide evidence to prove
that Ballinger, not Taft, had actually written the letter that cleared him and that
supporting documents provided by Attorney General Wickersham had not
reached President Taft until after he had signed the letter; the documents were

then predated. It appeared to the public that the administration had engaged in a cover-up, attempting to hide one lie with another. Despite the evidence of duplicity, however, the committee voted seven to five along party lines to clear Ballinger. Although the administration had won a tainted victory, the press, fueled by information made available by Brandeis, kept the case open to public scrutiny until Ballinger resigned his post in March 1911.

As the Ballinger-Glavis affair unfolded, Brandeis came to see that the real issue was democracy. "The loyalty that you want is loyalty to the real employer, to the people of the United States. This idea that loyalty to an immediate superior is something commendable when it goes to a forgetfulness of one's country involves a strange misconception of our government and a strange misconception of what democracy is. . . . We are not dealing here with a question of the conservation of natural resources merely; it is the conservation and development of democracy."[11] What Brandeis wanted to see was honesty and integrity in government and officials who understood accountability and their obligations as part of a larger governing body. "They [government officials] cannot be worthy of the respect and admiration of the people," he said, "unless they add to the virtue of obedience some other virtues—the virtues of manliness, of truth, of courage."[12] Individuals in positions of authority needed the courage to act responsibly, even at the risk of their positions, so that the interests of the public could be served and protected.

During the 1912 presidential campaign, Brandeis, who was nominally a Republican, cast his support behind Democrat Woodrow Wilson. Feeling that he and Wilson were kindred spirits in their economic and moral philosophies, Brandeis wrote a letter congratulating the former New Jersey governor on his nomination. Wilson, whose campaign lacked a clearly defined program on the problem of big business and monopoly, invited Brandeis, known for his views on the topic, to lunch. In the years preceding his nomination, Wilson, initially an economic conservative, had come to view corporate bigness as a threat to individual competition and a moral system that praised opportunity, hard work, and perseverance as prerequisites for middle-class success. Brandeis, who had always favored a competitive, small business–oriented economy that offered opportunities to those with talent and ambition, offered to help Wilson articulate a political program to compete with Theodore Roosevelt's. Roosevelt's program, known as the "New Nationalism," sought to restore opportunity by regulating monopoly through powerful federal agencies.

Brandeis's earlier legal battles had convinced him that concentrated economic power could have a negative effect on a free society. Like Lester Frank Ward, he believed that reason and morality could limit the social Darwinian notion that survival of the fittest was best. The solution to the menace inherent in the power of big business was to establish rules in the marketplace that would maintain competition and prevent the strong from destroying the weak. Such steps, argued Brandeis, needed to be taken to protect not only economic democracy but also the political democracy that depended on it. Otherwise, economic power would destroy liberty as well. As the cooperation between Brandeis and Wilson grew during the campaign, the issue of debate increasingly focused on "bigness." Whereas Roosevelt argued that monopoly was inevitable and beneficial (for reasons of efficiency) and that its excesses could be mitigated by federal regulation, Brandeis and Wilson argued that there was an inherent evil in monopoly (bigness) that impelled it to destroy smaller competitors. Brandeis aptly summed up their differences:

> The Democratic Party insists that competition can be and should be maintained in every branch of private industry; that competition can be and should be restored in those branches of industry in which it has been suppressed by the trusts; and that, if at any future time monopoly should appear to be desirable in any branch of industry, the monopoly should be a public one—monopoly owned by the people and not by the capitalists. The New Party [Progressive Party], on the other hand, insists that private monopoly may be desirable in some branches of industry, or at all events, is inevitable; and that existing trusts should not be dismembered . . . but should be made "good" by regulation. . . . We believe that no methods of regulation ever have been or can be devised to remove the menace inherent in private monopoly and overweening commercial power.[13]

Brandeis and Wilson offered voters a "New Freedom" rooted in restored competition.

After Wilson became president, he continued to rely on Brandeis's advice as he worked to implement his new domestic program, especially in the areas of banking and antitrust law. The hearings of the House Committee on Banking and Currency (the Pujo Committee) conducted between May 1912 and January 1913 had revealed how a few powerful New York financiers controlled the nation's banking and stock exchange systems and possessed the power to control prices, cash, and credit. Sensationalized in the press, the committee's findings provoked a public outcry for regulation. Ultimately persuaded by Secretary of State William Jennings Bryan and Brandeis that the banking system needed to be democratized and its currency issued and controlled by the government, Wilson convinced Congress to enact the Federal Reserve Act in December 1913. The new law created twelve regional banks with the power to lend money to private banks at rates set by the Federal Reserve System, issue new Federal Reserve notes backed by the government as the medium of exchange, shift funds to meet increased demands for credit and make more money available for loans to small businesses, and establish a

Federal Reserve Board appointed by the president to supervise and monitor the system. It did not, however, take steps to regulate banks or the stock exchange.

The findings of the Pujo Committee crystallized Brandeis's thinking on the topic of banking and prompted him to write a series of articles on "The Money Trust" that appeared in *Harper's Weekly* in late 1913 and early 1914 and were later published in book form as *Other People's Money and How the Bankers Use It* (1914). Brandeis had actually thought about doing an analysis even before the Pujo Committee investigation and had sketched the outlines of such a study to his friend Norman Hapgood in 1911. In writing to Hapgood, Brandeis commented,

> The honest financiers who are using, as bankers and insurance company managers, etc., the money of others, realize that they hold the money in trust for its owners and must be fair to the beneficiaries. They do not realize, however, that the power which the control of other people's money gives them to grant or withdraw credit, is a trust for the public—a power to be exercised impartially as the applicant for credit is entitled to it. They exercise their power regardless of that trust . . . and it amounts practically to their playing the industrial game with loaded dice. . . . By controlling the money of other people at the same time that they are engaged in industrial and other occupations, they suppress competition and get other advantages by means that are illegal.[14]

Brandeis believed that the existing banking system was a trust controlled by a small group of financiers using other people's money. Because they wielded tremendous and potentially dangerous power, the extent of that power would have to be controlled by the government. But Brandeis realized that the public still did not have the knowledge to deal with the problem effectively. Perhaps he could enlighten them.

Using the Report of the Pujo Committee as a starting point, Brandeis immersed himself in research. He was soon able to formulate a description of the money trust as he found it. Control of business operations in America had become concentrated in the hands of a few giant investment banking houses. At the top of this financial pyramid stood J. P. Morgan and Company, the National City Bank, and the First National Bank of New York, which controlled corporations with over $22 billion in resources. They, in turn, were joined, through joint ownership and interlocking directorates, by a second tier of banking firms. To Brandeis, this integrated banking system controlled economic operations to such an extent that almost no business enterprise of any significance could be undertaken without their consent and participation. These dominant investment houses had gradually gained control over industrial corporations, life insurance companies, and banks and trust companies.

He likened the system to a financial oligarchy that fostered monopoly and stifled business enterprise. To break this moneyed power, Brandeis proposed a series of reforms: prohibition of interlocking directorates, publication of bankers' commissions and profits, elimination of the banker as the middleman in the sale of securities, and the prevention of any connection between railroads and companies with which they had business dealings. But Brandeis's charges fell largely on deaf ears. A provision outlawing interlocking directorates that was eventually included in the Clayton Act of 1914 proved to be inadequate, and financial power continued to increase, spurred on by World War I. Brandeis received a measure of redemption, however, after the collapse of the banking system and the onset of the Great Depression, when Congress passed the Securities Act in 1933 requiring investment bankers to file statements of disclosure and provided criminal and civil penalties for wrongdoers.

The articles that Brandeis wrote on the money trust came out too late to have much of an impact on the banking bill but had a decided impact on the administration's antitrust legislation. Brandeis had actually sketched the outlines of his thinking on the topic in a memorandum to Wilson in January 1912. His antitrust program had three major points: remove vague wording (terms like "combination," "monopoly," "trust," "conspiracy," and "restraint") used in the Sherman Act, facilitate the enforcement of the law by the courts, and create a board or commission to aid in the administration of the law. Those suggestions were evident in Wilson's special message to Congress on the operation of trusts and monopolies in January 1914. In that address, Wilson delineated the points that would become the Clayton Antitrust Act. It was necessary, he said, to outlaw interlocking directorates in corporations, set up a federal commission to provide business with guidelines, and establish penalties for malpractices. The final bill reflected those points. Because it was impossible to define all the potential violations of antitrust law, Brandeis encouraged Wilson to support the creation of a strong regulating agency, the Federal Trade Commission, which would have the power to initiate prosecutions against unfair trade practices not defined by law.

The capstone of Brandeis's legal career came with his surprise appointment to the Supreme Court in 1916. The nomination delighted reformers but upset many conservatives. The sitting president of the American Bar Association (ABA) and six former ABA presidents publicly opposed the nomination. Some critics charged that Brandeis had used ruthless and unscrupulous tactics as an adversary in court. Many others assailed him because he failed to conform to the conservative judicial stereotype. Some resented his aloofness, others his combative and argumentative style, and still others his antiestablishment persona as the "People's Attorney." Led by President Wilson, however, the pro-Brandeis supporters held firm and eventually triumphed. As Wilson noted during the court fight,

> I have tested [Brandeis] by seeking his advice upon some of the most difficult and perplexing public questions about which it was necessary for me to form a judgment. I have dealt with him in matters where nice questions of honor and fair play, as well as large questions of justice and public benefit, were involved. In every matter in which I have made test of his judgment and point of view I have received from him counsel singularly enlightening, singularly clear-sighted and judicial, and, above all, full of moral stimulation.[15]

In the end, that seemed to be the verdict of the majority.

During his twenty-three years on the Supreme Court, Brandeis consistently argued in support of his belief that law should accommodate changing social and economic need. He left a record as a constant defender of freedom of speech, assembly, and religion as well as the protection of civil liberties. His dissenting opinions have become classic defenses in the struggle to liberalize judicial interpretation of the Constitution. In one especially eloquent dissent in *Olmstead v. United States* (1928), Brandeis condemned the use of wiretapping by federal authorities in violation of state law and admonished the federal government for assuming that, in the administration of the criminal law, the ends justified the means. During the 1930s, he saw his long-standing belief in judicial self-restraint in the review of legislative acts to allow flexibility for social experimentation realized when the courts upheld New Deal programs such as collective bargaining, minimum wages, unemployment insurance, regulation of securities and stocks, and restraints on holding companies.

Brandeis earned a national reputation as a reformer for his battles as the "People's Attorney" and for his influence as a political adviser to Woodrow Wilson before beginning a long and illustrious career on the Supreme Court. His reform vision, however, offers a consistency to all stages of his life. He wanted no less than to reconcile the law with a rapidly industrializing society, guarantee economic opportunity, and protect American democratic values. Because the law had become a bulwark guarding the rights of property and the courts functioned as defenders of the status quo, Brandeis argued for change. The law would have to be made to serve the public rather than the private interest, and the courts would have to accommodate change rather than block it. This was especially true in the area of protective labor legislation. As he demonstrated in *Muller v. Oregon*, the meaning given to law should evolve in relation to social need. For that to happen, sociological evidence would have to be considered in legal interpretation and human rights given preference over property rights.

Louis Brandeis, circa 1916. Library of Congress, Prints & Photographs Division.

Brandeis, according to his biographer, perceived "the perils of our industrial revolution"—"the development of corporate and cartel industry as menacing employees, competitors, capitalism, democracy—the state itself."[16] As a result, he became convinced, despite his theoretical distrust of big government, that unchecked economic power would have to be curbed by government action. This rule would have to be followed when granting municipal franchises, licensing public utilities, or allowing the formation of quasi-monopolistic transportation companies. It would entail government action to break up predatory trusts, government control to prevent the manipulation of money and credit, and government regulation to halt unfair business practices. If that could be done, then the rights of the public—as consumers and taxpayers—could be protected, economic opportunity restored, and competitive capitalism maintained. Curbing economic power would diminish its political influence as well. Once the power to blunt civic responsibility, compromise public virtue, and inhibit accountability was removed, democratic government could thrive. Brandeis believed that a better society was possible —one in which individuals could develop as citizens and human beings.

NOTES

1. Eric F. Goldman, *Rendezvous with Destiny: A History of Modern American Reform* (Chicago: Ivan R. Dee, 2001), 134–35.

2. Melvin I. Urofsky, *Louis D. Brandeis and the Progressive Tradition* (Boston: Little, Brown, 1981), 49.

3. Philippa Strum, *Louis D. Brandeis: Justice for the People* (Cambridge, Mass.: Harvard University Press, 1984), 41.

4. Urofsky, *Louis D. Brandeis and the Progressive Tradition*, 23.

5. Urofsky, *Louis D. Brandeis and the Progressive Tradition*, 25.

6. Alpheus T. Mason, *Brandeis: A Free Man's Life* (New York: Viking Press, 1956), 140.

7. Mason, *Brandeis*, 181.

8. Mason, *Brandeis*, 247.

9. Mason, *Brandeis*, 247.

10. Mason, *Brandeis*, 251.

11. Strum, *Louis D. Brandeis*, 137–38.

12. Mason, *Brandeis*, 281.

13. Melvin I. Urofsky, *A Mind of One Piece: Brandeis and American Reform* (New York: Charles Scribner's Sons, 1971), 76.

14. Louis D. Brandeis, *Other People's Money and How the Bankers Use It*, ed. Melvin I. Urofsky (Boston: Bedford/St. Martin's Press, 1995), 16.

15. Urofsky, *A Mind of One Piece*, 122.

16. Mason, *Brandeis*, 644.

SOURCES

Brandeis, Louis D. *Other People's Money and How the Bankers Use It*. Edited by Melvin I. Urofsky. Boston: Bedford/St. Martin's, 1995.

Gal, Allon. *Brandeis of Boston*. Cambridge, Mass.: Harvard University Press, 1980.

Mason, Alpheus Thomas. *Brandeis: A Free Man's Life*. New York: Viking Press, 1956.

Paper, Lewis J. *Brandeis*. Englewood Cliffs, N.J.: Prentice-Hall, 1983.

Strum, Philippa. *Louis D. Brandeis: Justice for the People*. Cambridge, Mass.: Harvard University Press, 1984.

Urofsky, Melvin I. *Louis D. Brandeis and the Progressive Tradition*. Boston: Little, Brown, 1981.

———. *A Mind of One Piece: Brandeis and American Reform*. New York: Charles Scribner's Sons, 1971.

Woloch, Nancy. *Muller v. Oregon: A Brief History with Documents*. Boston: Bedford/St. Martin's, 1996.

9

Lincoln Steffens Muckrakes the Business of Politics

As the nineteenth century drew to a close, many Americans had become convinced that the rapid growth of modern industrialization and the accompanying surge of urbanization and immigration had created a society burdened with social problems and plagued with social injustice. Among the first to call for reform of the current state of affairs were a group of journalists that President Theodore Roosevelt would label "muckrakers." These investigative reporters, writing for a new generation of popular, mass-circulated magazines and using the literature of exposure, began to direct public attention to a series of scandals and corrupt actions. Their descriptions of bribery, tax dodging, franchise grabs, and monopoly control of the marketplace seemed to confirm a growing suspicion that hallowed democratic ideals had become divorced from reality. In turning the spotlight on the corporate malefactor, the licentious politician, and the franchise boodler, they gave focus to progressivism and provided a great deal of impetus for the election of reform-minded politicians and the passage of reform-oriented legislation. Perhaps the most influential of these new journalists was Lincoln Steffens. His series on "machine" politics and "boss rule" for *McClure's* magazine helped start a crusade for political reform of local and state government. Steffens, however, became the most famous of the muckrakers for more than his sensational revelations. He offered readers a sociological explanation for corruption as he challenged them to do something about it.

Lincoln Steffens was born in 1866 in San Francisco, California. His father, Joseph Steffens, was a Canadian of German and Irish descent who had been raised on a farm in northwestern Illinois. After graduating from a commercial college in Chicago, Joseph Steffens worked as a schoolteacher and then as a clerk in a paint company before deciding to move westward in search of new opportunities. After traveling across the country as a scout for a wagon train, he settled in San Francisco and worked as a bookkeeper for an oil, paint, and glass company. In that city, he met and married Elisabeth Louisa Symes, originally from England, in 1865. The elder Steffens advanced quickly, first to manager of the firm's Sacramento office, where the family moved in 1870, and then to full partner. Over the next several decades, his achievements continued as he attained the positions of director and vice president of the California National Bank of Sacramento and president of the Board of Trade and became a leader in Republican state politics. Financial success eventually allowed him to purchase a Victorian mansion that became a showplace in the city. When he sold the property to the State of California in 1903, it became the governor's mansion.

A product of this privileged environment, Steffens grew up as a pampered youth. Given a pony to ride and the independence to do so, as he fondly recalled years later in his classic *Autobiography*, he roamed the surrounding Sacramento countryside as a youthful observer of life. Such freedom, however, seemed to encourage a lack of discipline, at least in school. Educated at private preparatory schools, young Steffens usually found himself at or near the bottom of his class. When his was fifteen, he had to repeat a year of school just to be allowed to go on to high school. When his attention still lagged, his parents sent him to a military academy. When that proved to be counterproductive, they hired a private tutor to prepare him for entrance examinations to gain admission to the University of California at Berkeley. By the time Steffens finally graduated from the university in 1889 (again at the bottom of his class) with a degree in history and a growing interest in philosophy, he had at least discovered a desire to learn more.

On graduation, Steffens turned down an offer from his father to join the family business and announced that he wanted to pursue graduate study in Germany. For the next three years, he studied philosophy (with a special emphasis on ethics) and psychology and pursued interests in art, music, and theater at universities in Berlin, Heidelberg, Munich, and Leipzig. With no career goal in mind and supported financially by his father, Steffens seemed to be studying to become an intellectual and happy as a professional student. At Leipzig, he met and secretly married Josephine Bontecou, a fellow student majoring in medicine and psychology. The daughter of a New York physician, Josephine was ten years older than Steffens. After further study at the British Museum in London and the Sorbonne in Paris and a final summons from his father to return home and get on with his life, the couple sailed for the United States. When the ship docked at New York Harbor in October 1892, there was a letter waiting for him from his father. As Steffens later recalled in his *Auto-*

biography (and the account may well have been embellished), it read, "By now you must know about all there is to know of the theory of life, but there's a practical side as well. It's worth knowing. I suggest that you learn it, and the way to study it, I think, is to stay in New York and hustle." Enclosed was a check for $100, which, his father said, "should keep you till you can find a job and support yourself."[1]

Finding his first job was not easy. After spending a month seeking an opening at business firms and brokerage and banking houses, Steffens used his father's connection to gain an interview with Robert Underwood Johnson, the owner/editor of *Century* magazine. After talking with Steffens and taking his measure, Johnson recommended him for a job as a reporter on the *New York Evening Post* edited by E. L. Godkin. A conservative, old-fashioned newspaper, the *Evening Post* provided sound, nonsensational news coverage and emphasized commercial topics. Under Godkin's editorial direction, the daily favored "mugwump" politics (honest government and civil service reform) and opposed Tammany Hall (the dominant political machine) and its immigrant supporters. Despite its constrictions, the *Evening Post* gave Steffens his first opportunity to observe the complex world of urban-industrial society.

Assigned to cover Wall Street, already the center of corporate and financial power, Steffens soon met the influential power brokers. Personable by nature, Steffens had a manner that put his subjects at ease and encouraged them to tell him what he wanted to know. Their openness seemed to kindle his interest in men and motives that would set him apart from other reform journalists. Especially noteworthy for his impact on Steffens's development as a journalist was James B. Dill, the Wall Street lawyer who had drafted a New Jersey law that allowed the state to become a safe haven in which corporations looking to evade the antitrust laws of other states could incorporate and escape possible prosecution. Steffens liked Dill because he was "honest" in the sense that he tried to conceal nothing. Dill admitted that he had manipulated the law by creating a loophole that allowed big business to evade the spirit of antitrust legislation and continue to operate against the public interest. As Steffens saw it, other businessmen were in the same way corrupt, but they refused to admit it. To make matters worse, these same hypocritical "good citizens" often justified their own immoral actions while condemning others for lesser crimes. This was true of most of the men Steffens met on Wall Street. Dill, on the other hand, understood the commercial world around him and refused to hide behind moral platitudes. Steffens was unable to grasp, at this early stage in his professional life, the full implications of this discovery, but a process of analyzing human nature had begun.

In late 1893, the editors at the *Evening Post* assigned Steffens to the Mulberry Street Police Station in lower Manhattan to investigate allegations of

bribery and vice in the Police Department. His editors hoped that any information he might uncover could be used by the newspaper to aid the efforts of
Reverend Charles H. Parkhurst, minister of the Madison Square Church and
president of the Society for the Prevention of Crime, who had undertaken a
crusade against Tammany Hall, the Police Department, and their collusion in
protecting vice. As Steffens told his father, the assignment was "beastly
work" that involved "police, criminals and low-browed 'heelers' in the vilest
part of the horrible East side amid poverty, sin and depravity."[2] Helping him
to understand this strange environment was Jacob Riis, veteran police reporter for the *New York Evening Sun* and author of *How the Other Half Lives*
(1890), a gripping description of conditions in the ghetto that utilized modern
photography to add poignancy to the story of the urban underclass.

Focusing on the saloon, the brothel, and the gambling den, Steffens soon
discovered that the police were involved in a ring of corruption. But he drew
distinctions. Although the average policeman participated in the corruption,
they were, to Steffens, not responsible for it. The evil resided, instead, in the
"system" and those who controlled it. The police "protected" illegal activities
and received a percentage of the illicit profit from vice, prostitution, and gambling as a reward. This was the "price" criminals paid for police corruption.
But beyond the police force were the political machine and its political allies
in both the Democratic and the Republican parties. These political leaders and
their legions of followers dealt in the spoils of office and the profits of vice
and were responsible for the corruption of the city, its politics, and its police.

Steffens's articles on police corruption helped sweep a reform ticket into
office in the municipal elections of 1894. The electoral triumph brought with
it a new bipartisan Board of Police Commissioners and a conscientious man
of action by the name of Theodore Roosevelt, who quickly took charge of reforming the department. Crooked officers were fired, illegitimate "pull" was
curtailed, and morality laws were enforced (including the closing of saloons
at night and on Sundays). Despite its best intentions, however, the reform administration suffered defeat at the hands of the machine in the very next election. What went wrong? Steffens was convinced he knew the answer. The
people who had demanded statutes on morality were the very ones who cried
most loudly against their enforcement. It was the "businessmen of New York"
who most opposed the closing of the saloons and the end of gambling and
prostitution. It was simply bad for business. Steffens placed the failure of reform in New York City on what he would later call "Anglo-Saxon hypocrisy,"
the actions of good, law-abiding citizens, not the crooks and the police. Crime
was a business and, as such, a part of American life. Curtailing the profits of
vice disrupted business. As Steffens perceived it, only when society stopped
condoning selfish behavior for profit could it expect to see law enforcement

free of corruption. Steffens had been a reporter only a short time, but he was already shattering myths that Americans held about themselves, their business practices, and their politics.

After five years as a reporter with the *Evening Post* and four more years as city editor for the staid *Commercial Advertiser*, Steffens accepted an offer from S. S. McClure to become managing editor of *McClure's* magazine. It was apparent almost from the beginning, however, that Steffens's talents as a reporter were wasted in his new position. He was a writer, and McClure sensed it, but one without a niche on the magazine's staff. In an attempt to remedy the problem, McClure ordered him to go find a story. The general idea that Steffens had was "to take confused, local, serial news of the newspapers and report it all together in one long short story for the whole country."[3] Drawing on an advertising bill the magazine had against the Lackawanna Railroad, he journeyed to the Midwest looking for material. Hearing that a young man by the name of Folk was "raising the deuce of a row about bribery in the board of aldermen" in St. Louis, Steffens traveled there in the summer of 1902 to check out the report. He met Joseph Folk, the circuit attorney pursuing the case, in a quiet corner of a hotel lobby. The two men were natural allies. Folk needed help and publicity in his campaign against corruption, while Steffens needed a compelling story. As they talked, Folk revealed to him the shocking evidence of municipal corruption he had uncovered. Steffens found himself drawn to the issue of exposure. "He [Folk] startled my imagination," said Steffens. Using the information that Folk provided, Steffens and local writer Claude Wetmore coauthored "Tweed Days in St. Louis" for the October issue of *McClure's* and in so doing created a national sensation.

The most important and shocking revelation to come out of Folk's investigation was that "good businessmen" corrupted "bad politicians" or that good business caused bad government in St. Louis. What Steffens and Wetmore tried to explain in their pathbreaking muckraking article was that businessmen, in desperate need of special privileges and public franchises, corrupted politics for their own selfish ends. Bribery became the businessman's necessity, while bribe money came to be regarded as the legislator's (alderman's, councilman's, and so on) legitimate entitlement. Folk helped Steffens see that bribery and corruption were systematic and systemic, that the city's best citizens were often linked with its worst, and that the result actually threatened democratic government. As Folk understood, bribery was more than just a violation of the law. It was a betrayal of the public trust. The authors of "Tweed Days in St. Louis" tried to show that local democracy had broken down. Five months later, Steffens drove this point home in his follow-up article, "The Shamelessness of St. Louis." He described the corruption that plagued St.

Louis as "boodle"—the practice by which bankers, lawyers, corporate managers, and business promoters bribed public officials to gain franchise grants,
municipal contracts, or low tax assessments. The ramifications of this were
complex. Boodle robbed the community, threatened free government, and
jeopardized the sovereignty of every citizen.

The warning in these articles was that municipal corruption could be found
anywhere. During the next several years, Steffens traveled to many other
cities (Minneapolis, Pittsburgh, and Philadelphia most prominently) and described their specific varieties of corruption for the readers of *McClure's*.
These articles would be collected and republished as *The Shame of the Cities*
(1904), a muckraking classic. Each article created a sensation and increased
Steffens's notoriety in the process. But as historian Louis Filler has noted, he
was "political muckraking's greatest authority" because he offered more than
mere sensation. He provided a hypothesis for the corruption of America's
cities and did so in a style that captivated readers. He always posed as "a naïf
who experiences reality in the presence of his readers, hoping to instruct them
even as he is himself instructed."[4] Readers increasingly turned to him for
remedies, but, barely a step ahead of his readers at this point, he could only
hope that an informed public would become righteously indignant, abandon
its moral apathy, and work to make government more democratic.

As progressivism moved from the city to the state level, Steffens followed.
Beginning in April 1904, he began a series of investigative articles on state
politics titled "Enemies of the Republic" in *McClure's*. Later collected and
published in book form as *The Struggle for Self-Government* (1906), the series, which included articles on Missouri, Illinois, Wisconsin, Rhode Island,
Ohio, and New Jersey, gave Steffens the opportunity to expand his theory on
the failure of popular government. His conclusion—that corruption had become institutionalized—was unsettling. "Our political corruption is a system," he stated, "by which our political leaders are hired, by bribery, by the
license to loot, and by quiet moral support, to conduct the government . . . not
for the common good, but for the special interests of private business." As he
had discovered in his series on the cities, it was not the bribe taker but the
bribe giver who was "the source and sustenance of our bad government." In
every place he looked, the corruption of politics by business was the same—
the same methods, motives, and purposes all being used to the same end.
"Just as in the city," he said, "the System in the State was corruption settled
into a 'custom of the country'; betrayal of trust established as the form of government." The repetitive acts of bribery and corruption chronicled by Steffens
formed a process that transformed representative democracy into "an oligarchy representative of the special interests" seeking special privileges. In
closing his article on Missouri, he offered "the captain of industry" a truth:

"That business . . . is not sacred; that not everything that pays is right; that, if bribery is treason (because it corrupts the source of law and justice and sells out the people), if the corrupt politician is a traitor, then the corrupting businessman is an enemy of the republic."[5]

As Steffens wrote the six articles that eventually became *The Struggle for Self-Government*, his mood darkened. His findings were beginning to dampen his inherent optimism. He even dedicated his second muckraking book "To His Majesty, Nicholas the Second . . . Emperor and Autocrat of all the Russians." Referring to the recent 1905 revolution and the tsar's broken promise to convene a legislative assembly with real power, Steffens sarcastically scolded the tsar for fearing representative government and failing to learn from the American experience. Americans liked to think that their charters and constitutions actually guaranteed them representative democratic government. But who did their current government really represent? To Steffens, the answer was corrupt business. The tragedy was that Americans could not discern the difference between the illusion of charter (cities) and constitutional (state and federal) government and the reality of actual government. The tsar had nothing to fear from a liberal constitution. He would just have to manipulate it to his advantage.

Although Steffens's tone in the introduction to his series on state government was bitter and suggested that he was losing faith in the American people, he had not yet reached that point. In preparing the articles for publication, he added a last line to each announcing the good news that in almost every state he had examined, popular reform movements were triumphing. The election of 1905 had seemingly made reform possible. In Missouri, Illinois, and Wisconsin, voters had elected reform governors to office. In Ohio, Cincinnati voters had thrown out boss George Cox. Similarly, voters in Toledo had elected reformer Brand Whitlock as their mayor, while those in Cleveland had returned the popular Tom Johnson to office as their city leader. The news lifted Steffens's spirits to the point that he remarked, "[W]e, the American people, carried ourselves at last, and the beginning has been made toward the restoration of representative democracy in all the land."[6] Despite his temporary euphoria over the election results in 1905, however, Steffens was slowly moving toward the conclusion that civic awareness alone would not be sufficient to bring about meaningful political reform. As a result, he began to consider the idea that civic awareness must be combined with a new morality before lasting change could be realized.

In 1908, the merchant Edward Filene and the Good Government Association of Boston recruited Steffens to study municipal conditions in their city and propose practical solutions to urban problems. He spent the following fall and winter in Boston conducting interviews, gathering sociological and statistical data, giving lectures, and attending receptions and dinners—all to gain a feel for the overall life of the city. His final report, "Boston—1915," was to be a constructive plan for the future. The exercise proved a failure. The planning committee, on which Steffens had only an advisory voice, offered very little in the way of recommendations. It even failed to confront substantive issues like taxation and municipal ownership. In the end, Boston's elite favored maintaining the status quo to experimentation. Steffens had wanted to draw Boston's commercial and civic leaders together to demonstrate that self-interest and public interest could and should work together to achieve real urban reform. As participants in the political process, he hoped that the city's leading businessmen might capitalize on the moral advantage that came with self-knowledge and contribute to civic improvement. Steffens thought that businessmen who had followed economic self-interest and unwittingly broke the law had something valuable to contribute. Because their business dealings had taught them what was "necessary" and their encounters with the legal system had shown them what was "wrong," they were already halfway to finding a cure. As Steffens described it, he wanted to "produce a city of people on to themselves, and so uncomfortably 'on' that they would either change the conditions or become a community of conscious crooks or, best of all, give up their old ideals and form new ideals which would fit modern life."[7] He seemed to be willing the impossible.

Steffens published his final muckraking book, *Upbuilders,* in 1909. It appeared while he was working on his Boston report and reflected his current thinking. As before, it was a collection of previously published articles written between 1906 and 1908. This time Steffens focused on five reformers: Mark Fagan, the mayor of Jersey City; Everett Colby, a state senator from Essex County, New Jersey; Ben Lindsey, the juvenile court judge of Denver, Colorado; Rudolph Spreckels, a reform-minded businessman from San Francisco; and William S. U'Ren, a "people's lobbyist" from Oregon. What these five individuals shared in common was their success in applying Christianity (the golden rule) as a means of solving social and political problems. Through their stories, Steffens hoped to illustrate the potential of what he called "applied Christianity" as an ethical basis for a new civic consciousness. It might be the way to restore government to its original unselfish purpose.

Steffens believed that men had a natural inclination to do good. If people could confront their selfish passions in a society corrupted by the "system," then they could change their social perspective and work for their fellow human beings and reform. It was simply "putting into practice in actual life . . . the doctrine of faith, hope and charity."[8] "If we loved our neighbor as ourselves," said Steffens, "we would not then betray, rob and bribe him."[9] These five men—these "upbuilders"—showed by their own life experiences that such a process was not as impractical as many would think. He hoped their stories would offer a vision of a better life.

Representative of this group was Ben Lindsey. He had come to understand the "system" by hearing cases in his juvenile court. According to Steffens, after investigating the causes of juvenile crime, Lindsey reached the conclusion that "boys are bad because, while they have lots of opportunity to do wrong, they have none to do good." In short, the problem was environmental. The cure for juvenile delinquency resided in improving the surroundings that children grew up in. For Lindsey, the answer was correction, not punishment. He felt that criminal justice, as it existed for minors, was heartless and thoughtless and actually created criminals. In its place, he "subordinated the machinery of justice to the good of the boy, and for routine and vengeance substituted sympathy and help." He softened his legal approach by forming a rapport with his "boys" and holding Saturday meetings with his probationers where he stressed a code of honorable conduct. He also became politically active trying to reform the society that produced wayward children. He fought saloon keepers who sold liquor to minors, lobbied successfully for a criminal statute making it illegal to contribute to the delinquency of a minor, and campaigned to make Colorado's child labor law effective. As a practicing Christian, Judge Lindsey was "re-introducing into life . . . and into all institutions which he can influence, the spirit of humanity." By serving as a model of the practice of Christian ethics, Lindsey and other everyday "upbuilders" were remaking law and institutions so that their primary function would once again be "the service of men and of the State."[10]

Despite the upbeat tone of *Upbuilders*, Steffens's hope for fundamental reform of the "system" was waning. He was trying to convince the American people that they were morally complicit in the failure of representative government. It was by their own apathy that government had ceased to represent them. Maybe the golden rule was unobtainable for society as a whole. Maybe middle-class hypocrisy prevented it. As he became increasingly disillusioned, Steffens began to think that the structure of government might need to be modified, perhaps in the direction of the public ownership of all public utilities and natural resources. Maybe the problem that had to be dealt with was not morality but the special legislation (privileges) granted by government to business. Maybe putting honest men into office without removing that which caused good men to do bad things was folly.

Steffens attempted to illustrate this point in a humorous story he told in his *Autobiography*. Asked to speak at a social gathering of civic leaders in Los Angeles, Steffens presented his well-known argument that business corrupted politics. "You cannot build or operate a railroad," said Steffens, "or a street railway, gas, water, or power company, develop and operate a mine, or get forests and cut timber on a large scale, or run any privileged business, without corrupting or joining in the corruption of the government." After he spoke, the first question he got was, "Who started the evil?" His initial answer was that the proper question would be "what," not "who." "If it was some Thing that hurt us," he said, "we could be Christians and forgive sinners; we could cease from punishing men and develop an environment in which men would be tempted to be good." But his listeners only wanted to hear that it was the politicians that created the corrupt conditions that good businessmen were subject to. Finally, a church leader in the group asked him who first— "way back, in the beginning"—started this evil system he described. "Ok, I think I see," said Steffens. "Most people . . . say it was Adam. But Adam . . . said that it was Eve, the woman; she did it. And Eve said no, no, it wasn't she; it was the serpent. And that's where you . . . have stuck ever since. You blame the serpent, Satan. Now I come and I am trying to show you that it was, it is, the apple."[11]

In 1906, Steffens split with McClure over business, artistic, and ideological disagreements and resigned from the magazine. Joining Ida Tarbell, Ray Stannard Baker, and several other colleagues who had similarly fled *McClure's*, he purchased an interest in the *American Magazine*. The new owners editorially promised their readers that the journal would "reflect a happy, struggling, fighting world, in which we believe, good people are coming out on top."[12] Editorial differences and a feeling that his position as an owner compromised his freedom as a critical journalist, however, caused him to sell his interest in the magazine after only a short time. He had decided, instead, to make his living as a freelance journalist.

In October 1910, an explosion ripped through the *Los Angeles Times* building, killing twenty people. The owner of the newspaper, Harrison Gray Otis, was widely known as an archfoe of organized labor. The two men accused of the bombing, John J. McNamara and his brother James, were officers in the International Association of Bridge and Structural Iron Workers. The union had a reputation for using dynamite in its disputes with contractors and employers. The two brothers were eventually arrested and placed on trial in October 1911 for murder. Although Steffens believed that the two labor leaders were guilty, he thought there was a greater question to be addressed. The public needed to understand the reasons behind the bombing, the injustices suffered by labor, and the causes of class hatred. In an effort to achieve that end, Steffens offered to be a mediator.

He proposed to "save" the McNamara brothers by making a bargain with the antilabor establishment. He would get the two men to plead guilty if the court would give them lenient sentences. Immediately following the trial, a conference would be held between the leaders of capital and labor where the two sides would hopefully agree to apply the golden rule and replace class warfare with industrial harmony. Steffens believed that if he could achieve this arrangement, he could convince his frightened middle-class readers (he had been hired by a newspaper syndicate to cover the trial) that they (society) were complicit in the process that exploited labor and drove it to revolution. For a while the plan worked well. Defense attorney Clarence Darrow, the McNamara brothers, the business leaders, and even Harrison Gray Otis all agreed. But public opinion and the churches did not. They did not understand, said Steffens, "that Christianity had been applied and worked."[13] Instead of forgiveness, they wanted revenge. In the end, the judge, who according to Steffens caved in to public opinion, went back on the agreement, gave a harsh public condemnation of the crime, and sentenced the two men to life in prison. For the rest of his life, Steffens carried a small gold cross on his watch chain with the inscription "the only Christian on earth."[14]

Defeated as a mediator, Steffens began to lose the respect of his public. As a muckraker, he had appeared as a hero. Now he looked only "quixotic." The McNamara case also tarnished his reputation with magazine editors who sensed that his politics were moving too far to the left. After 1911, they increasingly rejected his manuscripts. His progressive friends called him a blunderer. Labor leaders considered his meddling as either "folly" or "treason." Capitalists saw him as an apologist for their radical enemies. Steffens had arrived at a turning point in his life. The events in Los Angeles and the decline of muckraking "destroyed his confidence in the social power of morality."[15] In summing up Steffens's state of mind at this point in his life and describing the trajectory of his future activities, one historian has aptly commented, "No longer was Steffens a liberal. He had seen too much. The McNamara case had set the stage, Greenwich Village was to teach the theory, and soon revolution would trigger the response."[16]

Steffens's personal life reached an emotional low point in 1911, when his wife, Josephine, died, followed not long after that by his mother and father. Devastated by the losses and seeking rejuvenation, he moved to New York's Greenwich Village, an old, working-class section of New York City that had become the new mecca for writers, artists, socialists, and bohemians with radical ideas. Presiding over this new cultural scene was Mabel Dodge, a wealthy, divorced socialite and freethinker who craved being at the center of attention. One contemporary journalist and friend described her as "the only woman I know who might fairly be called 'God-drunk.' . . . She was always talking about 'It'; . . . the unseen cause of all seen things . . . the Infinite."[17] Steffens, who suggested that she convert her apartment into a salon where anyone and everyone could gather for weekly discussions, rightly sensed that she possessed the magnetic personality and social skills needed to make the evenings a success. Topics covered the intellectual spectrum from psychology and avant-garde art to socialism and anarchism, and conversations were "charged with a sense of discovery and the anticipation of the coming liberation of man and society."[18] "[M]ore cynical in their liberalism and more experimental in their vision" (and much younger than Steffens, who was then forty-five), these young radicals seemed unhindered by the intellectual constraints of their parents' generation.[19]

Steffens shared a house on Washington Square in the heart of Greenwich Village with John Reed, a young Harvard-educated writer. A Steffens protégé, Reed would later follow his mentor to Russia and gain notoriety as the author of his own romanticized account of the Russian Revolution, *Ten Days That Shook the World*. Immersion in this countercultural milieu helped Steffens regain his exuberance for living and forced him to begin to look at things in new ways. As he submerged himself in this group, he lost touch with mainstream American reform and political progressivism that was nearing its peak. The new prophets were Marx and Freud. Steffens had read enough Marx to understand that the class system was the root of social injustice, but Freud offered new perceptions of how society worked. Steffens became intrigued with the social and political implications of psychoanalysis. He later recalled thinking how "absurd" had been his "muckraker's descriptions of bad men and good men and the assumption that showing people the facts and conditions would persuade them to alter them or their own conduct." He found that Freudian theory agreed with Marx's insistence that "to change men's minds one must change their environment."[20] Steffens was ready to become a revolutionary.

In late 1914, Steffens traveled to Mexico to study the Mexican Revolution. The escalating conflict in Mexico provided Steffens with his first opportunity to observe a violent social upheaval and began his own intellectual fascination with the possibility that revolutionary change might be the only remaining way to establish a truly democratic social order. Steffens made two trips to Mexico between 1914 and 1916, gained personal access to constitutionalist leader Venustiano Carranza, and spent three months traveling with Carranza's government aboard a special military train. The revolution fascinated him but, in the end, only confused him. It did not follow Marx's blueprint. "It had occurred," said Steffens, "in a backward country with an undeveloped industrial system, among an unorganized, illiterate people who knew nothing of socialism and little of labor unions. It had no clearly defined socialist purposes; it was all mixed up—politics, economics, civil wars, graft."[21] Having learned little, he left the country with the revolution unfinished.

The Russian Revolution, however, seemed more monumental, and Steffens saw it as his story to cover. He traveled to Russia in 1917 and again in 1919 to observe firsthand the rush of social and political change. For Steffens and many others on the left wing of American politics, the impact of the Bolshevik Revolution was "stunning." Like the Mexican Revolution, the revolutionary course in Russia failed to follow a prescribed pattern. It appeared as "a series of random events finally dominated by Lenin . . . who recognized a unique opportunity, moved to fill the political vacuum and, as he said, picked up power where he found it, lying in the streets." What fascinated Steffens and other American radicals was that Lenin had shown how a brilliantly led minority party could bypass politics and seize power and then hold and consolidate that power. For Steffens, the process triggered a "psychological revolution." "Nothing that I used to think could stand in the face of that Russian experience," he noted some years later. "I could not have talked fast enough to anyone," he said, "to mention in a flash as I 'saw' it the details of the wreck of my political philosophy in the war and the revolution and the threads of the new, and better, conceptions which lay mangled but traceable in the debris." After interviewing Lenin in 1919, Steffens announced that he had "seen the future; and it works."[22]

The 1920s were lost and found years for Steffens. He suffered for his outspoken support of the Bolshevik triumph in Russia. Middle-class magazines found him too radical and would publish only anonymous editorial pieces written by him. Uncomfortable with the reactionary climate in the United States following World War I, he chose to live in Europe until 1927. He occasionally returned for lecture tours, to see family members, or to work to obtain amnesty for political prisoners. He was often harassed on the lecture circuit and not even welcome in his hometown. The owner/editor of the *Sacramento Bee* called him "a Radical and a Red of the deepest dye" and stated that the proper place for him was "in jail."[23] He remarried in 1924 and the following year began work on his autobiography. He thought his life could serve as an instructive example of the process of "unlearning" ingrained political and social processes of his society. Completed in 1931, the book is a classic recounting of a lifetime spent in search of a democratic-humanistic ideal. Steffens died in 1936.

Steffens is important to the topic of American reform as both an intellectual and a journalist. Some might critique his social thought as superficial. They might dismiss as naive his appeal (and that of muckrakers in general for that matter) for a new public activism to effect fundamental political change. They might also debate the influence of muckraking on the accomplishments of reformers during the Progressive Era. But perhaps such criticism says more about our own contemporary political cynicism than it does about his/their turn-of-the-century naïveté or effectiveness. One might also take issue with Steffens (along with the other muckrakers) for failing to provide solutions to the complex problems he exposed. This conclusion also seems unfair. If he appeared to wander intellectually, it was because he never ceased asking questions or stopped engaging in political analysis. But insight can point to solutions, and his muckraking books provide perceptive analyses of business, politics, and human nature. His writings offered contemporary readers a nuanced critique of capitalism and the profit motive, challenged the legitimacy of corporate and political elites, and posited a liberal prescription for a truly democratic society.

As a journalist, his constant inquisitiveness, his optimism, his innate liberalism, and his commitment to advocacy made him a model for investigative reporting. In assessing the general accomplishments of the muckraking movement, historian Vernon L. Parrington noted that it "indoctrinated" the American middle class "in the elementary principles of political realism," exposed the incestuous relationship between business and politics, and "revealed the hidden hand that was pulling the strings of the political puppets." Muckraking journalists "tarnished the gilding that had been carefully laid on . . . [the] callous exploitation" of the people and "brought under common suspicion the captain of industry who had risen as a national hero from the muck of individualism."[24] The same could be said for Steffens in particular. Few men did as much "to reveal America to itself in all its contradictions, all its humbugs, its vices, its hypocritical acceptances of necessary corruptions so long as they were hidden from the light."[25] He aided the fight against corruption and helped focus and direct the movement that became known as progressivism. In doing so, he contributed significantly to the development of a reform consciousness in American society.

NOTES

1. Lincoln Steffens, *Autobiography*, vol. 1 (New York: Harcourt, Brace and World, 1958), 169.

2. Patrick F. Palermo, *Lincoln Steffens* (Boston: Twayne Publishers, 1978), 27.

3. Steffens, *Autobiography*, vol. 2, 368.

4. Robert Stinson, *Lincoln Steffens* (New York: Frederick Ungar, 1979), 76.

5. Lincoln Steffens, *The Struggle for Self-Government* (New York: Johnson Reprint Corp., 1968), 4–5, 11, 38–39, 42.

6. Stinson, *Lincoln Steffens*, 68.

7. Steffens, *Autobiography*, vol. 2, 612.

8. Lincoln Steffens, *Upbuilders* (Seattle: University of Washington Press, 1968), 152.

9. Palermo, *Lincoln Steffens*, 74.

10. Steffens, *Upbuilders*, 99, 100, 152, 183.

11. Steffens, *Autobiography*, vol. 2, 572-74.

12. Palermo, *Lincoln Steffens*, 66.

13. Palermo, *Lincoln Steffens*, 81.

14. Russell M. Horton, *Lincoln Steffens* (New York: Twayne Publishers, 1974), 85.

15. Palermo, *Lincoln Steffens*, 97.

16. Horton, *Lincoln Steffens*, 86–87.

17. Horton, *Lincoln Steffens*, 87.

18. Palermo, *Lincoln Steffens*, 83.

19. Horton, *Lincoln Steffens*, 89.

20. Palermo, *Lincoln Steffens*, 83–84.

21. Justin Kaplan, *Lincoln Steffens: A Biography* (New York: Simon and Schuster, 1974), 212.

22. Kaplan, *Lincoln Steffens*, 218, 233, 250.

23. Kaplan, *Lincoln Steffens*, 266.

24. Vernon Louis Parrington, *Main Currents in American Thought: The Beginnings of Critical Realism in America, 1860–1920*, vol. 3 (New York: Harcourt, Brace and World, 1958), 407–8.

25. Parrington, *Main Currents in American Thought*, 331.

SOURCES

Filler, Louis. *Crusaders for American Liberalism*. Yellow Springs, Ohio: Antioch Press, 1964.

Horton, Russell M. *Lincoln Steffens*. New York: Twayne Publishers, 1974.

Kaplan, Justin. *Lincoln Steffens: A Biography*. New York: Simon and Schuster, 1974.

Palermo, Patrick F. *Lincoln Steffens*. Boston: Twayne Publishers, 1978.

Steffens, Lincoln. *The Autobiography of Lincoln Steffens*. 2 vols. New York: Harcourt, Brace and World, 1931.

——. *The Shame of the Cities*. New York: Hill and Wang, 1963.

——. *The Struggle for Self-Government*. New York: Johnson Reprint Corp., 1968.

——. *Upbuilders*. Seattle: University of Washington Press, 1968.

Stinson, Robert. *Lincoln Steffens*. New York: Frederick Ungar, 1979.

10

Harvey W. Wiley and the Ethics of Pure Food and Drugs

One of the dilemmas of the late nineteenth century was how to regulate drugs and food. Scientific and medical theories on the subject were lacking, chemical analysis primitive, and precedents for federal or state regulation almost nonexistent. In the absence of adequate scientific knowledge and official guidance, quackery in the sale of drugs flourished. Patent medicine manufacturers were not required by law to put labels on their products, and ingredients and formulas remained closely guarded secrets. Consumers literally purchased medicines at their own risk. Newspapers and magazines advertised the various cure-alls, and popular endorsements, then as now, proved to be effective sales tools. As companies competed for customers, they made more and more preposterous curative claims for their "medicines." In reality, these nostrums were ineffective or harmful (many contained dangerous habit-forming ingredients such as alcohol, morphine, and cocaine) and dishonestly advertised.

In an effort to bring some order out of the competitive chaos, drug manufacturers organized the Proprietary Association of America in 1881 to serve as an effective lobby in state and national legislatures. In time, this influential organization came to symbolize the "drug trust" and, like its industrial counterparts, soon controlled prices, centralized distribution, and limited competition. Facilitating the operation of the trust was an environment where the public was ill informed about medicines. Doctors were either ignorant of or apathetic to the problem, while legislatures were either compromised by the lobby or preoccupied with other issues. As a result, there existed no check on current practices. Compounding the problem were the numerous popular newspapers, magazines, and medical and religious journals that willingly accepted deceptive patent medicine advertisements. To make sure that the press remained accommodating to the drug trust, F. J. Cheney, the proprietor of Hall's Catarrh Cure, devised what became known as the "red clause." This clause, in essence a muzzle on the press, was inserted in advertising contracts in red ink to point out that advertising agreements could be voided if any hostile regulatory legislation was enacted in a state where a patent medicine advertisement appeared. The intention was to force newspapers and magazines to oppose such laws to protect crucial advertising revenues. By joining the drug lobby in state legislatures, the press could give the impression that public opinion was against any proposed regulation.

Just as difficult as regulating drugs was the effort to maintain the purity of food. As food processing during the nineteenth century shifted from the home to the factory, competition intensified. In the process, ethical standards declined, and companies debased their goods in an effort to stay competitive. To reduce production costs, some food manufacturers added chicory to coffee, mixed husks and dirt with ground pepper, and sold a mixture of glucose and hayseed that had been flavored and colored as raspberry jam. Although such adulterations generally did not threaten the consumer's health, they were dishonest. A more serious problem, however, related to food preservation. In an attempt to reduce spoilage during the lag time between production and consumption, food was increasingly refrigerated. Because this process had not been perfected by the 1890s, manufacturers increasingly turned to chemical preservatives such as borax, salicylic acid, and formaldehyde. By the late nineteenth century, the use of such additives was increasing at an alarming rate. Regulatory legislation was woefully deficient in responding to this growing tendency. Lack of enforcement hampered state laws. A state could not even enforce its regulations against an out-of-state manufacturer. The only legal means open to a state in such a case was to prosecute the in-state retailer who marketed the goods. As a result, the consumer lacked adequate protection, and the retailer faced the onerous burden of assuming fault for a disreputable manufacturer. Differing state laws also forced manufacturers who sold in a national market to cope with a myriad of restrictions.

One individual who became appalled at the unethical and harmful practices of drug and food manufacturers and convinced of the need for federal regulation to control those problems was Harvey W. Wiley, the chief chemist in the U.S. Department of Agriculture. Harvey Washington Wiley was born in 1844 in a log cabin farmhouse near Kent, Indiana, the sixth of seven children born to Preston Wiley and Lucinda Maxwell Wiley. Both parents were staunch members of the Church of the Disciples, an offshoot of Presbyterianism, and Harvey's father served as a lay preacher in addition to being a farmer. The family environment reflected their religious zeal. The Sabbath

Harvey Washington Wiley, circa 1905. Library of Congress, Prints & Photographs Division.

was strictly observed and all frivolity on that day severely restricted. Wiley, who remembered the day as being filled with Sunday school and church, memorizing Bible verses, and listening to long sermons, later remarked that he found the old Presbyterian faith to be an excellent character former. Harvey's parents stressed learning almost as much as faith. His father occasionally taught a subscription school, and Harvey started his own education at the age of four. Although his early education at neighborhood and district schools was sporadic, he learned to read from *McGuffey's* readers and to do mathematics from *Ray's* arithmetic. His meager formal education, however, was supplemented by extensive reading. He had access to books on history, literature, science, and philosophy from a traveling township school library. His father also owned a collection of books that included the Bible and Shakespeare. Preston Wiley also subscribed to several leading periodicals that included the *National Era* and the *Atlantic Monthly*. Harvey vividly remembered reading *Uncle Tom's Cabin* in serialized form in the *National Era*. The novel had perhaps even more significance, as Harvey's father was an abolitionist and helped transport many runaway slaves to Lancaster, Indiana, a station on the Underground Railroad four miles from the family farm in the southern part of the state.

In 1863, Wiley entered Hanover College in Indiana. After interrupting his studies for a year to serve briefly in the Union army as a member of the 137th Regiment of Indiana Volunteers, he graduated in 1867. By the time of his graduation from college, Wiley had decided to pursue a career in medicine. Needing money to do so, he accepted a position in a public school in Lowell, Indiana, and then, in the summer of 1868, apprenticed with a friend from his army days who had become a physician in Kentucky. With the influence of an uncle, Wiley gained an appointment as a tutor in Latin and Greek in the preparatory department at Northwestern Christian University (later Butler University) in Indianapolis. He soon gained a promotion to a position as adjunct professor of languages and before long was also teaching algebra, anatomy, and physiology. Wiley continued to study medicine on his own while teaching and, in 1869, received a lucky break when the Indiana Medical College opened and accepted its first students. After two four-month terms, teaching in the morning at the college and taking medical classes in the afternoon and evening, Wiley, having already satisfied his apprenticeship requirements, became doctor of medicine. Interrupting his plans to open a medical practice in Indianapolis, Wiley accepted a position at a high school (primarily because of the $1,200 salary) and began teaching natural science.

Just before the school year opened, Wiley attended a meeting of the American Association for the Advancement of Science held that year in Indianapolis. The experience increased his zeal for science to such an extent that it ended his career in medicine before it had begun. He now wanted to be a scientist. In January 1872, Wiley received another lucky break. Dr. Ryland T. Brown, who taught chemistry at both the Medical College and Northwestern Christian, accepted a position as a chemist in the Department of Agriculture in Washington, D.C. Wiley was asked to take his place and was formally elected to the chair of chemistry that May. In September, evidently to prepare himself for further academic advancement, Wiley took a sabbatical and enrolled as a special student in the Lawrence Scientific School at Harvard. Here he learned qualitative and quantitative analysis, worked for the first time in a chemical laboratory, and demonstrated a remarkable aptitude in the field of analytical chemistry. After only one academic year at Harvard, Wiley was awarded a bachelor of science degree to go along with a great deal of inspiration he received from the experience. Not long after resuming his academic post in Indianapolis, Wiley accepted a prestigious appointment as professor of chemistry at newly opened Purdue University, a position he held from 1874 until 1883.

Always looking for ways to augment his professional training, Wiley asked for a leave of absence from Purdue in 1878 to study abroad at the University of Berlin. While there, he attended only the lectures that sounded interesting and sought no academic degree. Important for his later career, however, were the classes he attended on food adulteration. Just as relevant were his visits to the government laboratory that examined food and drink. He was fascinated with the elaborate processes that the Germans utilized to detect impurities. He learned to use a polariscope and even purchased a spectra apparatus that he intended to use on his return to Purdue.

After returning to Indiana, Wiley began an in-depth study of sugar and sugar substitutes, such as manufactured glucose, obtained by the hydrolysis of cornstarch. He soon began lecturing on the importance of protecting the consumer from fraud through the deceptive use of these new products and started a campaign to have the Indiana legislature pass legislation to prevent adulteration. Wiley did not oppose the sale of sugar substitutes; he only recommended that such products be properly named and carry labels listing their composition. By 1883, Wiley had become one of the leading sugar chemists in the country and had begun to develop a scientific reputation as well as a keen interest in food adulteration.

In 1883, Wiley accepted an offer to become chief chemist in the U.S. Department of Agriculture in Washington, D.C., at a starting salary of $2,500. For the next decade, he worked to promote the domestic sugar industry and to provide practical information to improve farming and continued to examine food adulteration and search for the best means of detecting it. Chemists in the Department of Agriculture had started to take an interest in food adulteration almost fifteen years before Wiley arrived. In 1869, Dr. Thomas Antisell had drawn attention to the widespread adulteration in food-stuffs. Ten years later, Peter Collier analyzed butter, oleomargarine, alcoholic liquors, and powders that were used to color coffee berries. After finding lead in the powders, he proposed that the adulteration of food and drugs be made a criminal offense. "Where life and death are at stake," he said, "no specious arguments should prevent the speedy punishment of those unscrupulous men who are willing, for the sake of gain, to endanger the health of unsuspecting purchasers."[1]

Soon after arriving in Washington, Wiley began to focus on the problem of foods and their adulteration and began to study various food products with an eye to protecting both producers and consumers through uniform methods of analysis and by establishing general standards of purity. Beginning in 1887, un-der Wiley's direction, the Department of Agriculture began to publish a series of reports as part of Bulletin 13: Foods and Food Adulterants and described the chemical composition and adulteration of dairy products, spices, fermented beverages, lard, baking powder, sugar, molasses, honey, tea, coffee, cocoa, canned vegetables, cereals, and preserved meats. Although pointing out numerous instances of adulteration, the general report (eventually consisting of ten volumes and 1,417 pages) was scientifically grounded, conservative in its recommendations, and nonsensationalistic in tone. The report included analysis of foods only, not drugs, and indicated Wiley's primary interest at the time. Re-alizing that the reports were too technical to have any impact on the public or on Congress, Wiley endeavored to have a shorter report written that would present facts on food adulteration in more popular form. He then obtained the appoint-ment of special agent Alexander J. Wedderburn, an experienced journalist and an outspoken advocate of pure food, to do the work. Issued in 1890, the study as-serted that fraud was so widespread that it affected almost every article of food and noted that the impact fell most heavily on the uneducated and poor. Addi-tionally, the report charged that fraud robbed the farmer of profits, injured the ex-port market for American foodstuffs, and undermined the morals of the people. Although the great majority of adulteration was not injurious to public health, it had made food generally less nutritious. Wedderburn did note, however, that poi-sonous adulterations were found that had "not only impaired the health of the consumer, but frequently caused death."[2] Wedderburn stated his conclusion di-rectly. State laws were insufficient to deal with the growing problem. National legislation was needed.

Initially, a number of commercial interests agreed with Wiley and his chemists that national legislation against adulteration should be enacted. Gro-cers looked to protect the honest businessman from competition from an adul-terer and to maintain public confidence. Agriculturists, such as those who produced dairy products, wanted to separate themselves from the producers of oleomargarine, while those who grew corn and raised hogs wanted to stop adulterers of lard. Still others, specifically those who had a concern for public health, supported federal action in the interest of consumers rather than producers. But the only congressional legislation that came even close to passage was a general antiadulteration bill introduced by Senator Algernon Paddock of Nebraska in 1892. The core of Paddock's measure was to forbid the addition of any poisonous or harmful ingredient to food or drugs that might injure the health of the person consuming it, make it a misdemeanor to "knowingly" traffic in adulterated food or drugs, and require that products carry truthful labels. Paddock appealed to his colleagues to enact such legislation, as it would stiffen commercial morality, protect the health and pocketbook of the consuming public, and assist the farmer by enhancing the image of American food products and prevent foreign discrimination. The senator claimed to have received "many thousands" of resolutions and petitions from citizen groups, state legislatures, grocery and drug associations, boards of trade, and farm organizations. Paddock's bill, which had been prepared with Wiley's input and argued with the latest scientific evidence on adulteration gathered by Wiley's office, passed in the Senate but was prevented from coming up for a vote in the House. Commercial interests, such as cottonseed oil manufacturers who sold compound lard and a number of manufacturers of mixed foods and drugs, feared they would be adversely affected if they were forced to label their products. The power of threatened special interests to block pure food legislation and, later, compromise its effectiveness would plague Wiley for the next twenty years.

Contributing to the failure, however, was an apathetic public. Contrary to the claims of Paddock, the public still embraced the practice of using patent medicine–based home remedies as alternatives to potentially risky and almost certainly expensive medical care. They also tended to oppose any general legislation as an unnecessary intrusion on the part of an overly paternalistic government. Wiley agreed that there was a lack of vocal public support for such a measure and a fear of government interference but was more intrigued by a possible psychological explanation for the public's unscientific attitude. He seemed to agree with P. T. Barnum's theory that Americans liked to be duped and "humbugged." Cynically making light of the public's gullibility, he commented, "To be cheated, fooled, bamboozled, cajoled, deceived, pettifogged, [and] hypnotized . . . are privileges dear to us all. Woe be to that paternalism in government which shall attempt to deprive us of these inalienable rights."[3] Somehow the public would have to be awakened from its lethargy and public opinion brought to bear in a more forceful manner on a reluctant and heavily lobbied Congress.

In September 1895, Henry A. Huston, a former student of Wiley and his successor at Purdue University, delivered an address to the Association of Official Agricultural Chemists (AOAC) in which he called for more research on foods. The timely speech led to the formation of a food standards committee of which Wiley was named chair. Thus encouraged, Wiley pushed ahead with studies of product compositions so that adulteration could be more readily detected. At the AOAC meeting in 1897, Wiley campaigned for the reintroduction of the old Paddock bill with modifications. The intent of the new measure was to require honest labeling, but a provision was included that would ban any ingredients that might injure the consumer. After seeing the bill introduced in Congress in December 1897, Wiley assumed leadership of the legislative committee of the AOAC to work with congressional leaders toward its passage. Throughout the entire legislative process, Wiley stressed the theme of the ethics of pure food: the belief that consumers had a right to know what they were buying. Wiley, at this time, was no prohibitionist. He believed that the ethics of pure food required honest labeling, but he did not want to deny the poor cheap food substitutes. "It is not for me," he said, "to tell my neighbor what he shall eat, what he shall drink, what his religion shall be, or what his politics. These are matters which I think every man should be left to settle for himself."[4] The hopes of the pure food advocates, however, were frustrated, as Congress once again refused to take any action on the measure.

In 1902, Wiley did something that finally got the public's attention and, in doing so, helped break the grip of special interests that had stymied federal pure food legislation for over a decade. He decided to conduct tests on the effects of a variety of food preservatives on humans by using human subjects as guinea pigs. For his study group, he selected twelve healthy volunteers from the staff of the Department of Agriculture and created a controlled experiment whereby he monitored the effects of various foods and drink on his subjects. Beginning in December 1902 and continuing until June 1903, the twelve volunteers were fed a regulated diet at a special "hygienic table" in the department. A daily record was kept of their weight, pulse, temperature, and the intake and outgo of food for each individual. During the first experiment, boric acid and borax were introduced into the food of some of the subjects and the effects on them recorded. Other tests with different squads of volunteers were made by adding salicylic acid and salicylates, sulfurous acid and sulfites, and benzoic acid and benzoates to food. The final experiments with formaldehyde brought the tests to a close in December 1904. The publication of the results, issued in five parts and totaling 1,499 pages, showed that all the ingredients tested were found to be harmful to the metabolism, digestion, and health of the volunteers. The report provided the strongest scientific evidence yet of the need for a pure food and drug act.

The preservative experiments helped clarify Wiley's thinking on food adulteration and stiffened his resolve toward more stringent regulation. Chemicals interfered with digestion. Healthy individuals could tolerate small amounts of such additives, but what were the effects of larger amounts taken over longer periods of time? What were the effects of unnatural chemicals on those with weak or unhealthy stomachs? What were the risks to a person who unwittingly used a chemical he never realized he was ingesting? Wiley had become convinced that the real evil inherent in food adulteration was deception to the consumer. As one historian aptly summed up Wiley's thinking, "It was *wrong* as well as unhealthy to include certain preservatives in food packages; it was *unethical* to claim efficacy for drugs that were really ineffectual compounds of water or alcohol; it was *immoral* to include drugs in a compound that might damage the heart or cause unpredictable addiction."[5] The only solution was truthful labeling of contents. "What we want," said Wiley, "is that . . . the innocent consumer may get what he thinks he is buying."[6] Wiley still did not think complete prohibition was warranted, but he now believed that preservatives should be restricted to uses of absolute necessity and that the burden of proving need (to prevent spoilage) and harmlessness should be shifted to the producer. In ardently championing the interests of consumers, however, Wiley's statements had the effect of frightening some commercial interests, such as the National Wholesale Liquor Dealers' Association (the rectifiers/blenders of whiskey), the Proprietary Association (patent medicine producers), and the National Food Manufacturers Association (the manufacturers of compounded food products), and intensifying their opposition to a general federal law.

The press gave extensive coverage to the human interest angle of the experiments (twelve men risking their bodies for the public good), and when one reporter dubbed the twelve volunteers the "poison squad," the name captured public attention and became the subject of popular songs and vaudeville jokes. In the process, the Bureau of Chemistry became perhaps better known than any other government department and Dr. Wiley something of a celebrity. While the "poison squad" experiments progressed, Wiley continued to lobby for pure food legislation, lectured widely on the topic of adulteration, and continued to publish the results of his experiments. Despite the heightened pressure for a pure food and drug law that the experiments generated, they still failed to provoke Congress to action.

Although Wiley had piqued public interest, he had not yet outraged the public. That would be accomplished by the muckrakers and at just the right moment. Leading this effort was Edward Bok, the editor of the *Ladies' Home Journal*. Bok had been one of the first to refuse to carry patent medicine advertisements in his magazine as far back as 1892. Now, almost ten years later, he began a series of editorials against patent medicine manufacturers and called on his readers to boycott their products. In the course of his journalistic assault, Bok made a careless mistake. He obtained a report from the Massachusetts State Board of Health that listed alcohol, opium, and digitalis among the ingredients in Dr. Pierce's Favorite Prescription. The company claimed that its medicine contained none of the drugs cited, charged libel, and demanded $200,000 in damages. Bok quickly discovered that the Massachusetts report was out of date and incorrect. He eventually had to pay $16,000 in damages and print a retraction. He learned he would have to be more careful.

Committed to the fight, Bok hired journalist Mark Sullivan to do an undercover investigation of the patent medicine industry and to write articles on the trade. Sullivan advertised for "experienced patent medicine men" and learned about the industry from interviewing these insiders. He purchased and photographed letters that had been written by sick and trusting consumers to quacks who quickly cheated them and then sold their letters in bulk to other nostrum dealers. He also obtained the minutes of the meeting of the Proprietary Medicine Association in which F. J. Cheney revealed how clauses in his contracts with newspapers and magazines bound them to fight on his side against unfriendly legislation. Soon Bok and Sullivan were publishing articles such as "Why Patent Medicines Are Dangerous" and "The Patent Medicine Conspiracy against the Press," and the public was beginning to pay attention. Especially aroused by the revelations of Bok and Sullivan concerning the amounts of alcohol in patent medicines was the Women's Christian Temperance Union (WCTU). As the voice of both an influential interest group and a large number of women, they became valuable recruits in Wiley's army.

Supporting the work of Bok and Sullivan was a similar journalistic crusade begun by Norman Hapgood, the editor at *Collier's*. On June 3, 1905, the magazine printed the famous full-page cartoon by E. W. Kemble "Death's Laboratory," which showed a human skull with teeth consisting of patent medicine bottles and grabbed everyone's attention. Hapgood followed this journalistic coup a month later with a long editorial titled "Criminal Alliances with Fraud and Poison." He then set journalist Samuel Hopkins Adams to work on a major exposé of patent medicine quackery. Adams was a perfect choice for the assignment. He had worked for nine years as a crime reporter for the *New York Sun* and then as a writer for *McClure's*, where he turned his attention to medical science. He knew the current state of modern diseases, understood the problems relating to public health, and grasped the process by which special interests could block legislation they opposed. He was ready to tackle patent medicines. The articles that he wrote for *Collier's* began to appear in serialized form on October 7, 1905, as "The Great American Fraud." The series, which gained Adams lasting fame as a muckraker, revealed that popular medicines like Peruna contained exceptionally high alcohol levels, while others, like Liquozone, a nostrum advertised as a universal antiseptic, contained 99 percent water. Adams soon moved on to a more dangerous category of "subtle poisons," and when he informed readers of the cocaine addictions that often resulted from catarrh powders and the deadly results that occurred from using the drug acetanilide, he triggered a sensation.

In December 1905, Wiley's "poison squad" experiments and the work of Bok, Sullivan, Hapgood, and especially Adams prompted Senator Welden B. Heyburn of Idaho to introduce a new pure food and drug bill. Wiley lent his prestige in support of the measure, and President Theodore Roosevelt joined proponents by inserting a brief but well-publicized personal plea for its passage in his annual message to Congress that same month. Stripped of an initial provision that would have made false advertising illegal, the measure still provided for the testing of drugs by Dr. Wiley's Bureau of Chemistry and required that manufacturers list ingredients on the labels of their products. The amended bill passed the Senate on February 21, 1906. It was then sent to the House, where lobbyists for the whiskey rectifiers, the food processors, and the manufacturers of proprietary medicines stood a good chance of defeating the bill by preventing it from coming to a final vote.

Sensing that opponents would intensify their efforts to block passage, Wiley marshaled as many forces as he could in support of pure food and drug legislation. Included in this list were the American Medical Association and the General Federation of Women's Clubs. Crucial in organizing the club women of America behind the bill was the role played by Alice Lakey. As the president of the Village Improvement Association of Cranford, New Jersey, she had convinced Wiley to come and speak to her group. She quickly became an energetic convert to the cause. In 1904, she persuaded the New Jersey State Federation of Women's Clubs to adopt a resolution calling for a pure food and drug bill and convinced the General Federation to appoint a pure food committee. This committee wrote thousands of letters, distributed circulars to every state, sponsored lectures, and presented exhibits (Wiley provided examples of adulterated food for the exhibits and even printed a popular pamphlet, *Some Forms of Food Adulteration and Simple Methods for Their Detection*) to promote general interest in the topic. The committee's goal, as stated by its chair, was "to waken the public conscience to the ethical question involved in this fight for the honest label."[7] When important votes loomed in Washington, the pure food committee arranged for telegrams to be sent from each state federation president to every member of that state's delegation in Congress. As allies, Wiley found federation women to be "enthusiastic, hard working, persistent and effective" and called them "the most efficient organization now existing."[8] Looking to broaden her crusade, Lakey also spoke before the convention of the National Consumers' League in 1905 and convinced its council to appoint a similar committee of which she became the head. With the participation of the General Federation of Women's Clubs, the National Consumers' League, and the WCTU, women became thoroughly engaged in the legislative battle.

Wiley contributed his own evangelism to the patent medicine fight by addressing numerous gatherings no matter what size. His writings, previously limited to professional publications, increasingly began to appear in more popular venues like the *Independent* and *Public Opinion* under such titles as "Fraud in Food Manufacture" and "Deception in Beverages." Wiley recounted in his *Autobiography* that he regarded the patent medicine business the "most wretched and disgraceful evil the pure food and drug law sought to remedy." As a result, he was not reluctant to share his own disturbing findings with the public. Most of the nostrums his department analyzed were, he noted, "nothing more nor less than alcoholic drinks" that "created appetites in the poor dupes who used them as vicious as drunkards' craving for rum." "Head powders" were in reality sinister habit-forming drugs that women and girls became addicted to in alarming numbers, "painkillers" and "pain relievers" functioned as depressants, and popular "women's remedies" were often poisonous. "Poor mothers," said Wiley, "doped their babies into insensibility at night with soothing syrups containing opium or morphine." He also noted that catarrh cures, which depended on cocaine and opium for their effectiveness, had a brisk sale. The most vicious of the entire list of medical frauds reported by Wiley was the class that preyed on incurables. Cancer "cures" were common. "Quacks did not stop at duping actual sufferers from the disease," said Wiley, "but worked craftily to convince every prospective customer that he had cancer somewhere or other in his anatomy." Consumption was just as exploited. Desperate patients with tuberculosis were usually willing to spend their last penny to recover their health, "and the fiends who preyed on them many times got their last cent in exchange for a mixture of cod-liver oil and poisonous drugs."[9]

Missing in the general debate over food preservatives and patent medicines was any specific mention of the conditions under which meat was prepared at the packing plant. The public had learned of "embalmed meat" during the Spanish-American War in 1899. Theodore Roosevelt even testified before a Senate committee that as a soldier in Cuba he had eaten canned meat that was spoiled. The public gasped, but, for the most part, magazine editors declined to pursue the story. Like their dependence on patent medicine advertising, they also carried the advertisements of the major meat packers—Swift, Armour, and Morris—that were regarded as powerful and respected companies.

When Algie M. Simons, a socialist newspaper editor in Chicago, wrote a pamphlet titled *Packingtown* (1899) that questioned the business and labor practices of the major meatpacking companies and suggested that those concerns had traded in spoiled meat, his account went largely unnoticed. Three years later, the state of Missouri prosecuted the major meatpacking companies for being members of a trust that controlled beef prices. During the investigation, testimony revealed that wholesalers commonly sold meat that was beginning to spoil. One St. Louis meat dealer testified that he had seen meat that had been "rubbed" to remove "whiskers," painted to restore color, and preserved with ammonia. Yet the Missouri investigation received little national publicity.

It was Samuel Merwin, a journalist for *Success* magazine, who really brought the discussion of impure meat to a crest. Emphasizing the pure food angle, Merwin raised the issue of whether the major meatpacking companies were deliberately selling diseased meat and cited instances of dead hogs being removed from the stockyards to be "rendered" into lard. If, as Merwin suggested, packers were selling diseased meat, then why were there no revelations of unsanitary conditions in the reports of government inspectors? To Merwin, the answer was simple: inspection was a sham. Inspectors looked at livestock, but they did not examine the process by which meat was prepared, nor did they examine the final product. Merwin's charges were significant, and public pressure mounted on President Roosevelt to review them. He sent James Garfield, the commissioner of corporations, to investigate, but Garfield's report exonerated the major meatpacking companies. That was where things stood until Upton Sinclair published *The Jungle*, in which he exposed the unsanitary conditions in the meatpacking industry and raised the public's fear of diseased and adulterated meat. Appearing in print when it did, the novel added urgency to the ongoing crusade against impure food and patent medicines.

The Jungle, first serialized in the socialist weekly *Appeal to Reason* in 1905 and then published in book form by Doubleday, Page and Company in 1906, caused a national sensation. Hoping to write the great American working-class novel, Sinclair spent seven weeks in Chicago's meatpacking district doing research and talking to anyone who might have useful information regarding working conditions, sanitation, and the government's inspection methods. He also met Adolph Smith of the *Lancet*, a respectable British medical journal, who was internationally known as an expert on meatpacking and had written articles condemning the methods of the Chicago meat packers. Smith confirmed much of what Sinclair had discovered. He also informed Sinclair that unsanitary conditions were unnecessary and that conditions in Europe were much better as a result of state regulation. But Sinclair was an ardent socialist. He looked to transform the capitalist system rather than re-form it and hoped to awaken the reading public to the oppressive working conditions in the packinghouses of Chicago and to the exploitation of the workers as the first step in that process. Although Sinclair did give passing mention to food and drugs—milk was "watered" and given a pale-blue color as a result of being treated with formaldehyde; tea, coffee, sugar, and flour were "doctored"; canned peas were colored with copper salts; and fruit jams were treated with aniline dyes—the public was outraged more by the grue-some details of the unsanitary conditions and descriptions of contaminated meat than by the plight of the workers. When Sinclair informed the public that hams were treated with formaldehyde; that sausages were made from rot-ten meat, rats, and other refuse swept from the factory floor; that diseased cat-tle were butchered, treated, and sold as clean meat; and that men had actually fallen into the rendering vats to be sold as lard, readers feared for their own health. Capitalizing on the already growing concern over contaminated food and dangerous drugs, the novel sold 25,000 copies in its first six weeks.

The ensuing public outcry revitalized the debate over the pure food bill that was languishing in Congress. The public now demanded protection, and Roo-sevelt was once again prompted to take action. This time he sent another com-mission, composed of James B. Reynolds, a settlement worker, and Charles P. Neill, a labor commissioner, to investigate the operations of Chicago's meat packers and to check Sinclair's allegations. In the meantime, Senator Albert Beveridge of Indiana introduced a meat inspection bill in Congress. When Reynolds and Neill returned from Chicago, the report of their findings shocked many, including President Roosevelt. Unlike Garfield's earlier whitewash of the industry, their investigation confirmed the main charges in *The Jungle*. A storm of indignation swept the country. Although the packers lobbied feverishly (and with some success) to weaken the legislation, they could not defeat it. Swept up in the furor, both the Pure Food and Drug Act and the Meat Inspection Act became law on June 30, 1906.

Although the muckrakers deserve most of the credit for the success of pure food and drug legislation in 1906, Wiley was the central figure in a campaign that spanned more than twenty years. As the head of the Bureau of Chemistry, he had established the systematic investigation of foods and their adulterants. He directed the development of new analytical methods, tested the effects of chemical preservatives on humans, led the national discussion on the topic, and served as the primary scientific liaison to politicians working to develop effective federal regulation. During the 1905–1906 session of Congress, Wi-ley, along with Samuel Hopkins Adams, conferred closely with supporters of the final bill and supplied the data that essentially made the case for regula-tion undeniable. A colorful personality with an eagerness to be heard in the public arena, he did more than anyone else to dramatize the need for action. He established a dialogue with a variety of groups to broaden support for federal action and was willing to compromise on details to obtain the larger principle. To Wiley, an imperfect law was better than no law at all. Although he tended to deemphasize the dangers that adulteration could pose to human health, he never shrank from assailing the dishonesty inherent in that process. As one historian put it, Wiley was "as fundamentalist in his chemistry as his father had been in religion."[10] He truly saw himself as a crusader for higher ethical standards in commercial life.

The Pure Food and Drug Act that Wiley and others had worked so long to obtain was less than perfect. Although the law required manufacturers to print lists of product ingredients on their labels, it failed to establish a standard-setting authority for foods. Earlier efforts to authorize the secretary of agriculture to establish food standards to guide manufacturers and the courts had been sacrificed for political compromise. Contested definitions of food purity would have to be determined by the courts. Standards for drugs were more precise, but there were loopholes. The U.S. Pharmacopoeia and the National Formulary set standards for the use of terms, but companies could market drugs that were different or even substandard as long as that information was clearly presented on the label. The law also failed to include a provision preventing the use of fraudulent advertising. The new statute did, however, reinforce the principle of government regulation and the hope that such regulation could bring about improvements in the quality of American health and life. Deception was now illegal. Consumers had gained protection from dangerous food and drug products and, with the Federal Meat Inspection Act, from the negative effects of unsanitary factory environments. The law gave Wiley's Bureau of Chemistry authority to perform more thorough food and drug testing. It also empowered the secretary of agriculture to identify violators and send the evidence to the appropriate U.S. district attorney. It remained to be seen, however, whether the regulatory bureaucracy would function as reformers had hoped.

Wiley, for one, struggled with his superiors to make the law as thorough as possible. The result proved to be an example of bureaucratic infighting at its worst. According to one historian, a "gigantic conspiracy, involving the heads of the Department of Agriculture, lobbyists, and President Roosevelt himself, was devised to rob the Bureau of Chemistry—that is to say, Dr. Wiley—of the power to do further damage to the food industries through propaganda and chemical analysis of the manufacturers' products."[11] Almost as punishment for his criticism of lax administrative policies in regard to enforcement, Wiley saw the power of his bureau diminish over time. He finally left the department in disgust in 1912. Out of government service, Wiley accepted an offer from *Good Housekeeping* to head the magazine's bureau of food, sanitation, and health. The new position allowed Wiley to maintain a public forum, and he continued to write roughly an article a month in which he offered his opinions on the enforcement of the Pure Food and Drug Law and shared his views on human nutrition. In 1929, he wrote *The History of a Crime against the Food Law*, in which he chronicled his disillusionment with the government's commitment to reform. False advertising and general negligence continued after Wiley's death in 1930 at the age of eighty-six. Finally, in 1938, Congress passed the Pure Food, Drug and Cosmetic Act. The new law set up authority for the establishment of definitions and standards of identity and quality for foods that would, for the first time, have the force of law. The law prohibited foods produced under unsanitary conditions and banned the use of containers that might render foods injurious to health. The law also required evidence of a drug's safety prior to marketing and mandated prescriptions for any drug that might be dangerous if used improperly. Wiley would have been pleased.

NOTES

1. Oscar E. Anderson Jr., *The Health of a Nation: Harvey W. Wiley and the Fight for Pure Food* (Chicago: University of Chicago Press, 1958), 70.
2. Anderson, *The Health of a Nation*, 75.
3. Anderson, *The Health of a Nation*, 80.
4. Anderson, *The Health of a Nation*, 127.
5. Robert Crunden, *Ministers of Reform: The Progressives' Achievement in American Civilization, 1889–1920* (Urbana: University of Illinois Press, 1984), 196.
6. Crunden, *Ministers of Reform*, 185–86.
7. Stephen Wilson, *Food and Drug Regulation* (Washington, D.C.: American Council on Public Affairs, 1942), 27.
8. James Harvey Young, *Pure Food: Securing the Federal Food and Drugs Act of 1906* (Princeton, N.J.: Princeton University Press, 1989), 185.
9. Harvey W. Wiley, *An Autobiography* (Indianapolis: Bobbs-Merrill), 205–7.
10. Crunden, *Ministers of Reform*, 197.
11. Louis Filler, *Crusaders for American Liberalism* (Yellow Springs, Ohio: Antioch Press, 1939), 168.

SOURCES

Anderson, Oscar E., Jr. *The Health of a Nation: Harvey W. Wiley and the Fight for Pure Food*. Chicago: University of Chicago Press, 1958.

Crunden, Robert. *Ministers of Reform: The Progressives' Achievement in American Civilization, 1889–1920*. Urbana: University of Illinois Press, 1984.

Filler, Louis. *Crusaders for American Liberalism*. Yellow Springs, Ohio: Antioch Press, 1939.

Wiley, Harvey W. *An Autobiography*. Indianapolis: Bobbs-Merrill, 1930.

Wilson, Stephen. *Food and Drug Regulation*. Washington, D.C.: American Council on Public Affairs, 1942.

Young, James Harvey. *Pure Food: Securing the Federal Food and Drugs Act of 1906*. Princeton, N.J.: Princeton University Press, 1989.

11

John Randolph Haynes and Direct Democracy

As many Americans struggled with the economic and social transformations brought about by a rapidly industrializing and urbanizing society during the late nineteenth century, they also felt increasingly ignored as participants in the political system. From the perspective of consumers, taxpayers, workers, and farmers, policymakers identified issues and established priorities in a political environment ever more susceptible to the influences of economic power. It seemed as though the special interests and the politicians they controlled had stymied any discussion of vital social and economic issues. Concluding that their elected representatives no longer represented their interests, many Americans became discontented and dissatisfied with a system of governance that rewarded the economically powerful at the expense of the needs of the people. Popular democracy appeared to be a sham.

Frustration with the existing political system drove individuals to look for ways to improve it. Some suggested the creation of new political parties to challenge Republican and Democratic defenders of the status quo. Others argued for reforms that included expanding the civil service system and reducing the amount of money in political campaigns. Still others suggested changes to existing election procedures, such as the universal acceptance of the secret ballot, the direct primary process of nominating political candidates, and the establishment of nonpartisan state and local elections. Yet others advocated expanding the franchise by granting the vote to women and allowing for the direct popular election of U.S. senators. A growing number, however, began to conclude that the decision-making process itself should be opened up. Maybe it would be better if voters were allowed to bypass unresponsive or irresponsible legislative bodies and govern directly. Known popularly at the time as direct legislation and more popularly since then as the initiative and referendum, voters could either create new laws or veto laws passed by their state or local legislative bodies. If a given percentage of registered voters petitioned for such action, their proposals would be placed on the ballot for popular approval or rejection. Ideally, legislation could then reflect the public rather than the special interest and human need rather than corporate power. The process would also allow minority viewpoints to gain a hearing. To further encourage political accountability and popular control of political institutions, many favored allowing for the recall of elected officials by a similar petition process as well.

The idea of direct legislation grew rapidly during the 1890s. J. W. Sullivan, printer, editor, and labor activist, led the intellectual discussion of how the initiative and referendum could enhance representative government with the publication of *Direct Legislation by the Citizenship through the Initiative and Referendum* in 1892. As one reformer noted, "It has done more . . . to crystallize and give definiteness of aim to the sentiment of really democratic leaders . . . than any other one thing. It made converts and they spread its circulation."[1] One of those influenced by the book was Eltweed Pomeroy, the owner of a small cooperative manufacturing firm in New Jersey that produced ink. Pomeroy organized the National Direct Legislation League in 1896 and edited the organization's national newsletter, the *Direct Legislation Record*, to inform those interested in the topic of activities occurring in the various states. Pomeroy's new organization also convinced the Populist Party to add the initiative and referendum to its platform in 1896, although the party declined to include the recall.

The early organizers behind what became known as the direct legislation movement urged supporters to create direct legislation leagues, draw up constitutional (state) or charter (city) amendments, have them submitted for legislative consideration, and lobby heavily for their adoption. Results soon followed. South Dakota became the first state to amend its constitution to allow its citizens the option of direct legislation in 1898. Over the next twenty years, twenty-two states passed laws establishing the initiative and/or referendum, and voters in sixteen of those states considered over 400 propositions on their state ballots during that same period. In California, one of the most active environments for direct democracy then and now, the leader was a medical doctor and self-made millionaire by the name of John Randolph Haynes. Haynes, described as a left-wing progressive by his biographer, was an idealist who believed in Christian socialism, a pragmatist who was willing to bargain and compromise to achieve immediate improvements to society, and an activist who devoted his time and money to the causes he believed in.

John Randolph Haynes was born in Fairmount Springs, Pennsylvania, on June 13, 1853. His father, James Sydney Haynes, had tried farming but eventually became superintendent of various coal mines in the anthracite region in the northeastern part of the state. The area was known for its ethnic strife and violence and would come to be symbolized by the Molly Maguires. Growing numbers of Irish Catholic miners who had detested their British landlords in Ireland felt once again exploited by the Protestant English mine owners and operators as they tried to eke out a hard, dangerous existence in the coal mines of America. When Irish miners opposed the drafting of soldiers into the Union army and clashed with mine owners who supported that policy in 1863, violence escalated. The region would remain in turmoil for another decade. Fearing for his safety, James decided to quit the mining business and move his family to Philadelphia in October 1863.

James Haynes had saved enough money for the family to live comfortably for a while, but bad investments soon impoverished the family. Hard times forced John Haynes, then only fourteen, to leave the private school he attended and go to work to help support the family. He painted barrels for an oil company, sold dry goods, and apprenticed as a carpenter. After a summer of long, hard work building houses in Oil City, Pennsylvania, he saved enough money to follow his older brother Francis and enroll in the University of Pennsylvania Medical School. While studying to become a physician (a three-year course of study), Haynes also attended the Auxiliary School of Medicine at the university, where he took classes in world history and literature as well as science and eventually earned a Ph.D. to go along with the medical degree he received in 1874 at the age of twenty-one. Not required to serve an internship, he worked in his brother's medical office for several months and then started his own practice in the poor Irish working-class district of Port Richmond. For the next twelve years, he worked seven days a week, making over a dozen house calls each day. Like Walter Rauschenbusch and Jane Addams, the experience of witnessing poverty on a daily basis was one he never forgot.

In 1882, Haynes married Dora Fellows, the daughter of a coal operator and close friend of the family who lived in Wilkes-Barre, Pennsylvania. When their only child, Sydney, died from scarlet fever at the age of three, the Hayneses abruptly decided to leave the damp climate of eastern Pennsylvania and move to the warmer environs of Los Angeles, California. In 1887, John, Dora, his parents, and three of his siblings all moved to southern California. Once in Los Angeles, John established a medical practice with his brother Francis, gained an appointment as a medical professor at the University of Southern California, began to publish articles in major medical journals, and helped found the Pacific Hospital along with his brother Francis and brother-in-law Walter Lindley. The Haynes–Haynes–Lindley partnership was soon one of the largest and most successful medical practices in the city, and Haynes could list among his patients some of the most influential families in southern California.

Haynes arrived in Los Angeles at a good time. The population was rapidly increasing (from 11,000 to over 50,000 during the decade of the 1880s), and the booming area offered seemingly limitless opportunities for speculative gain. Haynes invested in real estate, purchasing house lots, buildings, and parcels of land throughout southern California. He developed other business interests as well. He invested heavily in a number of banks, oil and railroad companies, and land development ventures. He also had a stake in mining operations in Arizona and South America and became a founding stockholder in more than a dozen new businesses. Haynes soon found himself on the board of directors of several corporations and became a civic booster. He joined the Chamber of Commerce and the League for Better City Government. The latter organization was a "mugwump" group of Los Angeles business and professional elite who looked to elect the "best" candidates to office and favored revising the city's charter to reduce municipal spending, define more clearly the responsibilities of city officials, and extend the civil service system to city employees. Business dealings enhanced the opportunity to make social connections as well. Haynes soon joined a number of elite social organizations that included the California, University, and Sunset Clubs and Scribes, a discussion club composed of journalists and others who met weekly to discuss topics over dinner. Haynes accepted membership in a variety of fraternal orders—the Knights Templars, the Sons of the Revolution, the Society of Colonial Wars, and the Scottish Rite Masons—and was involved with several cultural organizations as well. Taken together, these professional, business, and social/cultural attachments provided the personal contacts that would allow Haynes access to the circles of influence and power in southern California. At the same time, his shrewd capitalistic instincts enabled him to begin to amass a fortune that would later finance his social reform interests.

The turning point in Haynes's life as a reformer occurred in January 1898, when he attended a lecture on Christian socialism delivered by Reverend William Dwight Porter Bliss, an Episcopal minister. Up to this point in his life, Haynes considered himself as "practically an anarchist" in his thoughts on solving society's social problems. What he meant was that he could not see "any way out of the existing order of things except to throw everything over and start fresh."[2] Bliss changed that. Influenced by the Christian socialist thinking of Frederick Denison Maurice and Charles Kingsley, Bliss founded the first Christian Socialist Society in the United States in 1889. He had also joined the Knights of Labor, membership that allowed him to view a socialist future from the perspective of workers imbued with the cooperative ideal. What Bliss wanted to do was Christianize secular socialism. Like Walter

Rauschenbusch, he wanted the church to embrace a more primitive Christianity in which the teachings of Jesus Christ, especially the Sermon on the Mount, would guide mankind to a cooperative commonwealth where workers would own the means of production in a noncompetitive environment. Middle-class Christian socialists like himself would preach the gospel and educate the workers to see the benefits of applying the teachings of Jesus to the industrial order. While society was slowly being educated to accept a non-Marxist (nonrevolutionary) version of socialism, leaders like Bliss would follow the path of expediency and advocate immediate reforms to ameliorate some of the worst social and industrial injustices in the meantime. Bliss's immediate reform agenda included direct legislation, the abolition of child labor and restrictions on the hours and regulations on the conditions affecting women workers, municipal ownership of utilities, woman suffrage, full employment, and graduated income taxation and increased taxes on land being held for speculation. It was hoped that nonsocialists, interested only in specific reforms, would join the crusade as well.

In 1897, Bliss organized the Union Reform League "to work for the coming of the Kingdom of Heaven upon earth" and urged the establishment of local branches that would be part of a national federation of all reformers, not just socialists.[3] When Bliss came to Los Angeles in 1898 to establish a chapter of his new organization, Haynes was swept away. His immediate conversion to activism was like a religious awakening. Inspired by Bliss's prescription for orderly, ethical social change, Haynes arranged a banquet and invited local clergymen and others to hear Bliss speak. The event led to the founding of a local chapter of the Union Reform League and the creation of a Committee of One Hundred, chaired by Haynes, to direct a campaign of action that would include scheduling lecturers, circulating publications, encouraging the local press to include articles on the topic, and lobbying local government to consider items on the organization's general reform agenda. When the Union Reform League reorganized the next year as the Social Reform Union and Bliss moved his office to Chicago, Haynes continued to be active as president of the California branch. Although the national organization lasted for only another two or three years before ideological bickering and apathy killed it, Haynes had discovered a long-term social reform goal, a specific and immediate plan of action, and a new enthusiasm for the possibility of change.

Direct legislation quickly became Haynes's top priority. He believed the reforms could be used to give voters more control over the political process and the actions of their elected representatives. As Haynes later recalled, "Many years [sic] observation of misgovernment in American cities . . . convinced me that the cure for the evils of democracy was more democracy—the bringing of the control over their affairs the nearest possible to the people."[4]

Haynes also believed that direct legislation could allow voters to obtain specific objectives that the current political system seemed unwilling to consider. He was also savvy enough to foresee potential political alliances down the road: with suffragists who could use the initiative to obtain the vote; with labor unions that sought protective labor legislation, anti-strikebreaking ordinances, or limits on the use of the court injunction in labor disputes; with prohibitionists who wanted to outlaw liquor; with single-taxers who envisioned increased opportunity by taxing those who speculated in land; and with socialists who favored public ownership of utilities.

In 1900, Haynes led a group of citizens who wanted to revise the city's charter and saw an opportunity to get the initiative and referendum included in the revised document. Elected to the fifteen-member board of freeholders who would make recommendations, Haynes arranged to be appointed to the legislative committee. The committee eventually submitted a draft of the initiative and referendum and added a provision for the recall even though no municipality in the United States had as yet adopted the idea. Haynes later confessed that none of the members of the committee were aware that the recall had been advocated in Populist circles and claimed the idea came to him after reading *The City for the People* by Frank Parsons. With a favorable vote from his committee, Haynes then used Parsons's persuasive argument in favor of direct legislation (Haynes presented each member with a copy of the book) to persuade the other members of the board of freeholders to follow suit. Before the new charter could be presented to the voters for popular approval, however, the California Supreme Court ruled that revisions to an existing charter could be proposed only as individual amendments. Simply put, the entire process had to be repeated.

In March 1902, the city council appointed a new charter revision commission to begin the task of "amending" the charter. This time, Haynes was not a member of the committee, but it did include several of his professional associates and close personal friends. Although the new committee worked from the draft of the previous board, Haynes took nothing for granted. He continued to champion direct legislation in speeches before civic groups and in newspaper articles. As a member of the executive committee of the recently formed Municipal League of Los Angeles, Haynes used his influence to have that body formally recommend direct legislation. He also hosted a formal dinner for the charter committee and invited Eltweed Pomeroy, president of the National Direct Legislation League, to be the guest speaker. At the conclusion of the dinner, the charter committee held an impromptu business session and adopted a motion in favor of including the initiative, referendum, and recall in the new charter.

The Direct Legislation League of Los Angeles, which Haynes had organized in 1900 and for which he currently served as president, led the political campaign for popular ratification of the charter. When the Municipal League abruptly decided to oppose the recall as too "experimental" and the conservative *Los Angeles Times* raised questions concerning its constitutionality, Haynes was ready to respond. He quickly authorized the printing of 30,000 small yellow cards urging voters to approve all the direct legislation amendments that supporters distributed to every voter coming to the polls. When the votes were finally tallied, the combined initiative and referendum amendment won by a majority of more than six to one and the recall by a majority of over four to one. The initiative allowed 5 percent of the registered voters to propose (by petition) laws at a regular election (15 percent to call a special election) and 7 percent to challenge a law passed by the city council (referendum). A simple majority of those voting on any ballot proposition was sufficient for approval. The recall required the signatures of 25 percent of the voters to call a special election to consider the removal of an elected official from office. Empowered, voters in Los Angeles proceeded to use all the direct forms of democracy. During the next decade, they considered seventeen ballot propositions (initiative or referendum) and approved ten of them. Included in the list was a measure creating a board of public works and another that authorized an investigation into the construction of the Owens River aqueduct project being developed to bring water to the city. Voters also used the recall to remove a city councilman for pandering to special interests at public expense in 1904 and to force Mayor Arthur C. Harper to resign just before a scheduled recall election in 1909 under charges that he used his office to protect organized vice.

Success in Los Angeles encouraged Haynes to organize the Direct Legislation League of California in 1902 to spearhead the campaign for inclusion of the initiative and referendum in the state's constitution. In 1902 and again in 1904, the league sent questionnaires to prospective candidates to the state legislature to obtain their views on direct legislation and to make those positions public. The league flooded the state with letters soliciting new members and money (Haynes paid most of the expenses himself) as well as endorsements from organizations like the State Federation of Labor. The league also presented a petition signed by 22,000 voters to the state legislature in 1903. During the following year, the league mailed 2,000 blank forms to the members of over 300 labor unions, asking them to petition state representatives and senators from their districts, and mailed 10,000 letters to voters urging them to do the same. The league requested 400 newspapers in the state to assist their efforts and asked 500 ministers for the names of ten to twenty "good men" in their communities who might favor the adoption of the initiative and referendum and might be able to exert some influence with their state legislators. Haynes made a direct appeal to the National American Woman's

Suffrage Association asking for support and urging the membership to consider the relevance of direct legislation to their cause, made personal trips to the state capital to try to persuade legislators, lobbied the county and state conventions of the two major political parties, and paid lobbyists to work in Sacramento. Despite these varied efforts, however, the 1903, 1905, and 1907 state legislatures refused to approve the league's proposed amendments.

Defeat in the California legislature, however, had given Haynes a lesson in power politics. Leading the opposition to direct legislation was the Southern Pacific Railroad. Known as the "Octopus," the corporation had a reputation as a ruthless manipulator of the political economy. William F. Herrin headed the Southern Pacific's "Political Bureau" and directed the activities of a powerful statewide political machine. Paid to protect the interests of the corporation, Herrin viewed direct legislation as a threat and was determined to block it in the legislature. Through the lavish use of retainer fees, free railroad passes, special shipping rates, and political campaign contributions, the machine was able to control party nominating conventions and, ultimately, legislative actions at the state capitol. As the editors of the *Los Angeles Express* aptly surmised, "W. F. Herrin and he alone can simplify the situation for Dr. Haynes, and unless [he] . . . becomes interested, the initiative and referendum will not be [favorably] considered."[5]

While Haynes continued to orchestrate the efforts of the Direct Legislation League and ponder ways to unblock the Southern Pacific–led impasse in Sacramento, he continued his active civic involvement in Los Angeles. In 1904, he began, through speeches and articles, a campaign to establish municipal ownership over all the public utilities (gas, electric, telephone, and transportation) in the city in addition to its municipally owned waterworks. Haynes criticized the existing private companies for providing inferior service and taking excessive profits and argued that private ownership of public utilities was the primary cause of the political corruption plaguing many American cities. To promote his ideas, Haynes joined a syndicate that undertook two short-lived experiments—formation of the People's Gas Company and the City Gas Company—in unsuccessful efforts to compete with the established gas company. In instances where it was not feasible for a city to build and buy out existing utilities or to operate a competing concern (as might be the case with streetcar lines), Haynes advocated regulation. Alarmed by the rising number of fatalities resulting from streetcar accidents, Haynes, in cooperation with the Voters League of Los Angeles (an organization formed in 1905 to work for civil service, municipal ownership, and direct legislation, among other reforms), led an effort to use the initiative to obtain a city ordinance requiring streetcar companies to install safer fenders on its cars. Specifically, what Haynes and the Voters League wanted were fenders that scooped up (rather than knocked down) pedestrians and cradled them in a basket until the motorman could stop the car. After collecting over 4,000 signatures, nearly enough to call for a special election on the issue, Haynes persuaded the city council to pass a fender ordinance in May 1906.

In the spring of 1907, Haynes joined in discussions that eventually led to the formation of a new political reform movement in California. Edward A. Dickson and Chester Rowell, two journalists who regularly covered the activities in the state legislature, called together a group of fifteen reform-oriented individuals with strong attachments to the Republican Party for a preliminary meeting in Los Angeles to consider organizing a new reform league. Spurred on by Dickson's and Rowell's vivid accounts of the buying and selling of votes that had taken place during the 1907 session of the state legislature, the group used the occasion to amplify the need for a long list of political reforms. Among the issues discussed at the meeting were public utility regulation, child labor legislation, penal reform, and woman suffrage. The highest priority of those attending the meeting, however, was, in the words of one of the participants, the "constructive destruction of the Southern Pacific machine."[6] As a result, political reforms—the direct primary, the direct election of U.S. senators, and the initiative, referendum, and recall—received most of their attention. Haynes, who attended the meeting, was sympathetic. He philosophically opposed the Southern Pacific as a monopoly and believed that it restrained trade, reduced competition, and corrupted politics. He also knew that obtaining a direct legislation amendment would be extremely difficult as long as the Southern Pacific could wield its influence in opposition. Hoping to bring the discussion into focus, Haynes proposed that the group adopt a specific agenda that included direct legislation. The majority, however, rejected his suggestion as premature. Instead, those in attendance decided to forgo specifics and focus on creating a statewide organization to oppose machine control of the state Republican Party.

When those in sympathy with these early reform soundings gathered for their first statewide meeting in Oakland on August 1, 1907, their numbers had grown to nearly fifty. They chose the occasion to formally adopt the name League of Lincoln-Roosevelt Republican Clubs (popularly known as the Lincoln-Roosevelt League) to symbolize the political heritage they sought to reclaim. These "California progressives" were, for the most part, a group with which Haynes was not entirely compatible. They tended to be cautious and conservative, regarded organized labor as an enemy of reform, and generally favored purified republicanism over expanded popular democracy. As a result, they again agreed to push direct legislation aside and concentrate their efforts on obtaining a direct primary law. They believed that such legislation would enable them to wrest control over the nomination of political candidates from the Southern Pacific–manipulated party conventions and enable honest, efficient, independent, reform-minded individuals to gain positions in state and local government. Support for the Lincoln-Roosevelt League grew quickly, and by the summer of 1908, the league claimed to have 100 newspapers behind it. In the elections that fall, a number of league-endorsed candidates won election to the state legislature.

Sensing that the reform climate in California was improving, Haynes worked to reinvigorate the Direct Legislation League and optimistically looked forward to having an initiative and referendum amendment accepted in the upcoming legislative session (1909). With a northern branch in San Francisco and a southern branch (directed by Haynes) in Los Angeles, the Direct Legislation League launched an energetic organizing campaign across the state. The organization mailed thousands of copies of a statement explaining its objectives to sympathizers in every township in California hoping that direct legislation committees would be established in those communities as well. Senator Jonathan Bourne of Oregon sent the Direct Legislation League 75,000 copies of an address made by him on the workings of direct legislation in his state (Oregon had adopted the initiative and referendum in 1902) that were distributed throughout California under his frank. A committee met with the managing editors of the leading newspapers to ask for cooperation and publicity and sent letters to hundreds of smaller newspapers in the state seeking similar support. Using a mailing list of citizens known to be favorable to direct legislation, the league solicited donations and cultivated personal contacts.

In addition to the grassroots organizing efforts, the officers of the Direct Legislation League made plans to maintain a headquarters in Sacramento while the legislature was in session. Haynes, supported financially by Los Angeles newspaper publisher Edwin T. Earl and wealthy San Francisco businessman Rudolph Spreckels, also formed a "People's Lobby" at the state capitol to monitor and publicize the voting records of various legislators. Haynes continued to be a tireless correspondent, constantly supplying information to various interested groups. When the legislature convened, the Direct Legislation League asked only for the initiative. Yet when the league-sponsored 8 percent (a figure later compromised to 12 percent) initiative amendment was introduced in the machine-controlled senate, it was defeated. Despite a tremendous organizing campaign and the endorsement of farm and labor groups, the state Democratic Party, numerous municipal and county Republican conventions, and well-known California reformers such as Francis J. Heney and James D. Phelan, the Southern Pacific machine still had the votes to block passage. The legislature did, however, pass a Lincoln-Roosevelt League–sponsored direct primary law that eliminated party nominating conventions. With that new device, reformers hoped to restrict Southern Pacific influence over the nominating process in 1910.

The Lincoln-Roosevelt League's gubernatorial candidate in 1910 was Hiram Johnson, who had risen to prominence as the prosecuting attorney in the sensational San Francisco graft trials of 1908 in which Mayor Eugene E. Schmitz and Boss Abraham Ruef were both indicted for extortion and convicted. The trials dominated the news and seemed to set records for legal improprieties. Witnesses were encouraged to give false testimony, jurors bribed, prosecution documents stolen, and private offices and safes broken into for incriminating evidence. When an appellate court freed Schmitz and Ruef on technicalities requiring a retrial, legal authorities criticized the court's action and raised questions concerning judicial integrity. During the trial, Freemont Older, the crusading editor of the *San Francisco Bulletin* who had begun the journalistic campaign that led to the indictment of Schmitz and Ruef, was kidnapped, while the star witness for the prosecution (a supervisor who had turned state's evidence) had his house dynamited. Then, on November 13, 1908, during Ruef's second trial, prosecuting attorney Francis J. Heney was shot and severely wounded in the courtroom by an ex-convict who was then found dead in his jail cell the following day from a revolver shot. At that point, Johnson volunteered to replace Heney, brought Ruef's second trial to a successful conclusion, and captured the public attention that led to his nomination for governor.

Johnson conducted a well-focused and well-orchestrated campaign and used his considerable oratorical skills to maximum effect as he repeatedly told ever-increasing crowds that he promised to kick the Southern Pacific machine out of politics in California. Taking advantage of the new primary law, Johnson won the Republican nomination along with almost the entire Lincoln-Roosevelt League–backed ticket. The league soon gained control of the regular state Republican Party organization as well. The climax of a campaign centered on antibossism came when the Johnson camp reproduced the infamous "Shame of California" photograph from the 1906 state party convention showing Boss Ruef (by then a convicted felon) with a congressman, a state supreme court justice, the party's gubernatorial nominee, and the chief lobbyist for the Southern Pacific Railroad as a billboard in hundreds of key locations around the state. It was more help than the reformers needed. Running on a broad reform platform that had been expanded to include direct legislation, the progressive Republicans were then swept into office in the fall elections. In just three and a half years, reformers had managed to topple the seemingly invincible Southern Pacific machine.

As soon as the election was over, the Republican State Central Committee called a planning session to set the upcoming legislative agenda. Haynes was appointed to the Committee on Direct Legislation, which was given the assignment of drafting amendments for the initiative, referendum, and recall and devising a strategy to pass them. The final drafts extended direct legislation to voters in all cities and counties as well as to voters at the state level. The initiative (for constitutional amendments and statutes) was based on a petition of 8 percent of all the votes cast for all candidates for governor in the previous general election and the referendum on a similar petition of 5 percent. With a progressive majority in the legislature, the combined initiative and referendum amendment was easily adopted. There was, however, a great deal of debate over the accompanying recall amendment. Even a number of those who favored the recall as it applied to elected officials wanted to exclude judges. Echoing the sentiments of those opposed to the exclusion of the judiciary, Haynes argued that judges were not incorruptible. "Why recall a Governor or other State official who is a drunkard, a knave or a fool," he argued, "and not a judge who is equally culpable?"[7] After a lengthy debate, the recall amendment (based on a 20 percent petition figure) also passed by a wide margin. All that remained was for voters to ratify the amendments at a special election to be held in October 1911.

Haynes and the Direct Legislation League took nothing for granted and immediately mobilized a campaign to ensure ratification. The league raised money (again mostly from Haynes), hired national organizer Judson King to direct the league's publicity efforts, scheduled speakers, mass-mailed literature to registered voters, and coordinated speeches by Governor Johnson in the larger cities and other speakers in the smaller towns. Haynes spoke in favor of the amendments at numerous venues throughout Southern California and accompanied reformer Francis Heney on an automobile speaking tour of the state. To further promote the reforms (and to underscore Haynes's role in the "people's rule" campaign), the editors of *California Outlook*, a progressive reform journal, placed him on the cover of their September 9 issue. As the campaign neared its end, both sides intensified the debate before civic groups and in newspapers, and speakers from both inside and outside the state were recruited to address numerous mass meetings. Opponents argued that direct legislation meant the end to representative government, the establishment of a tyranny of the majority in state politics, and the triumph of radicalism and incompetence. Proponents countered with the argument that only "misrepresentative" government was being threatened, that people could be trusted to decide important issues, and that direct legislation would protect individuals from corporate greed and political domination. In the end, the vote was one-sided. The initiative–referendum amendment carried by a count of 168,744 to 52,093, while the recall amendment passed by an even wider margin of 178,115 to 53,755. Although California was not the first state to embrace direct democracy, journalist and political observer George Creel rewarded Haynes for his decade-long crusade by bestowing on him the title "father of the Initiative, Referendum, and Recall."[8]

Although the passage of the direct legislation amendments in 1911 was the major triumph in Haynes's life as a reformer, he continued to take an active part in a number of reform bodies, such as the American Association for Labor Legislation and the American Indian Defense Association, that reflected his special interest in legal protections for women, children, miners, and Native Americans. He also contributed money to the National Consumers' League, an organization devoted to protecting women workers, outlawing child labor, and legalizing birth control. As for governmental changes beyond direct legislation, Haynes supported the idea of proportional representation, a system that would give political minority parties seats on the city council in proportion to the votes they received in an election. Much of his time in the years immediately following the adoption of the initiative, referendum, and recall in California was spent spreading those ideas to other states. Considered an authority on the topic, Haynes was often asked to share his experiences and offer his advice. One of his speeches, "Direct Government in California," was printed as a U.S. Senate document. Hoping to use direct legislation to support his other reform interests, he helped found the National Popular Government League in 1913 as a vehicle to work for the implementation of public ownership via the initiative process.

After the adoption of direct legislation in California, Haynes increasingly devoted his attention to the public development of hydroelectric power, a hotly contested issue in Los Angeles. The public power debate centered on how the city should distribute the electrical power that would be produced once the municipality's aqueduct and water delivery system in the Owens valley was completed. Should the city allow private development of this resource or build its own electrical distribution system? Appointed to the Public Service Board (later renamed the Board of Water and Power Commissioners) in 1921, Haynes became the dominant spokesperson for that department until his death in 1937. A series of successful bond issues eventually made municipal ownership a reality, while federal legislation authorizing the construction of Boulder (Hoover) Dam allowed the city to expand its authority by overseeing the distribution of water diverted from the Colorado River. In his involvement in the campaigns for both direct legislation and public management of water and power, Haynes "demonstrated his belief that it was best to leave the business of controlling the actions of government and public utilities to the public itself."[9]

Not everyone studying the topic of direct legislation today believes, as Haynes did, that direct democracy is sound policy. Their criticisms are both practical and philosophical. They argue that the initiative process has been co-opted, taken over by activists and professional signature gatherers who sell their services to wealthy sponsors (willing to bankroll their own pet initiatives in campaigns that are under no spending limitations) and wealthy interest groups (willing to spend freely to achieve their own policy goals). In the latter case, the same forces that compromise legislators have merely found a new venue. They also complain that governors can use the initiative to further their own political agendas when they find their bills stalled in the legislature and that legislators can do the same when they find themselves in the minority. Critics also tend to take the position that direct democracy, especially the use of the initiative, is alien to the spirit of the U.S. Constitution and the established legislative system of checks and balances. They find the initiative poorly suited for making complex policy decisions that have far-reaching consequences for government and society. As they see it, bypassing the legislature negates the opportunity for deliberation and compromise. They also fault the process for allowing a state's constitution to be too easily amended, for triggering lawsuits that ultimately force the courts (the least accountable branch of government) to decide sensitive political questions that the legislature was denied the opportunity to make, for congesting the ballot, and for generally confusing voters with often poorly written and deceptive propositions. Implied in their criticism is a dismissal of the notion that there is such a thing as a rational and informed electorate.[10]

One can only guess at how Haynes would have responded to these critics. After the adoption of direct legislation in California, he spent a good deal of his time guarding the initiative, referendum, and recall from opponents who periodically tried to compromise the reforms by increasing the percentages of signatures required on petitions, restricting the signature gathering process by prohibiting the hiring of paid petition circulators, limiting the number of times an initiative proposition could be placed on the ballot within a specified period of time, and exempting certain subjects (especially taxation) from the initiative. Haynes was able to block each of these attempts but had to pay lobbyists in Sacramento during the 1920s and early 1930s to keep him informed of possible legislative challenges and to work to stop them. Haynes had confidence in an informed electorate and would probably have approved of changes aimed at heightening voter awareness by disclosing the sponsors of initiative propositions in public advertisements and revising the voters' pamphlet to make it more informative and readable. Philosophically, Haynes would have objected to the notion that the initiative was, in reality, a system of laws without government. He always argued that the initiative and referendum were not alternatives to representative government but merely safeguards against the unresponsiveness and irresponsibility of legislators. He would have liked the argument that the initiative, referendum, and recall are actually three more checks in our existing system of checks and balances.

Haynes has been given only modest attention in most histories of the Progressive Era despite his considerable accomplishments and influence. His radical philosophical views and general preference to work in the political arena as a nonpartisan, independent activist have made him difficult to categorize or compartmentalize. He was a socialist (although he never joined the Socialist Party) committed to striving for a classless utopian commonwealth but doing so as an active capitalist and member of the upper class he was working to (peacefully) eliminate. Like many "progressives," Haynes was a moralist and an idealist, but, unlike most, he was also a pragmatist and a realist. Inspired by Bliss, he developed a social democratic vision of the future that was rooted in an optimistic belief in human progress and an unswerving faith in the power of popular democracy. At the same time, he used a keen understanding of the dynamics of modern interest-group politics and a knack for political compromise to become an influential power broker in California politics for nearly forty years. Haynes was, however, very much a part of the larger reform-oriented Progressive Era. As a "radical" who saw the need for piecemeal improvements to the social order, he, like other nondoctrinaire socialists, "infused into . . . [the reform] movement an altruistic zeal and a higher purpose."[11] He pushed more moderate reformers to broaden their reform vision and accept the need for more far-reaching changes than they would otherwise have advocated. In doing so, he helped "radicalize" the overall progressive agenda. Haynes's greatest individual contribution to the study of American reform, however, was in expanding citizen participation in civic affairs and recognizing the importance of political empowerment as a means for bringing about social change.

NOTES

1. Steven L. Piott, *Giving Voters a Voice: The Origins of the Initiative and Referendum in America* (Columbia: University of Missouri Press, 2003), 4.

2. Tom Sitton, *John Randolph Haynes: California Progressive* (Stanford, Calif.: Stanford University Press, 1992), 26–27.

3. Tom Sitton, "California's Practical Idealist: John Randolph Haynes," *California History* 67 (March 1988): 4.

4. Piott, *Giving Voters a Voice*, 153.

5. Piott, *Giving Voters a Voice*, 160.

6. Kevin Starr, *Inventing the Dream: California through the Progressive Era* (New York: Oxford University Press, 1985), 236.

7. Sitton, *John Randolph Haynes*, 93.

8. Sitton, *John Randolph Haynes*, 93.

9. Sitton, "California's Practical Idealist," 17.

10. For two recent studies that are highly critical the initiative process, see David S. Broder, *Democracy Derailed: Initiative Campaigns and the Power of Money* (New York: Harcourt, 2000), and Richard J. Ellis, *Democratic Delusions: The Initiative Process in America* (Lawrence: University Press of Kansas, 2002).

11. Tom Sitton, "John Randolph Haynes and the Left Wing of California Progressivism," in *California Progressivism Revisited*, ed. William Deverell and Tom Sitton (Berkeley: University of California Press, 1994), 17.

SOURCES

Bird, Frederick L., and Frances M. Ryan. *The Recall of Public Officers: A Study of the Operation of the Recall in California*. New York: Macmillan, 1930.

Crouch, Winston W. "John Randolph Haynes and His Work for Direct Government." *National Municipal Review* 27 (September 1938): 434–40, 453.

Deverell, William, and Tom Sitton, eds. *California Progressivism Revisited*. Berkeley: University of California Press, 1994.

Piott, Steven L. *Giving Voters a Voice: The Origins of the Initiative and Referendum in America*. Columbia: University of Missouri Press, 2003.

Sitton, Tom. "California's Practical Idealist: John Randolph Haynes." *California History* 67 (March 1988): 3–17.

———. *John Randolph Haynes: California Progressive*. Stanford, Calif.: Stanford University Press, 1992.

Starr, Kevin. *Inventing the Dream: California through the Progressive Era*. New York: Oxford University Press, 1985.

12

Alice Paul and the Campaign for Human Rights

The organized movement to obtain woman suffrage in the United States dates to 1848, when Elizabeth Cady Stanton and Lucretia Mott called the first women's rights convention in Seneca Falls, New York. The meeting was, in reality, a public protest against the existing inferior political, economic, and social position held by women in American society. The Declaration of Sentiments, the primary document to come out of that assemblage, proposed many reforms in favor of equal human rights. Reflecting the logic and rhetoric of the Declaration of Independence, the list of grievances included demands for changes to the legal definitions governing marriage and divorce and related legal determinations regarding child custody, property ownership, and earned and inherited income; an end to the monopolization of educational, occupational, and professional opportunities; and the right to vote. Similar meetings were held periodically during the 1850s. The Civil War, however, brought these discussions to a halt, and many women turned their attention to the war and their efforts to relief work. At the end of the conflict, as Congress committed itself to establishing citizenship and voting rights for black men, rights for women were ignored.

By 1870, when the discussion for women's rights had again gathered momentum, two separate organizations—the National Woman Suffrage Association (NWSA) and the American Woman Suffrage Association (AWSA)—debated the strategies to be used for obtaining equal citizenship and voting rights for women. Led by Elizabeth Cady Stanton and Susan B. Anthony, the NWSA championed a radical program of fundamental change to improve the status of women (their periodical was *The Revolution*) and advocated a federal constitutional amendment establishing a woman's right to vote. Competing with the NWSA was the more moderate AWSA, led by Lucy Stone and

Julia Ward Howe, which favored the enactment of voting laws for women at the state level (their publication was *The Woman's Journal*). The AWSA sought to make woman suffrage appear less threatening and more consistent with traditional American values. Both groups engaged in national organizing and educational campaigns. Although both associations supported suffrage referenda in the states, the NWSA also lobbied Congress. Despite their tireless efforts, however, congressional hearings were rarely held, and the question of suffrage for women was called for a vote only once (in 1887) and rejected. Much more work would have to be done.

In 1890, the leaders of the two organizations suppressed their differences and joined forces as the National American Woman Suffrage Association (NAWSA), with Elizabeth Cady Stanton as president, Lucy Stone as head of the executive committee, and Susan B. Anthony as vice president. Their strategy was to continue to demand a federal amendment but to focus primary attention on building support for woman suffrage at the state level as a catalyst for federal action. A change in organizational emphasis brought about a new rationale as well. Instead of demanding the vote as a natural right, NAWSA, looking to adopt less offensive tactics, shifted to a more pragmatic course and argued that women would use the vote to help create a better society. Women would add a needed moral balance to politics and lead the crusade for temperance, protective legislation for women and children, and better (honest) government. But tangible progress was slow. After Wyoming entered the union as a suffrage state in 1890 and Colorado (1893), Idaho (1896), and Utah (1896) soon followed, no other state added its name to the suffrage list for the next fourteen years. Despite more than 400 campaigns to persuade state legislators to submit suffrage amendments to the voters and over 300 campaigns to convince state party leaders to add woman suffrage planks to their party platforms, efforts had proved futile.

The lack of tangible results caused an increasing number of women activists to become disillusioned with NAWSA's strategy. Even the passage of suffrage amendments in Washington (1910) and California (1911) failed to convince many suffragists that the existing state-centered organizing effort was the best plan of attack. Some regarded the old tactics as "tired" and suggested a shift toward a greater emphasis on work at the federal level. Others argued for more aggressive (less genteel) action and favored using demonstrations like the woman suffrage parade to command publicity and complement federal action. Still others were eager to utilize the political power of women voters in the western states as leverage to help achieve a federal suffrage amendment. Characterized increasingly by younger women but often in concert with some older members, these "new suffragists" would soon form the core of a more militant wing of the woman suffrage movement.

Inspiration as well as a plan of action for these new suffragists actually came from the more aggressive British woman suffrage movement. Led by Emmeline Pankhurst and her two daughters, Christabel and Sylvia, and organized as the Women's Social Political Union (WSPU), the British suffragettes began a militant campaign in 1903. Their plan was to persuade the public to vote against any candidate for Parliament who did not support granting the vote to women. Beginning with "questioning" members of Parliament and the Cabinet when they appeared in public, they gradually escalated the militancy of their protest to include window smashing, rock throwing, arson, sabotage, physical attacks on Cabinet members, and even suicide. In the process, they made woman suffrage a national issue in Britain. The key was demonstration and confrontation. When they were arrested for their actions, these British suffragettes chose to go to prison rather than pay their fines. In prison, they began hunger strikes and endured tremendous physical hardships that included forced feedings and brutal beatings. Over 1,000 members of the WSPU were eventually imprisoned for their participation in these protests. The movement also produced its own martyr when Emily Wilding Davison threw herself in front of the King's galloping horse on Derby Day in 1913 and was trampled to death. In describing her reaction to the forcefulness of the English suffrage movement, Inez Hayes Irwin, who wrote a contemporary history of Alice Paul and the National Woman's Party, undoubtedly expressed the feelings of many American suffragists in stating, "When . . . the first militant of Mrs. Pankhurst's force threw her first stone, my heart went with it. . . . At last the traditions of female patience . . . had gone by the board. Women were using the tactics that, through all the ages men had used; the only tactics that were sure to bring results; rebellion and violence."[1] Although radical American suffragists never advocated a policy of militant violence, they learned valuable tactical lessons from the suffragettes. It seemed imperative that the party in power be held responsible for legislative inaction, that maximum use be made of publicity, and that newsworthy protests be staged to focus national attention on the suffrage issue and the demand for a federal amendment.

One American who witnessed firsthand the actions of the British suffragettes and became drawn into the struggle while in England was Alice Paul. Born on January 11, 1885, in Moorestown, New Jersey, a small Quaker community in Burlington County near Philadelphia, Alice was the oldest of four children of William and Tacie (Parry) Paul. Her father was a successful banker and real estate investor who also served on the board of trustees of several local businesses. Her mother was the daughter of one of the founders of Swarthmore College. Both parents were devout Quakers and adhered to traditional Quaker beliefs that included equality between the sexes. The family atmosphere was disciplined (neither music nor dancing were allowed in the Paul household) and emphasized achievement and service. Alice attended a Quaker school in Moorestown and remembered accompanying her mother to suffrage meetings at a neighbor's home. She read voraciously, especially in the classics, and took a special interest in the social commentaries of Charles Dickens. Her love of literature lasted throughout her life, although a story is told that she denied herself the pleasure of reading during the hectic suffrage campaigns because she did not want to be distracted from her crusade. The Paul family was well-off financially, and, despite her father's death when she was sixteen, continued financial support from her mother would later enable Alice to devote herself full time to her suffrage work.

Paul's formal education began at Swarthmore, where she chose biology as her undergraduate major. Her commitment to this discipline, however, was not deeply rooted, and she never really considered a career in science. During her senior year, though, she developed an interest in politics and economics and was awarded a College Settlement Association Fellowship at the New York School of Philanthropy (later the Columbia University School of Social Work). After graduating from Swarthmore in 1905 and completing her fellowship the following year, she enrolled at the University of Pennsylvania and earned a master's degree in sociology with minor fields in economics and political science in 1907. While at the University of Pennsylvania, she became more attuned to the problems facing women as a result of their legal status and eventually completed a doctoral dissertation on that topic titled "Towards Equality" in 1912. Paul interrupted her graduate work in 1907 to accept a second fellowship to study social work at the Woodbrooke Settlement for Social Work in Birmingham, England, a central training school for Quakers interested in the field of public service. She realized, however, that this would not be her final calling. "I knew . . . that I was never going to be a social worker," she said, "because I could see that social workers were not doing much good in the world. . . . You knew you couldn't change the situation by social work."[2] While in England, however, Paul found the cause that would consume her attention for the next twelve years.

Paul's life-changing experience occurred when she went to hear Christabel Pankhurst speak on woman suffrage at the University of Birmingham. When a rowdy, mostly male audience forced university officials to cancel her speech, Paul was both shocked and angered. Far removed from the nonconfrontational environment of her Quaker youth, this experience underscored the entrenched prejudice against women in society and triggered Paul's direct involvement in the struggle for woman suffrage. In the fall of 1908, she participated in her first suffrage parade and began an association with the WSPU that lasted for two years. As an active member of the WSPU, she quickly became versed in the tactics of militant British suffragism. Her participation in demonstrations led to her arrest and imprisonment. While in prison, she joined fellow suffragettes in a hunger strike to protest their treatment. Paul, who had previously exhibited little political activism and had not joined any American suffrage organization, had now become committed to an ideal.

One of the women whom Paul met while in England was Lucy Burns, an Irish American from Brooklyn, who would become her closest collaborator in the radical American suffrage campaign. After graduating from Vassar College, Burns briefly attended graduate school at Yale before moving on to study languages in Germany at universities in Berlin and Bonn. But Burns, like Paul, found herself drifting without any real focus. During a vacation, she traveled to England and met the Pankhursts. Quickly developing a strong attraction to the suffrage cause, she shifted her studies to Oxford to accommodate her new interest. When Burns found that activism proved a stronger calling than academics, she threw herself into suffrage work. She joined the WSPU, began speaking on street corners, and helped circulate petitions to Parliament. In the process, she was arrested and sentenced to prison four times. Paul met Burns in a London police station where they had been arrested for disrupting Parliament. Paul noticed that Burns had a small American flag pinned to her lapel, and she introduced herself. As the two young women quietly shared their suffrage experiences and discussed the state of the suffrage movement in America, it became evident that they shared similar hopes for the movement at home. Unbeknownst to either at the time, it was a propitious meeting and the beginning of a fruitful alliance as leaders of the radical wing of the suffrage movement in the United States. They would make a good team. In describing the two women years later, one suffragist remarked, "They are both political-minded. . . . Both saw the situation exactly as it was, but they went at the problem with different methods. Alice Paul had a more acute sense of justice, Lucy Burns, a more bitter sense of injustice. Lucy Burns would become angry because the President or the people did not do this or that. Alice Paul never expected anything of them."[3] Paul and Burns were also, as one historian has suggested, good examples of the new suffragist. "As a group, these women were singularly independent and aggressive. They confronted society on its own terms, found those terms unacceptable and determined to follow the path that they perceived led most directly to their emancipation, regardless of the barriers encountered."[4]

In 1910, after being released from Halloway Prison in England, Paul returned to the United States and resumed graduate study at the University of Pennsylvania, completing her doctoral degree in 1912. Burns remained in Scotland as an organizer for the WSPU until 1912, when she too returned home. Both had gained valuable experience, and both believed that the general program of the British suffragettes had practical applications to the suffrage movement in the United States. Both were convinced that the time was right to apply what they had learned. Paul believed the British suffragettes were correct in directing their opposition at the government. "It is not a war of women against men," she said, "but a war of women and men together against the politicians."[5] Paul and Burns agreed that holding the party in power responsible for the fate of a federal suffrage amendment in the United States made good practical sense. With six suffrage states by 1911 and two million women voters in those states, they thought they had the political leverage (if it could be mobilized) needed to press their case at the federal level. Critics of the plan would argue that in holding the entire party responsible for inaction, women would wind up voting against pro-suffrage congressmen and senators. Paul disagreed. As it was there was no incentive to force suffrage-state congressmen to work to influence their recalcitrant colleagues in the party. If, on the other hand, their own seats were placed in jeopardy, then, for the success of the party or for the sake of their own political careers, they would have to actively promote woman suffrage.

To begin their rather radical campaign, Paul and Burns proposed to the leadership of NAWSA the creation of a more intensive congressional lobbying agency in 1912, but their idea was rejected. Unwilling to accept that verdict, Paul and Burns appealed their case to the revered Jane Addams, who agreed to argue on their behalf if they would accept modest changes in the tone of their proposal. The strategy worked. Paul was appointed chair of the Congressional Committee (an all but moribund federal lobbying arm of NAWSA) and Burns vice chair. They now had an organizational base from which to work. The leadership of NAWSA must have expected little in the way of results from the new powerless committee, which had no staff and a nonexistent budget.

The first step in Paul's aggressive plan of action was to hold a massive suffrage parade down Pennsylvania Avenue in Washington, D.C., on March 3, 1913, the day before President Woodrow Wilson's inauguration. The idea was to apply immediate pressure on the incoming president to force him to address the issue and to jolt an apathetic Congress and public into awareness by means of a dramatic public display. Paul and Burns quickly selected a small group of dedicated feminists to round out their committee and began to solicit funds and volunteers. Hoping to take advantage of the large numbers of party supporters in the capital for the event and the huge crowds (estimated to be 500,000) of onlookers, Paul designed a masterful demonstration. On the day of the parade, 8,000 women participated. At the head of the spectacle, as a modern-day Joan of Arc, was beautiful Inez Milholland (Boissevain). Riding a white horse and wearing a flowing white dress and carrying a banner that

Alice Paul, circa 1912. Library of Congress, Prints & Photographs Division.

read "Forward Out of Darkness, Forward Into Light," she led a procession of twenty-six floats, ten bands, and six sections of marching units that included many socially prominent women. The predominantly male crowd watching the parade, however, was not appreciative. Beginning with jeers and taunts, they disrupted the parade and roughed up many of the women marchers in the process. The unruliness of the crowd and the inability or unwillingness of the police to control it forced the War Department to call in the cavalry to restore order. Although outraged by the actions of the mob, Paul regarded the chaotic outcome as irrelevant. She had accomplished her goal. Suffrage was front-page headline news across the country, and the Wilson administration had been placed on alert. The event also generated a great deal of needed enthusiasm among suffragists and sympathizers and increased interest in Paul's committee. For the moment, the leaders of NAWSA decided not to rein in Paul's efforts.

Immediately after the suffrage parade, Paul and the Congressional Committee began an intensive lobbying campaign. Their initial action was to send the first of many deputations to President Wilson requesting that he include woman suffrage in his political agenda. Wilson, who met cordially with the delegation, professed that the suffrage question had never been brought to his attention before. He told them that, at that moment, he had no opinion as to its merits and that he needed time to study the matter. While Wilson equivocated, the Congressional Committee coordinated an assembly of delegates (one from every congressional district in the country) that met on April 7, 1913, the opening day of the special session of Congress. After the ceremonial gathering, the women delegates, each carrying resolutions and petitions from their districts, sought out their senators and representatives to lobby on behalf of a federal suffrage amendment. It marked the beginning of an unceasing process. During the summer, Paul directed another assemblage of pilgrimages from around the country and then escorted the "pilgrims" through the streets of Washington to the Capitol, where they presented petitions bearing the signatures of over 250,000 supporters.

Paul's new program of direct action continued to take a variety of forms. Her group launched *The Suffragist*, a weekly magazine intended for a national audience. Rheta Childe Dorr, who edited the publication, also arranged frequent press conferences to generate publicity. She also made it a practice to confront President Wilson and other public officials with pointed questions. Designed to elicit provocative responses, it was hoped that such candid commentary might be picked up and circulated by other magazines looking for a story. By the end of 1913, the Congressional Committee had led organizing campaigns in half a dozen eastern states, organized a Men's League for Woman Suffrage, distributed over 120,000 pieces of literature, and raised over $25,000 in donations. The boldness, independence, and success of Paul's organization, however, soon began to threaten many in the leadership of NAWSA. Disputes over tactics (political confrontation versus political cooperation) and control of financial resources eventually led to a split that many saw as inevitable. Unwilling to endure the constraints of the more conservative leaders in NAWSA, Paul withdrew her group from the larger body in

March 1914 and began to function independently as the Congressional Union.

Paul's next move was to map out a strategy that would pit the suffragists against the Democratic Party (the party in power) in the off-year elections in 1914. During the early part of that year, the Democratic Party had taken several actions that placed it in opposition to the demands of Paul's Congressional Union. First, the House Democratic caucus voted 123 to 57 to accept a resolution declaring suffrage a state's rights and not a federal issue. Second, the Democratically controlled Senate rejected a proposed federal woman suffrage amendment by a vote of 35 to 34 (far less than the two-thirds majority necessary for passage). Third, President Wilson, aware of the mood of his party, announced that he, too, believed that suffrage should be left to the states. To convince politicians that their position on suffrage was "inexpedient," Paul and the Congressional Union declared political war against the Democratic Party in the nine western states where women had by then gained the franchise. "The question," said Paul, "is whether we are good enough politicians to take four million votes and organize them and use them." "[W]hen . . . the political parties are made to realize that opposition to suffrage means their defeat . . . that suffragists can actually affect the results of a national election, our fight will be won."[6] The campaign to organize women in the suffrage states and mount a vigorous campaign against all Democratic candidates in those states marked a shift in suffrage tactics. Enfranchised women were being asked to help their unenfranchised sisters by abandoning their loyalty to party in favor of gender solidarity.

The Congressional Union proceeded to send two organizers into each of the nine western states where women had won the vote. One organizer assumed responsibility for operating a headquarters, attending to the press, delivering literature, and directing speakers. The other stumped the state, speaking in support of a federal suffrage amendment and the Congressional Union and urging women to vote against Democrats as a sign of unity with women not yet enfranchised. Despite being denounced by threatened politicians and vilified in the party press, Paul's organization had made suffrage the issue everyone talked about. Of the forty-three Democratic candidates the Congressional Union campaigned against, only twenty were elected to office. Many of those who regained their seats did so with diminished majorities. Although there were many valid explanations for the election results—a stronger, reunited Republican Party and traditional losses incurred by the incumbent party in off-year elections—the Congressional Union had added a new factor to the political equation and one that newspapers across the country included in their postelection analyses. Obvious gains had been made. The Congressional Union "had grown markedly in members, money,

and importance, both in the suffrage movement and in the women's movement."[7] It had also instilled a degree of unease in the Democratic Party as it
looked forward to the next general election in 1916.

Although the Congressional Union drew encouragement from the 1914 political campaign, NAWSA charged that Paul's strategy was counterproductive
and that her intrusion in the election had been a failure. The public animosity
between the two suffrage organizations intensified after Carrie Chapman Catt
resumed the presidency of NAWSA in 1915 after a twelve-year absence. Catt
strongly objected to the idea that the party in power should be held responsible for the failure of Congress to pass a suffrage amendment. As she saw it,
the suffrage cause had friends in both major parties, and to achieve the two-
thirds majority required in both houses to pass a constitutional amendment,
bipartisan support was necessary. In 1916, in response to the ineffectiveness
of her own association and the aggressiveness of the Congressional Union,
Catt advanced her own blueprint for victory called the "Winning Plan."
NAWSA's leadership would continue to focus on federal action but recognize
that solid organizational work at the state level was essential in gaining the
necessary support for a national amendment and, ultimately, in carrying it
through state legislatures for ratification. Toward those ends, NAWSA would
energize its federal efforts with a nationwide publicity campaign while continuing to lobby vigorously in Washington. State branches, in turn, would step
up their activity on several fronts. They would continue to pressure state legislatures in states that already had suffrage to send resolutions to Congress. In
states where there was a chance for an amendment, they would push for a
popular referendum. In other states, they would press legislatures for partial
suffrage, such as participation in presidential primaries. In the South, they
would lobby for the right of women to vote in primaries. In each instance,
state branches would have the support of the national body.

Unfazed by NAWSA's criticisms, Paul continued to come up with new ideas
to keep her membership active. The first of these was a plan to establish
branches of the Congressional Union in states where none existed. By the end
of the year, the Congressional Union had organized in nineteen states, and its
membership had grown to nearly 4,500. By the end of 1916, that number had
increased to thirty-six branches, and a year later all forty-eight states had been
organized. Paul's stated purpose, contrary to what Catt and the leaders of
NAWSA might have perceived, was not to duplicate the efforts of NAWSA to
obtain state suffrage amendments. Paul remained focused on her larger campaign to make suffrage a national issue and to generate a nationwide demand
for a federal amendment, but she truly believed that achievement of this goal
required political pressure at the state level. The second plan, in actuality a culmination of the first, was to hold the first national convention of women vot-

ers to coincide with the Panama-Pacific Exposition in San Francisco in September 1915. "We want to make woman suffrage the dominant political issue from the moment Congress reconvenes," said Paul. "We want to have Congress open in the middle of a veritable suffrage cyclone."[8] The climax of the convention, highlighted by three days of meetings and speeches, was the completion of an 18,000-foot-long petition bearing 500,000 signatures. Paul, always looking for ways to attract public attention, chose Sara Bard Field, a popular suffrage speaker, to deliver the petition to Congress, but only after making a 3,000-mile trip across the country in an automobile named the "Suffrage Flier." When Field finally arrived in Washington in December 1915, Paul arranged to have her present the petition to Congress and to meet with President Wilson, who had recently announced his intention to vote for suffrage in a referendum in his home state of New Jersey.

On April 8, 1916, the executive committee of the Congressional Union met at their new headquarters in Cameron House, located directly across Pennsylvania Avenue from the White House, to hear Paul announce the next step in her political program. What she proposed was the formation of a women's political party to act as a balance of power in the upcoming presidential campaign. Paul had concluded, based on her study of recent election results, that a swing of only 9 percent of the vote in the suffrage states would throw the election to the other party. With the support of the executive committee, Paul immediately sent a delegation of twenty-three organizers on a tour of the western states aboard a train called the "Suffrage Special" to whip up support for the new party. As a result, more than 1,500 delegates from those states attended the formal convention launching the National Woman's Party (NWP) in Chicago on June 5–7, 1916. In an effort to garner maximum publicity, the NWP scheduled the convention to conclude the day before the opening of both the Progressive and the Republican party conventions in the same city. The new party would be strictly independent, with membership limited to enfranchised women, and its sole purpose would be to promote a national suffrage amendment. In a speech directed at the male representatives of the major parties who had been invited to attend the convention, delegate Anne Martin summed up the sentiments of Paul and the NWP in stating, "We do not ask you here to tell us what we can do for your Parties, but what your Parties can do for us."[9] Members of the NWP appeared before the resolutions committees of the Democratic and Republican parties, and although both major parties included suffrage planks in their platforms for the first time, they stopped short of endorsing a federal amendment (as the Progressive, Socialist, and Prohibition parties had done).

Immediately after the convention, the NWP began to pressure Republican presidential nominee Charles Evans Hughes to come out in support of a federal amendment and encouraged state NWP and Congressional Union members to "flood Hughes with telegrams from every possible source."[10] The lobbying appeared to work as Hughes departed from his party's platform and endorsed a federal suffrage amendment on August 1. Bolstered by the announcement, the NWP jumped into the presidential campaign exactly as it had in 1914. The 1916 effort, however, was complicated by external events as the major issue in the campaign was the war in Europe and the possibility of American involvement. Although the NWP attempted to counter the Democrats' popular refrain, "He Kept Us Out of War," with their own slogans—"He Kept Us Out of Suffrage" and "A Vote for the Democratic Party Is a Vote Against Women"—most voters (and many suffragists) seemed to favor Wilson and peace rather than Hughes and preparedness and the implications of that policy. Paul considered withdrawing from the campaign to cut possible losses but decided not to do so. "If we withdraw our speakers from the campaign," she stated, "we withdraw the issue from the campaign. We must make this such an important thing in national elections that the Democrats will not want to meet it again."[11] The final results were a disappointment for Paul and the NWP. Although the election was close (Wilson collected 277 electoral votes to Hughes's 254), only two of the twelve suffrage states voted against Wilson despite the efforts of the NWP. Ironically, many attributed Wilson's victory to the women's vote on the peace issue.

The difficult 1916 campaign also had a tragic note. Inez Milholland, who worked as a roving speaker for the NWP, collapsed during a speech in Los Angeles on October 22 in which her last words were, reportedly, "Mr. President, how long must women wait for liberty?" Her death (evidently from complications resulting from pernicious anemia) only weeks later at the age of thirty gave the NWP its own martyr. From that moment on, her final words appeared as a standard-banner at all NWP protests and rallies. The NWP even created an image of Milholland mounted on her white horse and wearing her white dress and carrying a banner with the legend "Forward Into Light" (as she had in the original suffrage parade) that became the official poster of the organization.

The electoral defeats of 1916 forced Paul to escalate the level of protest. Beginning in January 1917, members of the Congressional Union (known as "Silent Sentinels") began picketing in front of the White House. Although even some supporters found the practice of picketing undignified, Paul knew that more drastic measures had to be employed if a federal amendment was to be passed before the next presidential election. To emphasize the diversity of support for a suffrage amendment, Paul planned a number of special picketing days when volunteers from various states, colleges, and professions would be represented. A series of theme days—Patriotic Day, Lincoln Day, and Labor Day—was also used to attract the attention of the press. Before the

United States entered World War I in April 1917, the public tended to sympathize with the picketers. But when Paul announced that her "antiadministration" policy would continue uninterrupted during the war, the public's attitude quickly changed to derision and abuse. NAWSA had immediately thrown its support behind President Wilson's war policy and hoped that by showing that women were "loyal Americans" by not protesting and working to support the war effort, they would be rewarded with the vote at the end of the conflict. Paul's Congressional Union, in contrast, refused to allow the war to deter the fight for suffrage. To Paul, woman suffrage and the war were separate issues. Women who wanted to work to support the war effort could do so, but they would have to do so through associations outside the NWP (the Congressional Union was absorbed by the NWP in March 1917). As the NWP formally put it, "[T]he problems involved in the present international situation, affecting the lives of millions of women in this country, make imperative the enfranchisement of women. . . . [O]rganized for the sole purpose of securing political liberty for women, [we] shall continue to work for this purpose until it is accomplished, being unalterably convinced that in so doing the organization serves the highest interests of the country."[12]

After Wilson's declaration of war, the pickets began to carry banners bearing quotations from the president's own speeches to highlight the hypocrisy of fighting for democracy abroad ("for the right of those who submit to authority to have a voice in their own government") while ignoring disenfranchised citizens at home. Paul intended the banners to embarrass the president and possibly have the suffrage amendment considered as a war measure. But an increasingly emotional public, whipped to a frenzy by wartime propaganda, had no toleration for such criticism. They ripped poles out of the hands of the picketers and destroyed their banners. Some of the picketers suffered physical injury in the process. At first, the police did nothing to disrupt the protest, but beginning on June 20, after an especially caustic banner greeted diplomatic representatives from Russia as they drove into the White House, the police began to arrest picketers. Charged with obstructing traffic, they were, at first, released without penalty. After another week of continued picketing, however, punishments increased to three nights in jail. Beginning on July 14, the sentences were drastically increased to sixty days in the Occoquan Workhouse, a facility noted for its small, dark, rat-infested cells and its fetid air and inedible food. These repressive tactics backfired; public opinion shifted in favor of the picketers. They had obviously been jailed on a pretext to remove them from public view, and their punishments seemed severe and heavy-handed. Despite attempts on the part of the Wilson administration to control the situation, events had seemingly spiraled out of control. Public outrage at the treatment of the women forced President Wilson to pardon all prisoners confined in the workhouse on July 21. Paul publicly thanked the president for his pardons but remained defiant. "The President can pardon us again . . . and again and again, but . . . picketing will continue and sooner or later he will have to do something about it."[13]

As the picketing campaign progressed, confrontations between suffrage picketers and angry crowds increased, as did the administration's displeasure. Crowds surrounding the women became rowdier and more moblike. Incidents of physical abuse against picketers multiplied as well. Suffragists who tried to hold on to their banners were frequently dragged along the pavement by onlookers who tried to take them away. Soon more and more uniformed servicemen began to take part in the harassment as self-appointed defenders of the administration (their participation in the disorders was eventually curtailed by military order). As before, assaults on suffragists went largely uncontested by the police. The confrontation intensified on October 20, when Paul was arrested in front of the White House. Her trial provided the authorities with the opportunity to single her out as the leader of the NWP and to mete out punishment accordingly. Sentenced to seven months in the Occoquan Workhouse, Paul began a hunger strike (other arrested NWP members would soon follow her example) and demanded that she and her jailed comrades be treated as political prisoners. After a week of confinement and for three weeks thereafter, Paul was force-fed three times a day. When she still refused to cooperate, she was first separated from the other prisoners and then transferred to the prison psychopathic ward in the District Jail. There she was subjected to interrogations by doctors from the District of Columbia's Institution for the Mentally Insane in a failed attempt to raise questions concerning her sanity and to discredit her leadership of the NWP. It was not until November 20, 1917, that legal counsel for the NWP was able to obtain a writ of habeas corpus that allowed Paul to be transferred to a regular hospital.

Even before Paul began her hunger strike, the NWP had decided on yet another way to heighten public awareness. They created a "Prison Squad" comprised of previously jailed picketers (dressed in clothing identical to their prison uniforms) who toured the country to inform the public about conditions in Washington. Their public testimony alarmed Democrats already worried about how this adverse publicity would impact approaching congressional elections. Finally, on November 28, without any prior notice, all the suffrage prisoners were released. Sporadic picketing resumed over the next two months but never again matched the intensity of the previous summer and fall. When arrests were made, the punishments were never as severe as they had been. The picketing campaign had proved to be an ordeal for Paul and her colleagues in the NWP. Thousands of women had picketed, approximately 500 had been arrested, and 168 had served debilitating prison sentences. The question on everyone's mind was whether the effort had been worthwhile.

Historians still debate whether it was the conciliatory approach of NAWSA (backed by approximately three million members) or the militant approach of the Congressional Union/NWP (supported by roughly 35,000 members) that ultimately forced the Wilson administration to alter its attitude toward suffrage. Paul felt, at the least, that the NWP created the sense of urgency that shortened the timetable for passage of a federal amendment. By late 1917, a change on the part of the Wilson administration had become apparent. When a New York State referendum on woman suffrage came up for a vote in November, President Wilson publicly endorsed it prior to its approval by the voters. Then, when the House of Representatives abruptly agreed to bring the question of a suffrage amendment (known commonly by then as the Susan B. Anthony amendment) up for a vote in January 1918, Wilson personally lobbied a dozen Democratic representatives to raise the number of supporters to exactly the two-thirds majority needed for passage. It was beginning to look as if Paul was right, that President Wilson, the leader of his party and the symbol of the control that the Democratic Party had over political and legislative questions at that moment, could use his political influence to prod his party to action on even the most contentious of issues.

When the Senate, where opposition to suffrage was even stiffer, continued to delay a vote on the suffrage amendment, Paul again raised the level of confrontation. Beginning on September 16, 1918, the NWP began burning copies of Wilson's "war for democracy" speeches in urns dubbed the "Watchfires of Freedom" in Lafayette Park across from the White House. Two weeks later, Wilson gave the Senate only thirty minutes' notice and then proceeded to the Capitol to address that body in favor of immediate action of the suffrage amendment. In a speech that must have given Paul a great deal of satisfaction, Wilson remarked,

> I regard the extension of suffrage to women as vitally essential to the successful prosecution of the great war of humanity in which we are engaged. . . . It is my duty to win the war and to ask you to remove every obstacle that stands in the way of winning it. . . . They [other nations] are looking to the great, powerful . . . democracy of the West to lead them to a new day . . . and they think . . . that democracy means that women shall play their part in affairs alongside men and upon an equal footing with them. . . . The executive tasks of this war rest upon me. I ask that you lighten them and place in my hands instruments, spiritual instruments, which I do not now possess, which I sorely need and which I have daily to apologize for not being able to employ.[14]

Although Wilson's speech only inched the Senate closer to passing the federal suffrage amendment, in tying the success of the war to suffrage, the president had vindicated the position assumed by Paul almost two years before. Final Senate approval of the woman suffrage amendment, a process delayed primarily by recalcitrant southern states' rights Democrats, came on June 4, 1919. Ratification by two-thirds of the states, a process that was equally hard fought, took more than fourteen additional months. The Nineteenth Amendment to the U.S. Constitution became effective on August 26, 1920.

After ratification of the suffrage amendment, many in the suffrage movement felt their goal had been achieved and abandoned further activism. That was not the case with Paul. Renewing her interest in the problem of legal restraints on women's rights and advancing her ability to confront them, she enrolled in law school in the 1920s and eventually earned LL.B., LL.M., and D.C.L. degrees. Regarding the right to vote as a triumph short of establishing full equality for women, Paul turned the attention of the NWP to lobbying for an equal rights amendment (ERA) to the Constitution. Paul drafted the first ERA and managed to have it introduced in Congress in 1923. The proposed amendment simply stated, "Men and women shall have equal rights throughout the United States and every place subject to its jurisdiction." (It was later modified to read, "Equality of rights under the law shall not be denied or abridged by the United States or by any state on account of sex.")[15] Dubbed the Lucretia Mott amendment by Paul to honor the nineteenth-century women's rights activist, the ERA immediately divided the women's movement. Many feminists, like Florence Kelley, who had worked closely with Paul on suffrage, saw the amendment as a threat to the body of protective labor legislation for women that had been painstakingly established during the Progressive Era. Instead of protections, Paul saw only restraints and argued that many state laws discriminated against women and that only a broadly based amendment could eliminate those discriminations. The ERA (which had never garnered much support in Congress) had something of a revival in the years immediately after World War II, when the argument was again made that passage would reward women for their patriotic work during wartime. Despite the renewed interest, however, the ERA never received anywhere near the two-thirds vote necessary for passage.

During the 1960s, the emerging women's movement changed the tenor of the debate. Although the 1964 Civil Rights Act prohibited discrimination in employment based on sex and seemed to allay the fears of working women and labor unions that prior protections would be undermined, feminists like Paul insisted that the ERA was still necessary to protect a woman's dignity as a human being and as a guarantee that recent civil rights legislation would be enforced. Paul continued to campaign for the ERA until 1972, when Congress finally approved the amendment and sent it to the states for ratification. But conservative reaction to the amendment was strong and well organized, and arguments that the ERA would undermine the family and disrupt traditional social patterns (would there be unisex toilets and women being drafted into the military?) alarmed many. When Paul died in 1977 at the age of ninety-two, she was convinced that the ERA (still three states short of passage) would be victorious. It was not to be. The ERA eventually went down to defeat in 1982, when the time limit required for ratification (previously extended to ten years) expired.

What differentiates Paul from many women in the more moderate wing of the suffrage movement and establishes her unique place in any history of American reform is the manner in which she perceived equality and the way she thrust women into the public sphere by calling out louder than almost anyone else for a radical redefinition of gender in order to equalize power relations in American society. Paul felt a strong kinship with Elizabeth Cady Stanton and the sentiment of the original Seneca Falls Declaration of 1848—that society was wrongly structured so as to deny women basic liberties, rights, and responsibilities and, therefore, prohibited women from becoming fully human. As she told an interviewer in 1976, she believed that "women of every experience and every walk of life . . . have this same feeling for building up respect for their own sex, power for their own sex, and lifting it up out of a place where there is contempt for women in general." In thinking about the type of women who joined the Congressional Union/NWP and what they might have had in common, she remarked, "It was a feeling of loyalty to our own sex and an enthusiasm to have every degradation that was put upon our sex removed. That's what I had anyway." When asked in 1976 what she thought of the current women's movement, Paul answered in the same spirit. "These people talk now," she said, "about equality for women, liberation for women, they are always talking about advantages to women—how you will get promoted, and how you will get more pay, and so on . . . which is a different feeling from the dignity of your sex that you are all trying to get, and the freedom." Elaborating further, she observed, "I think if we get freedom for women, then they are probably going to do a lot of things that I wish they wouldn't do; but it seems to me that isn't our business to say what they should do with it. It is our business to see that they are free."[16]

During the battle for suffrage, Paul had ignored issues like birth control and reforming marriage and divorce laws because she thought it necessary to concentrate her energies on one goal. Winning the vote was, indeed, important, but Paul subsequently realized that it was, in itself, not inclusive enough to guarantee complete equality between the sexes. In describing why she chose to begin a new fight for an ERA, Paul stated that she wanted "to try to follow up the whole emancipation program of 1848 and bring it to conclusion."[17] She envisioned an America where women no longer confronted legal, economic, and professional disabilities and inequities that rendered them second-class citizens.

NOTES

1. Christine A. Lunardini, *From Equal Suffrage to Equal Rights: Alice Paul and the National Woman's Party, 1910–1928* (New York: New York University Press, 1986), 6.

2. Amelia R. Fry, "Conversations with Alice Paul: Woman Suffrage and the Equal Rights Amendment," Suffragists Oral History Project, Online Archive of California, http://ark.cdlib.org/ark:/13030/kt6f59n89c (Berkeley: University of California, 1976), 20.

3. Inez Haynes Irwin, *The Story of Alice Paul and the National Woman's Party* (Fairfax, Va.: Denlinger's Publishers, 1977), 18.

4. Lunardini, *From Equal Suffrage to Equal Rights*, 17.

5. Lunardini, *From Equal Suffrage to Equal Rights*, 18.

6. Lunardini, *From Equal Suffrage to Equal Rights*, 61, 62.

7. Lunardini, *From Equal Suffrage to Equal Rights*, 69.

8. Lunardini, *From Equal Suffrage to Equal Rights*, 71.

9. Lunardini, *From Equal Suffrage to Equal Rights*, 89.

10. Lunardini, *From Equal Suffrage to Equal Rights*, 92.

11. Irwin, *The Story of Alice Paul and the National Woman's Party*, 183.

12. Irwin, *The Story of Alice Paul and the National Woman's Party*, 207.

13. Lunardini, *From Equal Suffrage to Equal Rights*, 122.

14. Lunardini, *From Equal Suffrage to Equal Rights*, 145.

15. Fry, "Conversations with Alice Paul," 266, 299.

16. Fry, "Conversations with Alice Paul," 183, 197.

17. Fry, "Conversations with Alice Paul," 261.

SOURCES

Clift, Eleanor. *Founding Sisters and the Nineteenth Amendment*. New York: John Wiley & Sons, 2003.

Dumbeck, Kristina. *Leaders of Women's Suffrage*. San Diego: Lucent Books, 2001.

Fry, Amelia R. "Conversations with Alice Paul: Woman Suffrage and the Equal Rights Amendment." Suffragists Oral History Project. Online Archive of California; http://ark.cdlib.org/ark:/13030/kt6f59n89c. Berkeley: University of California, 1976.

Irwin, Inez Haynes. *The Story of Alice Paul and the National Woman's Party*. Fairfax, Va.: Denlinger's Publishers, 1977.

Lunardini, Christine A. *From Equal Suffrage to Equal Rights: Alice Paul and the National Woman's Party, 1910–1928.* New York: New York University Press, 1986.

Stevens, Doris. *Jailed for Freedom: American Women Win the Vote.* Edited by Carol O'Hare. New York: New Sage Press, 1995.

Zimmerman, Loretta Ellen. "Alice Paul and the National Woman's Party, 1912–1920." Ph.D. diss., Tulane University, 1964.

Index

Adams, Samuel Hopkins, 176; exposes patent medicine quackery, 172–73

Addams, Jane, 81, 112, 116, 117, 120, 183, 202; activist for woman suffrage, 103; analyzes the political machine, 101–2; college address on the role of women, 91–92; college years, 92–94; considers socialist critique of capitalism, 101; develops interest in Christian social reform, 95; efforts for international peace, 104–5; expands reform interests, 98–100; ideas regarding women as potential voters, 102; importance to the history of American reform, 105–6; influence of parents on, 92; launching the Hull House settlement, 96–98; medical maladies after college, 94; radicalized by the Pullman Strike, 100; supports Progressive Party, 103–4; visits Toynbee Hall, 95–96

Adkins v. Children's Hospital (1923), 122

African Americans, 4; problems confronting, 6–7; violence against, 7, 59–60, 68, 71

Agricultural Wheel, 49

Alpha Suffrage Club, 70

Altgeld, John Peter, 117

American Bar Association (ABA), 141

American Economic Association, 17, 79

American Federation of Labor: attitude toward women and child laborers, 109

American Journal of Sociology, 18

American Medical Association, 173

American Woman Suffrage Association (AWSA), 197–98

Anglo-Saxon race, 5

Anthony, Susan B., 67, 197, 198

Association of Official Agricultural Chemists (AOAC), 170

Baker, Ray Stannard, 75–76

Ballinger, Richard A., 136–38

Barnett, Ferdinand L., 70

Barnett, Samuel, 95

Barrett, W. H., 59, 64

Batten, Samuel Zane, 82–83

Bellamy, Edward, 52, 101

Besant, Walter, 95

Beveridge, Albert, 176

black capitalism, 59

Bliss, William Dwight Porter, 80, 83, 184–85, 195

About the Author

Steven L. Piott is professor of history at Clarion University of Pennsylvania. He holds B.A. and M.A. degrees from the University of Utah and his Ph.D. from the University of Missouri. His published works include: *The Anti-Monopoly Persuasion: Popular Resistance to the Rise of Big Business* (1985); *Holy Joe: Joseph W. Folk and the Missouri Idea* (1997); and, *Giving Voters a Voice: The Origins of the Initiative and Referendum in America* (2003). He is a former Fulbright Teaching Fellow at Massey University in New Zealand.